IQBAL

By the same author

IQBAL

The Life of a Poet,
Philosopher and Politician

ZAFAR ANJUM

RANDOM HOUSE INDIA

Published by Random House India in 2014
Second impression in 2015

Copyright © Zafar Anjum 2014

Random House Publishers India Private Limited
7th Floor, Infinity Tower C, DLF Cyber City
Gurgaon – 122002, Haryana

Random House Group Limited
20 Vauxhall Bridge Road
London SW1V 2SA
United Kingdom

ISBN 978-81-8400-586-8

Typeset in Adobe Caslon Pro by R. Ajith Kumar

Printed and bound in India by Replika Press Private Limited

A PENGUIN RANDOM HOUSE COMPANY

For
Dr Syed Hasan
and
all those great souls who are inspired by Iqbal's message

'I have lost hope in the older men, and I have a message for tomorrow. Therefore, help the youth to comprehend my works and fathom the depths of my thought with ease.' —Iqbal, *Javed Nama*

'All the details of the life and the quirks and the friendships can be laid out for us, but the mystery of the writing will remain. No amount of documentation, however fascinating, can take us there. The biography of a writer—or even the autobiography—will always have this incompleteness.'—V.S. Naipaul

'How much do we need to know about a writer, personally? The answer is that it doesn't matter. Nothing or everything is equally satisfactory. Who cares, in the end? As Northrop Frye has said, the only evidence we have of Shakespeare's existence, apart from the poems and plays, is the portrait of a man who was clearly an idiot. Biography is there for the curious; and curiosity gives out where boredom begins.'—Martin Amis

'The commonplace that a biographer has found the "key" to a person's life— usually something arbitrary like the death of a sibling or moving house—is implausible. People are too complicated and inconsistent for this to be true. The best a biographer can hope for is to illuminate aspects of a life and seek to give glimpses of the subject, and that way tell a story.' —Patrick French

Contents

List of Illustrations

1. Iqbal's father, Shaikh Noor Muhammad
2. Iqbal's teacher and guide Syed Mir Hasan
3. Allama Iqbal with his son Javed Iqbal
4. Allama Iqbal with Javed Iqbal in 1930
5. Iqbal's wife Sardar Begum
6. Javed Iqbal
7. Karim Bibi, Iqbal's first wife
8. Munira Bano, Iqbal's daughter
9. Allama Iqbal in Spain
10. Iqbal in London, 1931
11. Iqbal offering prayers in the Qartaba Masjid (Spain)
12. Iqbal in his room with his favourite hookah
13. Iqbal in Aligarh
14. Allama Iqbal in Allahabad, 1930
15. Iqbal at a party during the Second Round Table Conference in London, 1931
16. Allama Iqbal with Sir Ross Masood and Syed Sulaiman Nadvi in Afghanistan, 1933
17. Iqbal at a reception hosted by the National League, London, in 1932
18-23. Portraits of Iqbal

The author and publishers would like to thank Dr Muhammad Suheyl Umar, director, Iqbal Academy Pakistan, Lahore, for his kind permission to reproduce these illustrations in this work.

Muhammad Iqbal's family tree

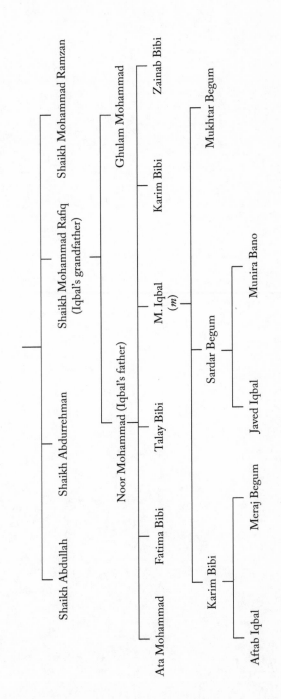

PROLOGUE

Why Iqbal?

One evening in April this year I was sitting with a friend in Blue Jazz Café in Singapore's Arab Street neighbourhood. My friend, who is a professor in a prestigious university in Delhi, asked me what I was currently working on. 'Iqbal,' I told him, 'a biography of Allama Muhammad Iqbal.'

'But why a biography of Iqbal?' He pressed me with a perfectly valid question. 'What is your connection with Iqbal?'

He had a point. It is true that I have no direct connection with Iqbal. The great poet was dead long before I was born. I'm not from Pakistan or the Punjab. I have never been across the border, not even to research this book (a variety of things prevented this). I am not even an Urdu scholar, though I was enrolled for a masters degree in Urdu at Delhi's Jawaharlal Nehru University. I was forced to drop out after a year due to insufficient attendance (my loyalties were divided: I was pursuing a course in journalism at the same time).

My friend and I talked for a long time about Iqbal, Urdu, Partition, and about how the idea that a state could be created on the basis of religion was a failed idea. If the idea of Pakistan as a land for Indian Muslims was such a good idea, then how come Bangladesh came to be separated from Pakistan, he argued. If Iqbal stood for the idea of Muslim nationalism, and not territorial nationalism, then it was already a failed idea, he railed on.

Later on, I thought at length about my friend's question: What is my connection with Iqbal? I believe that my bond with Iqbal and his poetry is deeper than that of just a lay reader and plain admirer of his scintillating and soul-stirring verses. I am attached to Iqbal by an umbilical cord that is both spiritual and intellectual.

The bond is not without its physical manifestations too. I grew up in a small town in Bihar and the school that I attended until my matriculation—Insan School—was founded by Dr Syed Hasan, a disciple of Dr Zakir Hussain, independent India's first Muslim President. Dr Hasan, who had a successful academic career in the USA, left everything behind to found a school in one of Bihar's most backward districts—Kishanganj, my hometown. And one of his inspirations was Iqbal whom he had met as a student.

My first tutor, Mahboob Alam Saheb—who has dedicated his life to the Urdu language as a teacher in a small village in West Bengal—was very fond of Ghalib's and Iqbal's poetry. From when I was young, he exposed me and my sister Soghra to Iqbal's inspiring verses. Famous lines from his poetry such as '*Khudi ko kar buland itna ke har taqdeer se pehle . . .*' and '*Tu Shaheen hai basera kar pahadon ki chattanoon me*' became part of our daily speech. Slowly, Iqbal seeped into us during languid summer afternoons and hurried winter evenings, while we did our school work.

When I came to Aligarh to attend university, I stayed in Allama Iqbal Hall as a boarder for five years. I also became one of the editors and contributors to the hall's magazine, *Iqbal*. The great poet, in an oblique way, became a real presence in my life.

Years later, when I trooped over to study at J.N.U. in Delhi, I was horrified to realize that Iqbal had been slowly erased from our memories. In Aligarh, his poetry was alive and his presence could be felt. This was not so in Delhi. I began to wonder how many people in India, both Hindus and Muslims, especially of the younger generation, knew about Iqbal today? Some might know him as a poet, but how many know that there is much more to Iqbal than his poetry. Neither his contribution to the philosophy of Islam nor his achievements as a politician are common knowledge. How many know about Iqbal's political role in the creation of Pakistan and why a patriotic poet like him came up with the idea of Pakistan?

The story you are going to read in these pages is an attempt to narrate Iqbal's life once again for those who have forgotten him. I don't claim it to be a comprehensive account, for to write such a book would require a lot of time and research, and in the time that I was given, I have tried my best.

I hope this book will satisfy those curious about Iqbal and spur them onto further reading. This humble effort is my spiritual homage to Iqbal and his universal message.

Zafar Anjum
Singapore
July 9, 2014

Introduction

> Come dear friend! Thou hast known me only as an abstract
> thinker and dreamer of high ideals. See me in my home playing
> with the children and giving them rides turn by turn as if I were
> a wooden horse! Ah! See me in the family circle lying in the feet
> of my grey-haired mother the touch of whose rejuvenating hand
> bids the tide of time flow backward, and gives me once more the
> school-boy feeling in spite of all the Kants and Hegels in my
> head! Here Thou will know me as a human being.
>
> —Iqbal, *Stray Reflections*

Allama Muhammad Iqbal, one of India's first patriotic poets,
whom Sarojini Naidu called the 'Poet laureate of Asia', remains
a controversial figure in the history of the Indian subcontinent.
On the one hand, he is seen as a Pan-Islamic philosopher and the
'Spiritual Father of Pakistan', and even the inspiration of the Iranian
Revolution. On the other, his patriotic and socialistic poems, and his
intellectual struggle against both the colonial powers and Islamic
fundamentalists places him in the ranks of the twentieth century's
major political thinkers.

Professor Yahya Michot,[1] fellow of Islamic Studies at the Oxford
Centre for Islamic Studies and the Faculty of Theology, Oxford
University, regards Iqbal as the last great Muslim thinker in the
lineage of Ghazali, Razi, and Shah Waliullah. Many scholars have
also highlighted Iqbal's fondness for his homeland (pre-Partition
India), and pointed out how he used Sanskrit vocabulary and figures

of narrative from Hindu folklore and mythology in his poetry.

In his own time, Iqbal's towering genius was aptly recognized by another genius born of Indian soil, Nobel laureate Rabindranath Tagore. The great poet said this of Iqbal: 'India just cannot afford to ignore Iqbal whose poetry has universal appeal.'

Like most of his peers, Iqbal received a traditional Eastern education in a madrasa under the guidance of the famous scholar Mir Hasan. He published his early poems in *Makhzan*, an Urdu journal edited by his friend Shaikh Abdul Qadir. The Anjuman-e Himayat-e Islam in Lahore was another forum for his poetry. He used to recite his poems at its annual gatherings. Some of the early poems that he recited at the anjuman's conferences were '*Nala-e Yatim*', '*Abr-e Guhar Bar*', '*Tasvir-e Dard*', '*Naya Shivala*', and '*Tarana-e Hindi*'. The last three were written to celebrate Indian nationalism.

In 1905, Iqbal travelled to Europe to study philosophy in Britain and Germany. Though he found Europe's achievements impressive, 'its racist and ultra-competitive culture' disturbed him. As noted by Pankaj Mishra, even before more famous critics of the West like Tagore and China's Liang Qichao, Iqbal was already writing in 1908:

> *Dayaar-e Maghrib ke rehne walon*
> *Khuda ki basti dukaan nahin hai*
> *Khara jise tum samajh rahe ho*
> *Woh ab zar-e kum ayaar hoga*
> *Tumhari tehzeeb apne khanjar se*
> *Aap khud khudkushi karegi*

> O, dwellers of the cities of the West,
> This habitation of God is not a shop,
> And that which you regard as true coin,
> Will prove to be only a counterfeit.
> Your civilization will commit suicide
> With its own sword.[2]

О

Iqbal started out as an Indian nationalist. Following the footsteps of Akbar Allahabadi, he celebrated India's multiculturalism, called Lord Ram 'Imam-e-Hind', and India the land of Chishti and Nanak. He also wrote paeans to its eternal beauty, the most famous being 'Sare jahan se achcha Hindustan hamara'. But while in Europe, the history of Islam seeped into his soul, and changed Iqbal forever.

The three years that Iqbal spent in Europe transformed his outlook. Not only did he begin to reject nationalism, he also heeded the religious questions that he had so far ignored. At that time, the Islamic world was threatened with imminent dissolution. While Turkey was in the throes of disintegration, Persia became the target of Russian ambition. Within a few years, the Turko-Italian War rang the death-knell of Tripoli. All these disappointing developments, in Iqbal's opinion, resulted from the great evil of nationalism. Henceforth, it became his bête noir.[3]

In 1908, during his return to India, Iqbal saw the coast of Sicily, which once was a beacon of 'Islam's greatest triumphs in Europe'. He saw it now as a 'tomb of Muslim culture':[4]

Hai tere asaar me poshida kiski dastaan
Tere sahil ki khamoshi me hai anadaaz-e bayan
Dard apna mujh se keh main bhi sar-a-pa dard hoon
Jis ki tu manzil tha, main us karvaan ki gard hoon
Rang tasveer-e kuhan me bhar ke dikhlade mujhe
Qissa aiyyam-e salaf ka keh ke tadpade mujhe
Main tera tohfa su-e Hindoostan le jaoonga
Khud yahan rota hoon, auron ko wahan rulwaoonga

Whose story is hidden in your ruins?
The silence of your footfall has a mode of expression.
Tell me of your sorrow—I too am full of pain;
I am the dust of that caravan whose goal you were.
Paint over this picture once more and show it to me;
Make me suffer by telling the story of ancient days.

I shall carry your gift to India;
I shall make others weep as I weep here.[5]

On a different note, struck by Europe's vitality,[6] Iqbal came to admire
the philosophies of Nietzsche and Bergson. Nietzsche's idea of the
Superman, of self-creation and self-assertion and Bergson's *elan
vital* inspired him to develop his own philosophy of *khudi*, in light
of Quranic teachings, the Prophet's traditions, and Arab and Persian
literature. 'The Western people,' he wrote, 'are distinguished in the
world for their power of action; and for this reason, a study of their
literature and philosophy is the best guide to an understanding of
the significance of life.'[7]

However, he diagnosed Europe's Achilles' heel as its materialism,
underpinned by Darwin's theory of the survival of the fittest. This led
him to believe that the West would destroy itself through excessive
competitiveness and unbridled expansion. In contrast, he believed
that Islam, which concealed the principle of true individualism and
humility, would come to humanity's rescue.

As his European sojourn made him 'hyperconscious of his
Muslim identity', he became increasingly convinced 'that the
progress of Indian Muslims lay not in imitating Europe but in
reforming and reviving the religious community they had been born
into.'[8] In Islam, Iqbal found a better model to combat excessive
competition, heartlessness, capitalism, and nationalism—all the
ills of the West. In Islam, Iqbal saw 'a successful opponent of the
race-idea, which is probably the hardest barrier in the way of the
humanitarian ideal.'[9]

To counterbalance European aggression, Iqbal began to advocate
Muslim solidarity as the political goal of the Islamic world. The main
poems he wrote on this theme, right after his return from Europe,
were *Shikwa* (1909) and *Shama-o-Shayer* (1912). When some
mullahs pointed out that his tone in *Shikwa* was too arrogant for
God's audience, he composed *Jawab-e Shikwa*, as a response to the
mullahs and to raise money for the Balkan Relief Fund in November

1912. *Khizr-e Rah* (1921) and *Tulu-e Islam* (1922) conclude the first phase of his Urdu poetry—both written as a reaction to the First World War and its aftermath.[10]

Meanwhile, soon after *Shama-o Shayer* (1912), Iqbal began to switch to Persian as the medium of his poetic compositions. Perhaps he was eager to reach a wider reading public beyond the Urdu-speaking Muslims of India. Persian became the tool 'that carried his message not only for the Muslim world but for all of humanity.'

Iqbal, later in life, wrote the following on his choice of Persian:

The language of Hind is sweet as sugar,
Yet sweeter is the fashion of Persian speech.
My mind was enchanted by its loveliness,
My pen became as a twig of the burning bush
Because of the loftiness of my thoughts,
Persian alone is suitable to them.[11]

Using Persian, Iqbal's message reached Iranian and Afghan readers, affording him some recognition outside India.[12] In 1933, on the shah of Afghanistan's invitation, he participated in academic deliberations in Kabul, along with Syed Sulaiman Nadwi[13] and Sir Ross Masood,[14] and helped formulate the country's education policy.

His poetry also influenced the Islamic Revolution of Iran. He inspired a generation of Iranian thinkers who created the intellectual basis of the Islamic Revolution of 1979. The Islamic Republic of Iran was 'the embodiment of Iqbal's dream', said Iran's supreme leader Sayyid Ali Khamenei in 1986. 'We are following the path shown to us by Iqbal,' he added. Another leader, Ali Shariati, in his book, *We and Iqbal*, compared him to anti-colonial activist Syed Jamal al-Afghani and the Indian poet Tagore. 'He fights with colonialism for the liberation of Muslim nations as Syed Jamal had done. He endeavours to save civilization as Tagore had tried to do from the tragedy of calculating reason and the pest of ambition,' he wrote.

Europe infused Iqbal's life with a singular mission—to revive the dynamism of Islam to save humanity from the ills of materialism. A transformed Iqbal stopped considering himself a poet; to his mind, he became a messenger who used poetry to awaken humanity, and especially Muslims, to its ills.

Iqbal's first poem in Persian was *Asrar-e Khudi* (*Secrets of the Self*), which was published in 1915. The book found readers in Iran, Afghanistan, and parts of Turkey and Russia. When R.A. Nicholson translated it into English in 1920, Iqbal became known in England and America too. Later on, the poem was translated into German and Italian.[15] Nicholson's translation brought Iqbal 'a rather tardy recognition in the form of a knighthood in 1922.'[16] Had Iqbal found a more influential supporter, as Tagore had found in W. B. Yeats and Ezra Pound,[17] he would have been better known in the West and could have possibly won the Nobel Prize.

After *Asrar-e Khudi*, Iqbal wrote another Persian poem, *Rumuz-e Bekhudi* (*Mysteries of Self-Denial*). A sequel to the former poem, it 'stressed the development of the human Ego or Personality and [held] Power and Courage as the ideals to be followed by Man to accomplish his great destiny.' In *Rumuz*, the poet places the service of mankind as the highest goal of mankind. *Rumuz* was followed by *Payam-e Mashriq* (*Message of the East*), a collection of odes and poems in reaction to Goethe's *Westostlicher Divan*, *Zabur-e Ajam* (*Psalms of the East*), and *Javed Nama* (*The Book of Eternity*). The last was a work styled on Dante's *Divine Comedy*.

Meanwhile, his Indian fans demanded of him poetry in Urdu. Responding to this call, he published a collection of Urdu poems, *Bal-e Jibril* (*The Wings of Gabriel*) in 1935 and *Zarb-e Kalim* (*The Stroke of the Rod of Moses*) in 1936. Through this, Iqbal achieved the status of the greatest Urdu poet in the twentieth century. Among Urdu poets, he is placed second only to Ghalib, who Iqbal himself admired as one of the language's greatest. In Persian, Iqbal created a name for himself in a language that was not his mother tongue;

he hadn't even visited Iran. Yet his Persian poems were widely read from Afghanistan to Iran.

* * *

In 1928, Iqbal delivered six lectures on Islam and philosophy in Madras, Mysore, Hyderabad, and Aligarh. These lectures were published in a collection titled *Six Lectures on the Reconstruction of Religious Thought in Islam*. Through his lectures, Iqbal intended to 'define and bring out the dynamic side of Islam'.

In order to do this, he created the concept of *khudi*, 'a unified and comprehensive conception of personality'. This became Iqbal's major contribution to the world of ideas. The Persian word 'khudi' means 'Ego' or 'Self'. It is not an Islamic word, nor derived from Islamic philosophy. For Iqbal, it came to be a mantra of action for any individual or nation to succeed. That was his message to the world. Iqbal believed in action and continuous struggle. One of his Persian couplets reads as follows:

Someone asked me,
Are you happy with the way this world is?
I said no.
The answer came,
Then go smash it up and make it the way you wish.

In his poetry, Iqbal has made the development of ego, or *khudi*, the essence of his message. Like the German philosopher Nietzsche, Iqbal rejected weakness and advocated the will to power:

A point of pure light which is called *khudi*,
Is a spark of life, under a covering of our clay.
By love it becomes lasting,
More living, more burning, more glowing.

Love enkindles its intrinsic worth,
And evolves its hidden potentialities.
Its nature acquires fire from love,
And learns to beautify the world by love . . .
Love is peace as war in the world,
It is the water of life as well as the sword of genuine steel . . .
Learn, therefore, the art of love and seek a beloved heart,
Seek to acquire the eye of the Prophet Noah and the patience of
Job.[18]

Khudi is Iqbal's universal message. It is not only for Indians or Pakistanis, it's for the entire world.

Was Iqbal's philosophy of *khudi* borrowed from or inspired by the works of German philosopher Nietzsche? There are undoubtedly similarities between the two views. But where they differ is in the goals of self-struggle. Iqbal advocated that this strength should be 'used for the service of humanity, and not for self-aggrandizement and vainglory.'[19]

About Nietzsche, Iqbal had a clear view. He declared in one of his Persian verses that Nietzsche had the heart of a Muslim and the brain of an infidel ('*Qalab-e Momin o dimagh-e kafir ast*').

In contrast to Nietzsche, in Iqbal's view, the Western man is not the Perfect Man. He might be the Superman of Nietzsche, having won over the land, the seas and the skies, but he is not the Perfect Man. Iqbal's Perfect Man is the one who leads mankind to the right path, who has the vision of Noah and the patience of Job.

When Iqbal published *Asrar-e Khudi*, many objected to his criticism of mysticism.[20] Even though Iqbal himself was a mystic, he was one after his own fashion. Iqbal denounced all mysticism that led to inaction, including Hafiz of Shiraz. He once wrote, '*Nikal kar khanqahon se ada kar rasm-e Shabbiri.*'[21]

The ideal sufi for Iqbal was Jalaluddin Rumi,[22] who could be aptly regarded as Iqbal's spiritual teacher. In one of his poems, Iqbal undertakes an imaginary journey with Rumi as his guide. They pass through the heavenly abodes of many saints and sages. They ask them questions and receive their wise answers. Remarkably, the first soul the poet and Rumi encounter is a Hindu saint Vishwa Mitra. This saint has dedicated thousands of years in devotion, has eyes brilliant with his spiritual knowledge, a black serpent around his neck and a halo of white hair. Vishwa Mitra asks Rumi: 'Who is this young man with you? His eyes betray an intense desire for life.' Rumi answers: 'This fellow is the seeker of truth. Though he lacks in maturity, his heart is full of a yearning. He is like an eagle who seeks to go round the seven heavens.' The sage is pleased to see the young seeker and asks him what condition prevails with the people of the East. 'An awakening of the spirit is visible among the Orientals,' Iqbal replies, 'as a result of which they do not feel helpless any longer, nor are they sunk in laziness and inactivity. I showed them the brilliance of the treasure bequeathed to them by their ancestors and this has moved in them a desire for noble achievements. They are no longer inclined to worship the idols of the West.'

When Iqbal asks Vishwa Mitra whether he has a message for the people of the East, the saint gives him the message of *amal* (action and work). After meeting Vishwa Mitra, Iqbal and Rumi meet Bharthari, and Zarathushtra, and then watch a dialogue between Gabriel (The Arch Angel) and Ibless (The Devil). When they come across Nietzsche, he asks Iqbal what nation he belongs to. 'Hindi [Indian],' Iqbal replies. 'You belong to an ease-loving nation,' Nietzsche says with a touch of disdain in his voice. 'The nation of which the wealthy members pass their nights in pleasure and the poor members die of hunger, can never remain alive—nations live by experience and ambition and by refraining.'[23]

There is universal acknowledgement of Iqbal's greatness as a poet. The problem starts when we come to his politics. Indian journalist and scholar Khushwant Singh once aptly said that if you forget Iqbal's politics, he was a great poet. However, Iqbal's message cannot be appreciated without understanding his politics. At the same time, one must note that Iqbal's politics was his response to his immediate circumstances. Otherwise, we might misconstrue his politics as only the ambition to create Pakistan.

Iqbal is credited with creating the idea of Pakistan. In truth, the two-nation theory was already common currency when Iqbal became its most vocal proponent. Iqbal the patriot embraced the Two-nation theory and devised the idea of a north-western Muslim province when he became convinced that Muslims faced extinction in India. He demanded the formation of a Muslim state in these words: 'I demand the formation of a consolidated Muslim state in the best interests of India and Islam. For India, it means security and peace resulting from an internal balance of power; for Islam, an opportunity to rid itself of the stamp that Arabian imperialism was forced to give it, to mobilize its law, its education, its culture, and to bring them into closer contact with its own original spirit and with the spirit of modern times.'

In his demand for a Muslim state, Iqbal, therefore, 'tacitly excluded the Muslims of Bengal, although they also formed a majority within their region and had in fact briefly enjoyed a separate state of their own.'[24] Iqbal's vision, however, did not remain limited to the Muslims of north-west India. In 1937, in a private and confidential letter to Jinnah, he wrote: 'Personally I think that the Muslims of north-west India and Bengal ought at present to ignore Muslim minority provinces. This is the best course to adopt in the interests of both Muslim majority and minority provinces.'[25]

Also, it must be noted that the truth is occluded when we say that Iqbal envisioned Pakistan, and Jinnah made his idea a reality. The truth is more complicated than that. The fact is that, initially, Jinnah hardly paid any attention to Iqbal's vision. Rather, Jinnah was suspicious of this entire project for a long time.[26] While Iqbal was announcing his call for Pakistan in Allahabad, Jinnah was in London at the Round Table Conference 'making a last-ditch effort on behalf of his cherished goals of constitutional reforms and protection of the rights of the Muslims within a unitary India.' It was the growing narrow-mindedness and violence of Hindu communalists and the shortsightedness of the other leaders within the Congress that gradually turned Jinnah into a zealous supporter of the idea of Pakistan.

Unlike Iqbal who was an idealist, Jinnah initially rejected the Two-nation theory. On August 11, 1947, in his very first speech to the constituent assembly of Pakistan, he did not say anything that implied that the Hindus and Muslims were two separate nations with two separate destinies. In fact, he did not even mention the word 'Islam' in his speech.[27] According to Jinnah, religion had 'nothing to do with the business of the State'. While Iqbal believed that Islam itself was no less a polity, Jinnah declared to his listeners:

'If you change your past and work together in a spirit that everyone of you, no matter to what community he belongs, no matter what relations he had with you in the past, no matter what is his colour, caste or creed, is first, second, and last a citizen of this State with equal rights, privileges, and obligations, there will be no end to the progress you will make. We should begin to work in that spirit and in course of time all these angularities of the majority and minority communities, the Hindu community and the Muslim community—because even as regards Muslims you have Pathans, Punjabis, Shias, Sunnis, and so on, and among the Hindus you have Brahmins, Vaishnavas, Khatris, also Bengalis, Madrasis, and so on—will vanish. We should keep that in front of us as our ideal and you will find that in the course of time Hindus would cease to be Hindus and Muslims would cease to be Muslims, not in the religious sense, because that is the personal faith of each individual, but in the political sense as citizens of the State.'[28]

Most probably Iqbal would not have seen it the same way. In his Allahabad address in 1930, he had asked the audience:

'Is religion a private affair? Would you like to see Islam, as a moral and political ideal, meeting the same fate in the world as Christianity has already met in Europe? Is it possible to retain Islam as an ethical ideal and to reject it as a polity in favour of national politics in which a religious attitude is not permitted to play any part?'

Yet, according to Iqbal's friend Edward Thompson, towards the end of his life the poet had developed reservations about the idea of Pakistan. I quote from one of his articles:

'In the *Observer* I once said that he [Iqbal] supported the Pakistan plan. Iqbal was a friend, and he set my misconception right. After speaking of his despondency at the chaos he saw coming "on my vast undisciplined and starving land" he went on to say that he thought the Pakistan plan would be disastrous to the British government, disastrous to the Hindu community, disastrous to the Moslem community. "But I am the President of the Muslim League and therefore it is my duty to support it".'[29]

Iqbal's first tragedy was that after his death, he was claimed as the national poet of Pakistan and was largely ignored in India. His second tragedy is that Pakistan, a country that was founded on the basis of religion, the second such nation in the world after Israel, practically forgot its own national poet. Similarly, in India, Iqbal remains a pariah and the majority of people know little about his life or his work.

Pondering why Iqbal's message has been lost to his countrymen, his son Dr Javed Iqbal writes that the left-wing 'intellectuals' of Pakistan have always regarded Iqbal as an obstinate barrier or a protective wall which has to be demolished before the Muslims can be made to accept their progressive views. The leftists 'pull Iqbal down whenever they get an opportunity.' On the other hand, he says, the right-wing 'intellectuals' of Pakistan, who claim to own Iqbal, represent him as a 'conservative' and a 'reactionary', and everything that is written on him by this group of 'intellectuals' fails to capture or interpret the exciting, dynamic, and forward-looking qualities of his thought.[30]

Yet, a third group considers Iqbal to be sympathetic to communism. He once said that if you simply add God to communist philosophy, it becomes Islam. Iqbal had the gall to put Marx on the pedestal of prophethood. He had even said that though Marx was not a prophet, he did produce a prophetic book, *Das Kapital*. No wonder then that Iqbal used the Russian Revolution of 1917 as a background in his poem '*Khidr Raah*' in which he conveyed to the working classes the importance of labour organization and class struggle:

Uth ke ab daure jahan ka aur hi andaaz hai
Mashriq-o Maghrib mein tere daur ka aghaaz hai

Get up now that the way of the world has changed
It is the beginning of your age in the East and West

To refute the charge of being a communist, Iqbal had written a letter that was published in the daily *Zamindar* on June 24, 1923:

'Someone . . . in some newspaper . . . has attributed Bolshevik ideas to me. Since in my opinion holding Bolshevik views amounts to the renunciation of Islam, it is my duty to refute this charge. I am a Muslim. It is my affirmed conviction, and this conviction is founded on sound and demonstrable reasoning, that the Quran has suggested the best cure for economic ailments of the different classes of human society . . .'[31]

Not just a communist, Iqbal has also been considered a communalist, especially in India. Was he communal? Did he hate the Hindus of India? Proud of his Brahmin ancestry, Iqbal believed in 'higher communalism', which precludes any feelings of ill will against any community while still stressing the uniqueness and specific character of each community.

Let us see what he said in his famous Allahabad address of 1930:

'The principle that each group is entitled to its free development on its own lines is not inspired by any feeling of narrow communalism. There are communalisms and communalisms. A community which is inspired by feelings of ill will towards other communities is low and ignoble. I entertain the highest respect for the customs, laws, religious and social institutions of other communities. Nay, it is my duty, according to the teachings of the Quran, even to defend their places of worship, if need be. Yet I love the communal group which is the source of my life and behaviour; and which has formed me what I am by giving me its religion, its literature, its thought, its culture, and thereby recreating its whole past as a living operative factor, in my present consciousness. Even the authors of the Nehru Report recognize the value of this higher aspect of communalism.'

The fact is that Iqbal's poetry was used by different groups to serve their own interests. His poetry had so many facets that he seemed to assume different roles in different phases of his poetry: He was a staunch nationalist, a vocal communist, an advocate of Hindu–Muslim unity, a humanist, a believer in Islamic revivalism, a freedom fighter, and an advocate of international brotherhood.

No Urdu poet has shed as many tears on India's misery as Iqbal. He had warned his countrymen by these words:

Watan ki fikr kar nadan musibat aane wali hai
Teri barbadiyon ke mashware hain aasmano me

Be worried about the fate of your country, you fool, I see trouble
    brewing as,
The skies are contemplating your destruction.

In order to understand Iqbal, we must see him at three levels: As an Indian, as a Muslim, and as a humanist advocating universal brotherhood. As an Indian, Iqbal's patriotism is indubitable. '*Saare jahan se achha Hindustan hamara,*' Iqbal declared blatantly. His poetry is full of patriotic fervour and a pride for India's ancient civilization. In one of his couplets, Iqbal represented Ram as the leader of the East. Even in *Javed Nama*, a book of Persian poems, Iqbal presents a scene that involves Jesus Christ and Gautama Buddha sitting in front of Allah—from a narrow Islamic perspective, this would be considered heresy.

Iqbal died in 1938, nearly a decade before India was painfully partitioned and Pakistan created. With the march of time, Iqbal slowly disappeared from political discourse. His vision was forgotten in Pakistan as the country swung between the birth pangs of democracy and the smothering grip of military dictatorship. Interestingly, that seems to be changing now. Many Pakistanis are showing a revival of interest in Iqbal. For example, Imran Khan, former cricketer and currently one of Pakistan's frontline political leaders, has expressed his love and admiration for Iqbal in his biography, *Pakistan: A Personal Journey* (Bantam Books, 2011). In this book, he devotes a chapter to Iqbal titled, 'Rediscovering Iqbal: Pakistan's Symbol and a Template for Our Future'.

'It is difficult to find a poet or thinker of Iqbal's calibre who has championed the cause of justice for the oppressed and wronged people of the world as passionately as he did,' writes Khan in his autobiography. 'If we follow Iqbal's teaching, we can reverse the growing gap between the Westernized rich and traditional poor that helps fuel fundamentalism.'

But no matter how much we analyse Iqbal's politics and poetry, and even his life, Iqbal the man remains veiled in mystery. This enigmatic mystic and seer had once said about himself:

> *Main khud bhi nahin apni haqiqat ka shanasha*
> *Gehra hai mere bahr-e khyalaat ka paani*

> I myself am not aware of my own true self,
> There's a great depth in the ocean of my thoughts

And this:

> *Iqbal bhi Iqbal se agaah nahi hai*
> *Khuchh iss mein tamaskhar nahi, wallah nahi hai*

> Even Iqbal is not aware of Iqbal,
> There is no joke in it, I swear by God

People may argue about Iqbal's status as an Indian or Pakistani, as a Muslim poet or a communist, or even a humanist. But in his own lifetime, Iqbal had outgrown all categories. He is a shared heritage for the whole world and we ought to celebrate him as such.

Dhoondta phirta hoon aye Iqbal apne aapko
Aap hi goya musafir, aap hi manzil hun mein

I keep looking, oh Iqbal, for myself,
As if I'm the traveller as well as the destination.

PART ONE
1877–1905

Beginnings

1

The Son of an Untutored Philosopher

I'm of a pure Somnathi extraction
My ancestors were idol worshippers
—Iqbal

In a wide green field, a crowd chases a pretty, white pigeon.[1] The pigeon circles above the heads of the chasing party. The crowd, in a mad dash, tries to capture the bird in flight. Now the bird flies high and now it descends down, teasing those who are sprinting after it. At last the pigeon swoops down into the lap of a tall and handsome 40-year-old man who accepts it as a gift from the heavens.

Shaikh Noor Muhammad, the man dreaming this dream, wakes up with a smile in a house near Do Darwaza Mosque in Kashmiri Mohalla in Sialkot,[2] a border town of the Punjab located by the Chenab river, at the foot of the Kashmir hills.[3]

It is a cold night in early November and he sees his wife Imam Bibi sleeping peacefully next to him under a warm blanket. She is expecting again and he interprets the dream to be a divine indication that he will be blessed with a son whose good fortune it will be to serve mankind.[4]

The tall Kashmiri Noor Muhammad, red of skin and with a penetrating gaze, is known for his simplicity in the community. He has a peaceful and affectionate nature. When he was growing up, he could not study at the *maktab*, the local school; but this did not stop him from teaching himself the alphabets. Because of his own efforts he becomes literate and is able to read books in Urdu and Persian.

He is the eleventh child of his father, Shaikh Muhammad Rafiq, the only child to have survived from his father's second wife. After him, another son, Ghulam Muhammad, was born. He grew up to be an overseer in the department of canals in the British government.

Noor Muhammad and his family have always lived together with his younger brother Ghulam Muhammad's family. The house near the Do Darwaza Mosque was bought in 1861 by their father Muhammad Rafiq and they have been living in this house ever since. It has been expanded over time to accommodate new members of the family.[5]

Noor Muhammad loves to spend a good deal of his time among sufis and Islamic scholars. By virtue of keeping such pious company, he has come to have a good grasp of *Shariat* and *Tariqat*. His knowledge of *tasawwuf* (mysticism) is so deep that his friends call him *Anpadh Falsafi* (Untutored Philosopher).[6] He regularly studies and recites the Quran which he considers to be the ultimate source of all bliss, worldly and for the hereafter.

By profession, he is a tailor and embroiderer. In his early career, he helped his father, Shaikh Muhammad Rafiq, in his *dhassa* and *loi* (blankets and shawls) business but when an official rents him a Singer sewing machine, a mechanical marvel of its time, he turns to tailoring. His wife, Imam Bibi, disapproves of the sewing machine when she learns that the machine was bought with illicit money. Noor Muhammad returns the machine to the official and he strikes out on his own as a cap embroiderer, and makes Muslim prayer caps. The enterprise becomes a success and soon he employs other workmen in his workshop. By virtue of his popular merchandise, people start addressing him as Shaikh Natthu Topianwale.[7] In the later stages of his life, he slowly loses interest in his business and takes a deeper interest in mysticism. He ignores his business and, with time, his business suffers decline.

Noor Muhammad's is a family of migrants in Sialkot. What he has heard is that his ancestors came from an old Kashmiri Brahmin family. One of his early ancestors, a Kashmiri Pandit, converted to Islam in the fifteenth century.[8] His gotra was Sapru.[9]

Even Noor Muhammad doesn't know how or why his family moved from Kashmir to Sialkot. But he has heard stories of migration from his father and from his grandfather. These are not very appealing stories. These are stories of poverty, desperation, and struggle.

His elders tell him that in the five thousand year old history of Kashmir, twenty-one Hindu families ruled over that famed piece of paradise on earth. Droughts, floods, palace intrigues, and civil war weakened this Hindu dominance in the eleventh and twelfth centuries. Finally, Zulqadir Khan Tatari's invasion finished the last family of Hindu rulers.

When Muslims became predominant in Kashmir in the thirteenth century, the Brahmins of the province did not pay much attention to the knowledge or languages of Muslims. The bias reflected a kind of social obscurantism among the Brahmins who considered Persian the language of the *malechch*[10] and prevented their community members from studying Persian or working for the government of the Muslim rulers. Those who defied this social practice were disowned by the community.

However, Kashmir's Sultan Zainul Abidin Budshah (who ruled between 1420 and 1470 AD) encouraged Hindus to study Persian and allocated many scholarships and allowances for Hindu students.[11] The first group of Brahmins in Kashmir who courted the Persian language and literature (which had become the court language in 1298) and earned the trust of their Muslim rulers were called Saprus. This word denotes a person who starts reading early.[12] For Kashmiri Brahmins, the word Sapru became a derogatory expression, used to describe fellow Brahmins who had left behind their customs to embrace Islamic languages and knowledge. Slowly, as the category Sapru crystallized into a gotra in the Kashmiri Hindu community.[13]

One of Noor Muhammad's early ancestors, known as Hazrat Baba Lol Hajj or Loli Haji (Lover of Hajj)[14] was one of Kashmir's famous sages. According to Kashmiri folklore, he performed Hajj several times on foot, and came to be known as Lol Hajj. He belonged to a village called Chaku Bargana Aadoon. For twelve years, he stayed outside Kashmir and trekked from country to country. It is said that he had left Kashmir because he did not enjoy cordial relations with his wife.[15] According to one legend, he was cross-eyed and bow-legged and hence a target of his wife's derision. Heartbroken, Baba not only left his family but also gave up on the world and turned into a mystic.[16]

When he came back to Kashmir, he received a divine signal to become a disciple of a sufi pir named Hazrat Baba Nasruddin.[17] Nasruddin, in turn, was a disciple of Hazrat Nooruddin Wali.[18] Baba Lol Hajj spent the rest of his life in the company of Baba Nasruddin and he is buried close to his master's grave.

Noor Muhammad does not know exactly when his ancestors migrated from Kashmir to Sialkot.[19] This migration most probably happened towards the end of the eighteenth century or in the early nineteenth century. This was the time when Afghan power was declining in Kashmir and Sikh power was on the rise. The Sikhs, having established rule in Punjab, drove out the Afghans from Kashmir with the help of Raja Gulab Singh. Between 1837–39, Gulab Singh extended his rule by seizing Ladakh and Baltistan from Tibet. Seven years later, the Sikhs lost Kashmir to the British in the Anglo–Sikh wars. Raja Gulab Singh offered the British 750,000 pounds (Rs 75 lakhs) to continue ruling Kashmir. In 1846, the two parties signed the Treaty of Amritsar—Kashmir was made an independent state under Raja Gulab Singh.[20]

Sikh rule over Kashmir (1819–1864) inaugurated a tragic phase for Kashmiris. After the Treat of Amritsar, the Dogra rulers who now possessed the state 'set upon a policy of unlimited cruelty on the helpless Kashmiris, with the result that many Kashmiri families migrated from Kashmir to the Punjab.'[21] The Sikhs had treated

Kashmiris like animals. For instance, if a Sikh murdered a Kashmiri, he was legally bound to pay a fine to the state which ranged between sixteen and twenty rupees. Four rupees were paid to the family of the victim if he was a Hindu and two rupees were paid to the victim's family if he was a Muslim.[22] The local people were burdened by heavy taxes. To escape their dire situation, many migrated to Punjab in a state of penury. In those days, the punishment for cow slaughter was hanging by death. If a Muslim was found to have slaughtered a cow, he would be dragged through the streets of Srinagar and then be hanged or burnt unto death. In 1831, during the reign of Kanwar Sher Singh, a deadly drought reduced the local population from eight to two lakhs.[23]

Fleeing such painful circumstances, one of the migrants was either Noor Muhammad's great-grandfather, Shaikh Jamaluddin, or his four sons, namely, Shaikh Abdurrehman, Shaikh Muhammad Ramzan, Shaikh Muhammad Rafiq, and Shaikh Abdullah. It is also possible that Shaikh Jamaluddin, along with his four sons, migrated to the Punjab through Jammu. Of the four brothers, three lived in Sialkot and Shaikh Abdullah lived in Mauza Jaith Eke.

Noor Muhammad's wife Imam Bi was known as Beji amongst the relatives.[24] She comes from a Kashmiri family from a village in Sialkot district. She is illiterate but god-fearing and devout, and is very particular about performing namaz. She takes care of the household affairs and folks in the neighbourhood respect her because of her helpful nature. Even though she is a housewife, she is a bit of a social worker. She can't help but settle neighbourhood disputes and when her friends ask her to keep their cash or ornaments in her safe custody she takes on this responsibility gladly. She also secretly helps the poor in her locality. It is no surprise that their son Shaikh Ata Muhammad[25] teases her by saying that she practices *gupt daan*, secret donations.[26]

Now that Imam Bi is pregnant again, Noor Muhammad wonders if it will be a boy or a girl this time. His dream of a pigeon falling into his lap gives him the intuition that this child will bring him good luck and will make a name for himself and his family.

Noor Muhammad closes his eyes and prays to Allah for his child's safe delivery and survival. Imam Bi and he had lost a child during childbirth earlier.

He recalls an incident that marks a painful phase in his family's history. It so happened that his brother had only girls, no boys. But like most mothers, his brother's wife desired boys too. Once, both Imam Bi and Ghulam's wife got pregnant nearly at the same time. Imam Bi gave birth to a boy whereas Ghulam's wife had a baby girl. Imam Bi knew that her sister-in-law had desired a male child. To cheer up her sister-in-law, she suggested an exchange of babies. The swapping of babies took place but unfortunately the male child died within a few months. Imam Bi bowed her head before Allah's will and returned the girl child to her sister-in-law.

On Friday, November 9, 1877,[27] when the dawn is yet to break, Noor Muhammad and Imam Bi are blessed with a son in one of the dark and narrow rooms of their house. Remembering his dream, Noor Muhammad names him Muhammad Iqbal,[28] indicating luck and fortune.

Noor Muhammad beams with happiness when he holds Iqbal in his hands for the first time. The cute little thing is fair, bonny, and ruddy like a cherry. With the tender love of a father, he kisses the boy on his forehead, folds him in a rug carefully, and returns him to his smiling mother. It is time for the *fajr* prayers and he needs this moment to thank Allah for this beautiful gift.[29]

2

A Pair of Leeches

The powerful man creates environments; the feeble have to adjust themselves to it.

—Iqbal

Could a pair of leeches change a child's fate?

In Iqbal's case, it did.

While Iqbal, the child, grows up well in an environment of love and affection among his extended family members in Sialkot, he encounters a health problem when he is about two years old. He suffers from an ailment and apparently it is something to do with his blood. In a family unused to modern medicine, it is believed that the child's health will be restored by having leeches suck out his infected blood.

Iqbal's mother, Imam Bi, opts for this traditional treatment. A pair of leeches is applied close to the child's right eye. The leeches suck away the infected blood and the child is cured but his vision is irreversibly damaged.[1] At the time of the treatment, it is not discovered but as Iqbal grows older he experiences a progressive decline in the vision of his right eye.[2]

This act of quackery will have unintended consequences that will force Iqbal to choose a path different from what he once wished to follow.

For now, Iqbal's father is more concerned about his education and his future. At the time of Iqbal's birth, twenty long years have passed since the Revolt of 1857, but the shadows of this watershed event have eclipsed the future of Muslims in British India. The Revolt has left the Muslim community in the grip of despondency, unsure of its future. Though both Hindu and Muslim soldiers, rulers, zamindars, and peasants revolted against the British occupiers, the brunt of British reprisals were largely borne by the Muslim community.

Sialkot, which was a small town compared to metropolises like Lahore or Bombay or Delhi, did not remain unaffected by the consequences of the revolt. After the British quelled the uprising, they hanged two officers and blew 139 soldiers to smithereens with their canons. Most of these victims were Muslims. The British also imposed a collective fine of fifty thousand rupees on the residents of Sialkot.

Even though Iqbal's father Noor Muhammad was not directly involved in the revolt, he, like all his contemporaries, senses that Indian Muslims face troubled times. His younger brother Shaikh Ghulam Muhammad has become a government servant. It is possible that Ghulam Muhammad has come under the influence of Sir Syed Ahmed Khan's Aligarh Movement[3] through which Khan had been trying to restore British trust in India's Muslims.

At this time, Indian Muslims face a situation of cultural and political decline. Persian and Arabic, their languages of literature and governance are no longer taught in educational institutions. Moreover, Christian missionaries, emboldened by British hegemony, begin to publicly dencounce Islam. Attacks are also being made on the honour of the prophet, Muhammad. In such an unfavourable milieu, Muslims begin to make their own arrangements for the religious education of their children to safeguard their culture. In the absence of government-aided religious schools for Muslim children, religious scholars—the ulema—open *maktabs* in mosques or operate them from their own houses.[4]

Sialkot has four such schools run by Moulvi Ghulam Murtaza,

Maulana Abu Abdullah, Ghulam Hasan, and Moulvi Muzammil where Arabic and theology are taught to children. Maulana Syed Mir Hasan's Madrastaul Uloom provides education in Arabic and Persian literature.[5]

When Iqbal turns six, Imam Bi sends him to a local mosque, Masjid Hassamuddin, to learn to recite the Quran. The instructor at the mosque, Umar Shah, teaches young boys and girls in the mosque's compound. Iqbal joins the rank of his pupils. The 6-year-old Iqbal is sweet but extremely precocious and naughty. He laughs a lot and makes others laugh with his pranks.

When Iqbal is a little older, Noor Muhammad brings him to Syed Mir Hasan's Madrastaul Uloom for enrollment. Hasan is not only a prominent proponent of the Aligarh Movement in Sialkot, he is also a vernacular Muslim teacher in the local Scotch Mission School. He was the one who had given Shaikh Noor Muhammad the moniker 'Untutored Philosopher'. When Iqbal is a little over four, Hasan takes note of the child's brilliance and precociousness, and persuades Noor Mumammad to send him off to Scotch Mission School to receive a modern education.[6]

Iqbal is in his early stages of education when Noor Muhammad's family becomes temporarily destitute. His business has declined and as a result, to supplement the family income, little Iqbal, along with his older brother Ata Muhammad, has to work in a *papier mache* factory. In return, they receive rotis to eat. This episode of misfortune briefly halts Iqbal's education.

Iqbal loves his elder brother intensely. His brother commands great respect in the household. His help will be crucial in the future for Iqbal's education in India and abroad. A tall and strong-bodied man with an awe-inspiring personality, Ata Muhammad is stern by temperament. Interestingly, he cools down as quickly as he loses his temper. He loves to dress up in Western clothes.

Ata Muhammad gets married into a Rathod family. With some help, he gets a job in the British Army as an engineer. Soon, he starts helping his father financially. This turns the family's fortune around.

After the brief lull, Noor Muhammad's business starts to flourish again and Iqbal goes back to school.[7]

In 1885, Iqbal passes his grade one exam from the Scotch Mission School. He stands first in his class. After passing this exam, Mir Hasan starts tutoring him in a room near Masjid Hassamuddin.

Iqbal enjoys a loving atmosphere at home. His mother Imam Bi plays an important role in his development. He loves her dearly. When Iqbal will grow up and study in Lahore, and later on in England and Germany, she will be the reason for his visits to Sialkot. She will eagerly wait for his letters from London.

Besides his mother[8], his sister-in-law too dotes on him. When she gives birth to a baby girl, Barkat Bi, little Iqbal loves her intensely and carries her around in his arms and feeds her. He also has two sisters now, Kareem Bi and Zeenat Bi, to play with and entertain.[9]

Young Iqbal develops a deep interest in poetry. He has a sweet voice and often buys books like Rumi's *Masnavi* and anthologies of Punjabi ballads. He reads them aloud lyrically to entertain the women at home in the afternoons and at night when they weave *azarbands*— cotton strings for pyjamas—to be sold in Noor Muhammad's shop.

Iqbal is also allowed to attend lectures about the metaphysical teachings of the Hispano-Arab philosopher Ibn Arabi (1165–1240), which are hosted at his house. This exposes the young mind to matters of mysticism and spirituality. Arabi taught that *tawhid*—the oneness of God—had two meanings: the spiritual and the philosophical. The spirual meaning demands that every Muslim seek union with God. The philosophical meaning signified the concept of *Wahdatul Wujood*—pantheistic monotheism. If the universe was the outer aspect of God, God himself was its inner aspect. In that sense, Arabi's views came to be regarded as a propagation of Greek pantheism. When Iqbal is growing up, followers of Sufism, including Iqbal's father, regard Arabi very highly. Yet, Iqbal will challenge Arabi's thesis as a young scholar in the coming years.[10]

Once, over dinner, while discussing a friend who has recently passed away, Iqbal's father faints at the mere thought that his friend might have been separated from his divine maker for too long. He remains unconscious for several hours that night. Incidents like this leave a deep imprint on the psyche of a young Iqbal who learns of Sufism directly from his father.

At the same time, Iqbal is serious and diligent towards his studies. A very intelligent and hardworking student, he often burns the midnight oil. Once his mother, whom he lovingly calls Beji, finds him working by the lamp. It is almost midnight. She calls out to him a couple of times but he does not reply. Concerned, she goes over to check on him only to find that the boy has fallen asleep studying.

Even though he is way ahead of his classmates in school in terms of his intelligence, he is not just a book worm. He also loves sports and his pranks and sharp repartee quickly endear him to his classmates.

Iqbal's wit slowly becomes legendary. Once he enters class late. When the teacher asks him why he is late, pat comes his reply: '*Janaab, Iqbal der se hi aaya karta hai.*' ('Sir, it takes time for good fortune to strike.') The teacher is hugely impressed by his presence of mind.

Once, Iqbal's teacher Mir Hasan leaves his house to run an errand. Iqbal is with him, and there is also a little child named Ehsaan. Hasan asks Iqbal to carry the child in his arms. Iqbal obliges but after going some distance, he gets tired. He puts the child on a shop's counter to relax for a while. When Hasan has gone a little ahead he turns back and to his surprise finds that Iqbal isn't with him. He makes his way back to find Iqbal catching his breath in front of a shop. Hasan asks him, pointing to the child, Ehsaan:

Is ki bardshat bhi dushwari hai?

Is he too much of a burden to carry?

Iqbal mouths a spontaneous line in response:

Tera Ehsaan bada bhaari hai!

This favour is far too heavy for me.

Rearing pigeons, kite-flying, and physical exercise in akhadas are some of Iqbal's extra-curricular interests. His interest in rearing pigeons will continue throughout his life. He sits on top of the roof and enjoys seeing the flight of pigeons for hours. He can tell a pigeon's type or breed from the way it flies—this is something he has picked up from Lalu Pehalwan, a local wrestling talent.

When Iqbal sees pigeons spreading their wings in the sky, he feels as if he too is in flight with them, exploring the skies. In the pigeon's flight he witnesses a kind of dignity that he finds enchanting.[11] In his later years, he will continue his love affair with pigeons, will rear pigeons of different breeds and will be fond of a particular pigeon from the land of Prophet Muhammad. He will even compose a poem in its memory when it will fly into the beyond.

3

Seeds of Mysticism

The question is not whether miracles did or did not happen. This is only a question of evidence which maybe interpreted in various ways. The real question is whether belief in miracles is useful to a community. I say it is; since such a belief intensifies the sense of the supernatural which holds together primitive societies as well as those societies (e.g. Islam) whose nationality is ideal and not territorial. Looked at from the standpoint of social evolution, then, belief in miracles appears to be almost a necessity.

—Iqbal, *Stray Reflections*

It is the dead of night and an 11-year-old Iqbal is asleep in his room. An unusual noise wakes him up. When he lifts his head off the pillow, he sees his mother going down the steps of their house. Curious, he gets up and follows her like an automaton to the front door of the house. The door is half ajar and streaming through it is a shaft of light.[1]

Iqbal finds his mother standing at the door; she is looking out. Standing behind her, he too looks out. A bizarre sight awaits him outside the door—his father, Noor Muhammad, is sitting in an open space, surrounded by a halo-like illumination.

He wants to go out to his father and touch and feel that halo that hovers over his head. When he tries, his mother holds him back.

'Son, go back to your room and sleep,' she whispers into his ears. He does not want to go back to his bed, without solving the mystery of this sight. It takes a little persuasion from his mother to make him return to his bed.

Early in the morning when Iqbal wakes up, the first thing he remembers is the curious incident of the night. He wants to quickly get up and run up to his father and ask him what was going on at night. Why was he sitting outside in the dead of the night all alone? What was the halo all about?

Iqbal reaches the place where he saw his father meditating at night. He finds his mother sitting next to his father. He is busy explaining his trance to her.

'A caravan from Kabul that was approaching the city is in great trouble, and has had to halt twenty-five miles away from our own town. This caravan has been travelling with an ailing person whose condition has become serious. This is preventing them from journeying further so I must go immediately to help them,' his father says.

His father collects some medicines and sets out in the direction of the caravan along with Iqbal. On the way he is worried about whether he'll be able to reach the patient soon enough. The tonga luckily reaches the caravan's camping site without any delay. Iqbal finds a brooding silence enveloping the site and people at the camp wear a worried look on their faces; they are concerned about the deteriorating condition of the ailing person. The caravan seems to be of an affluent family that must be making its way to the city for the patient's treatment.

When they arrive at the site, Iqbal's father seeks out the leader of the caravan and asks to be taken to the sick fellow. The men who receive him stand baffled: how could this stranger know about the condition of the patient? No one could have informed him of the man's illness. No one in the caravan knows the stranger who demands to see their patient.

Awed, they escort Noor Muhammad to the patient. Iqbal follows his father into the tent. The sick man lies on a makeshift bed, moaning and crying in pain. His condition is undoubtedly serious. He suffers from a horrible disease that has eaten up portions of his limbs. Anyone can see that his body is slowly being consumed by the disease.

His father dips his hand in his bag and takes out an ash-like substance. He smears the affected parts of the patient's body with this ashen dust.

After the treatment, he gets up, rubbing his hands in satisfaction. 'The patient will live and be healed of his ailment soon,' he tells the leader, 'but only God has the power to restore his lost limbs.'

The people surrounding the mysterious healer are too awed to believe the words of this stranger messiah. Iqbal himself, though he does not confide in his father, is skeptical about the entire episode.

In the next twenty-four hours, the patient's condition improves miraculously. He expresses confidence that he will be cured. The people in the caravan are joyous to hear this good news.

The leader offers a substantial fee to Noor Muhammad but he refuses the offer and they return home.

A few days later, the caravan reaches Sialkot and the patient is found cured of his suffering.[2]

Mystical experiences like this begin to shape Iqbal's fecund mind—this is a phase of his learning that comes straight from his father's teachings.[3]

Iqbal's father, being deeply spiritual, has spent a few months in seclusion under the influence of a sufi or wali. Whatever he gains from the experience, he passes it on to Iqbal.[4]

Once a beggar appears at the family's doorstep. The insolent fellow is asked to leave but he refuses to budge. This behaviour enrages Iqbal, who is just entering adolescence. He walks up to and slaps the poor man. The effect of the whack is such that the 'harvest of his beggary spills from his hands'.

Iqbal's father is at home and watching his young son behave in this rude manner, tears begin to roll down his cheeks. He beckons Iqbal to come near him. 'What did you do to that poor man?' the old man asks, admonishing Iqbal on this bad conduct.

'What you just did to the poor man is disgraceful behaviour for a Muslim youth,' he reprimands him. 'I am convinced now that I have failed as a father to raise a young man of character. On the day of Ressurection the beggar will cry and the Prophet will ask me why the young Muslim entrusted to my care, that heap of clay, did not become a man?'[5] Noor Muhammad begins to sob, shaking his head in disbelief.

Iqbal feels so ashamed at his arrogant act that he wants to go and bury himself in the ground. I will remember this lesson, he resolves in his heart. Throughout his life, Iqbal will be kind to the poor and the destitute.

Besides teaching his son to be humane and compassionate, Iqbal's father insists on one more thing—he must study the Quran. Everyone in the family reads the Quran daily and so does Iqbal. Once his father tells him a secret: 'Whenever you read the Quran, read it as if it were revealed to you. When you read the Quran, imagine that Allah is talking only to you.'

Iqbal takes note of this instruction from his father. All his life, he will read the Quran on a regular basis and he will read it with complete dedication, he makes a commitment to himself.

For his father, Iqbal is a 'bud burst forth from Muhammad's branch'. Once, his father asks him for compensation for the hard work he has put into Iqbal's upbringing. When Iqbal asks him what that compensation could be, his father says: 'The compensation of my labour on you will be that you serve the cause of Islam.' To Iqbal's contentment, his father will confirm on his deathbed that Iqbal has adequately compensated his efforts with his inspiring poetry.

4

The Birth of a Poet

A prophet is only a practical poet
—Iqbal, *Stray Reflections*

Sialkot is known in the Punjab as a city of enterprising people. The spirit of its enterprising soil seeps into the bloodstream of Noor Muhammad. By 1889, Noor Muhammad's family is doing well financially. He has bought a two-storey building adjacent to his paternal house. He has also bought and added two shops to the back of the house that opens into the Bazaar Chudigaraan. He adds another shop to the property and redevelops the building into a three-storey structure. Besides these developments, he also acquires another house in Bazaar Chudigaraan and rents it out.[1] Iqbal grows up navigating his way through the dank and narrow lanes and bylanes of Bazaar Chudigaraan.

In 1891, Iqbal finishes middle school and enters class nine. At this time, he is fourteen or fifteen years old. He is already using expressions that are in a certain *behr* or *wazan* (metre). As he becomes close to Syed Mir Hasan, his scholar teacher, he starts to compose poetry more frequently and takes guidance from his teacher.[2]

Urdu has become so popular in the Punjab that every city holds literary discussions and boasts of poetry recitation groups. Sialkot too occasionally holds small gatherings of Urdu poets called mushairas. Iqbal starts writing ghazals for the locally held mushairas. He has been participating in them since he was in class eight. He also has developed an ear for music—he is aware of its technical aspects—and particularly loves Indian classical music—a trait that probably accounts for the music and rhythmic harmony in his poetry.

At this stage, Iqbal has begun to be aware of his powerful personality. He often writes this inscription in his books: 'Steal not the book for fear of shame / Look down and see my powerful name—Muhammad Iqbal.'[3]

In 1893, when he is sixteen, two crucial events occur in Iqbal's life. First, he passes the matriculation exam in first division, winning a medal and a scholarship; secondly, at the insistence of his family he is married to Karim Bi. She comes from a wealthy Kashmiri family in western India, the eldest daughter of Dr Ata Muhammad, the state surgeon of Gujarat. Karim Bi's father is a wealthy but devout man. Iqbal's family, in a stroke of pragmatism, fixes this match keeping in my mind the wealth and influence of Dr Ata Muhammad, who is known all over the state.

Though Iqbal was not ready to be married, he had to obey the wishes of his family.[4] The marriage takes place despite the age difference between the bride and groom—Iqbal is sixteen years old whereas Kareem Bi is nineteen.[5] In the coming years, their loveless marriage will result in painful estrangement and two children. They will officially separate after twenty long years.

On May 4, 1893, when Iqbal is about to start on his wedding procession from Sialkot to Gujarat, he receives news of his matriculation results.

The two events act as countervailing forces in Iqbal's life: one allows him to move to the next stage of his educational journey and the other imprisons him in a relationship that is not of his choice. The latter will bedevil his future, restrict his carefree soul, and torment his heart. His matrimonial obligations will prevent him from pursuing relationships with two beautiful women he meets in Europe.

On May 5, 1893, he takes admission in Scotch Mission College for intermediate classes. He adopts the *takhallus* 'Iqbal' during the first year of his F.A. (Grade 12).

His earliest poems are published in Delhi's *Zabaan* magazine in the issue of November 1894. The last couplet of one of his published ghazals in *Zabaan* is:

Garam hum par jo kabhi hota hai woh bu't Iqbal
Hazrat-e Daagh ke ashaar suna dete hain

Whenever that idol gets cross with me, Iqbal
I recite to her the couplets of respected Daagh

Emboldened by his early success, Iqbal decides to approach Daagh Dehalvi, ustaad to the nizam of Deccan, and the most famous Urdu poet of his era, for mentoring. Though they are thousands of kilometres apart from each other, the relationship of master and disciple is established through correspondence.[6] Iqbal sends Daagh some of his ghazals for correction. Daagh accepts him as his student and sends back Iqbal's poems with comments and advice.[7]

There is nothing extraordinary in this mentor-mentee relationship: Daagh is so popular as a poet throughout India that hundreds of emerging poets send him their compositions for advice by Dak. The demand for Daagh's mentorship is so high that he has to establish a separate department with dedicated staff to look after the flood of poetic correspondence.

After a brief correspondence, Daagh concludes that this young poet from Punjab is extraordinarily talented. He writes to him that there is not much he can do to improve Iqbal's compositions. Consequently, the correspondence does not last very long. Regardless, Daagh will remember Iqbal throughout his life and so will Iqbal.[8]

Though the two will never meet in person, Iqbal will continue to address Daagh as his mentor.[9] Iqbal expresses his strong desire to meet Daagh in the following manner:

Yehi hai jo shauq-e mulaqat-e hazrat
Toh dekhenge ek bar mulk-e dakan bhi

If this is the intensity of desire to meet His Highness
I will surely visit the Deccan at least once

In a ghazal published in 1896, Iqbal pays tribute to Daagh in the
following words:

Naseem o Tishna hi Iqbal kuchh nazaan nahin un par
Mujhe fakhr hai shagirdi-e Daagh-e sukhandaan ka

It's not that only Naseem and Tishna are proud of him, Iqbal
I too am proud of being a disciple of Daagh, the master of verses

And in yet another ghazal of the same period, he has this to say
about his master:

Janaab-e Daagh ki Iqbal yeh saari karamat hai
Tere jaise to kar dala, sukhandaan bhi sukhanwar bhi

You owe it to the miracle of Daagh, O Iqbal
That a worthless poet like you has become a master versifier

In 1895, Iqbal passes the F.A. exam in second division from Scotch
Mission College.[10] After this, for higher education, he has to move
to Lahore since Scotch Mission College does not offer B.A. classes
at this time.

Iqbal is reluctant to leave his family and friends behind in Sialkot
and proceed to Lahore for higher studies but his teacher Syed Mir
Hasan prevails upon him, prodding him to make the move. He agrees
to do so with a heavy heart.

Iqbal will remain close to his teacher Hasan for as long as Hasan
lives, and in 1923, when the British government decides to knight

Iqbal, he will insist that he will only accept the title if his teacher Mir Hasan too is honored with a title. To please Iqbal, the British government confers the title of 'Shamsul Ulema' on Hasan.

This is how Iqbal will pay tribute to his teacher when he dies:

Mujhe Iqbal us Sayyid ke ghar se faiz pahuncha hai
Pale jo uske daaman me, wahi kuchh ban ke nikle ga

I, Iqbal, have benefitted from the house of that Sayyid [Mir Hasan]
Those whom he nurtured, have achieved some status in life

5

A Scholar in Lahore

It is determination, not brains, that succeeds in life
—Iqbal, *Stray Reflections*

September, 1898. A tall, well-built, fair-skinned Iqbal with a drooping moustache alights from a passenger train at the Lahore Railway Station. His face has an awe-inspiring quality to it. The young man adorns a white shalwar-kameez over which a small waistcoat fits snugly; on his head he wears a Roman cap.

His friend Shaikh Gulab Deen is at the station to receive him. They hug each other and then Gulab Deen takes his friend to his house at Bhati Darwaza.

Lahore has been the political and cultural capital of the Punjab for centuries—it served as a regional capital for the Shahi kingdoms in the eleventh century, the Mughal empire in the sixteennth century, and the Sikh empire in the early nineteenth century. It is the capital of the Punjab region under the British Raj in the mid nineteenth and early twentieth centuries. This city of gardens has a rich historical heritage, and is a city of poets and writers, mosques and temples. It boasts of Mughal structures like the Badshahi mosque, the Lahore fort, Shalimar gardens, and the mausolea of Jehangir and Noor Jehan.

In this megacity, Iqbal takes admission in the B.A. Class of the well-known and prestigious Government College. Set in a beautiful campus, the college building faces an open field with lemon and orange trees. A variety of tall trees provide a leafy shelter to college students who, in summers, fill the green openness with their gossip and chatter.

Iqbal stays at his friend's place for sometime and then moves to room number one in Quadrangle Hostel. For the next four years, Iqbal will stay in this hostel. In all these years, he would not bring his wife along to stay with him, nor would he fetch her when he settles permanently in Lahore a few years later.

The college has about two to two hundred and fifty students— making it easy for students to become acquainted with each other and forge close relationships with their teachers. Given Iqbal's intelligence and wit, it is not difficult for him to strike up friendships with students at the college. He already knows a few students from Sialkot. Here, in the course of his B.A. studies, Chaudhury Jalaluddin and Ghulan Bheek Nairang—his fellow students with a literary bent of mind—become his close friends.

Being a senior student, Iqbal lives in a cubicle in the western section of the hostel whereas Nairang stays in a dormitory on the eastern side. After school hours, both Iqbal and Nairang spend a lot of time together. In summer nights, Iqbal puts up his cot outside Nairang's dormitory.

His room in the hostel becomes the rendezvous of friends and a centre for poetry recitations. Iqbal's friendly temperament attracts many of his boarding house mates, who throng to his room, chat and smoke hookah with him. In summers, he sits draped in a cotton vest and a *tehband*,[1] and in winters, he throws a blanket over himself. He loves smoking hookah. To entertain his friends and visitors, he indulges in all kinds of gossip. His humorous disposition makes his company irresistible. Known for his banter, Iqbal does not let any chance for repartee slip by. It is, however, not just humour and gossip that is the hallmark of Iqbal's mehfils. Literary discussions are also held and poems are read and composed in his hostel room.

At this stage of life, everyone sees Iqbal as an agreeable friend and a capable poet but no one has any hint of the greatness that God will bestow upon him in his later life.

Even though his friends do not consider him an extraordinary poet, he shares some of his grand plans with them. During the smoke-induced discussions, for example, he often presents one of his magnificent schemes inspired by Milton's *Paradise Lost* and *Paradise Regained*. His ambition, as a poet, is to narrate the incidents of Karbala so colourfully and powerfully that his composition will rival Milton's masterpieces. Even though this aspiration remains unfulfilled, it shows how a young Iqbal harboured grand poetic ambitions.

During his college days, Iqbal sometimes visits the relatives of his friends who live in Lahore. Ziauddin Ahmed is Iqbal's class fellow and he, along with Nairang, are fond of wrestling. These two engage in wrestling exercises—a common sport of the day—in an akhada dug in a corner of Ziauddin's family house. Sometimes, Iqbal joins them and wrestles with Nairang.

* * *

For his B.A., Iqbal studies English, Philosophy, and Arabic. He attends English and Philosophy classes at Government College but for Arabic language and literature he has to go to Oriental College.[2] The teachers at the college include Maulana Faizul Hasan Saharanpuri, Maulana Muhammad Hussain Azad, and Moulvi Muhammad Deen.

In 1896,[3] Iqbal passes his B.A. exam with distinction in Arabic and English and is honoured with medals. He and his class fellow Fazal Hussain both pass the exam in second division.[4] Among the Muslim examinees, Iqbal stands first, followed by Fazal Hussain.[5]

Iqbal opts for philosophy for his M.A. and during his stint as a masters student, he becomes a close friend of his teacher, Professor Thomas W. Arnold. Arnold, who had left Aligarh College and was respected for his scholarship by the founder of the college, Sir Syed

Ahmed Khan, had joined Government College in 1898 as Professor of Philosophy. A famous Orientalist, Arnold is the author of the groundbreaking work, *The Preaching of Islam* (1892) which he had completed in Aligarh. In his book, he had argued that Islam did not spread by the force of the sword alone. The spread of Islam also happened through peaceful means. No Western scholar before Arnold had attempted this line of argument. This work endeared Arnold to the Muslim intellectuals of India, and he was held as 'the best living example of the West's praiseworthy character.'

Arnold's warmth for Iqbal and his respectful understading of Islamic culture draws Iqbal to him. Arnold is so impressed by Iqbal that he tells his friends that a student like Iqbal turns a teacher into a researcher, and a researcher into an even greater researcher. Arnold treats him like a friend. Their friendship and respect for each other will become a crucial factor in drawing Iqbal to England a few years later.

In 1899, Iqbal secures a third division in his M.A. exam. However, he is the only successful student in this subject in the entire University. He receives a gold medal for 'topping' as the only candidate for the subject in the state of Punjab.

While Iqbal pursues his M.A. in Philosophy, he also attends law classes simultaneously at the Lahore Law School. He fails in the first exam in jurisprudence held in December, 1898. One year later, he seeks permission to write the exam again without attending law classes, but his application is rejected.

In 1904, Arnold leaves his job in the college and moves back to England but he leaves only after kindling in Iqbal a desire to take up further studies in England. When Arnold departs for England, Iqbal pays a tribute to his teacher and friend in the form of a farewell poem—'*Nala-e Firaaq*' ('A Lament for Separation').

* * *

Lahore, being a cultural centre, brims with poets and writers. Poetic soirees are quite common in the city. The city's rich patrons of arts organize evenings of poetry recitation. Some cultural associations also organize poetry recitations where poets new and old entertain anyone who would care to come and give them an ear.

In his early days in Lahore, Iqbal does not participate in any mushairas even though Lahore can boast of a few notable ones.[6] One evening in the November of 1898, some of his class fellows drag him to a mushaira at Hakim Aminuddin's residence in Hakiman's Bazaar, a well-known majlis that attracts a fairly large number of participants and audience. Well-respected poets such as Arshad Gorgani (a member of Delhi's royal family and a teacher of Persian in Ferozpur's government madrasa) and Mir Nazir Hussain Nazim are also present at the function. To appreciate and laude the poets there is a large crowd of spectators. With a pounding heart a 22-year-old Iqbal climbs on to the stage and for the first time recites the following verse:

Moti samajh ke shaan-e karimi ne chun liye
Qatre jo the mere arq-e infa'al ke

His Grace gathered them as pearls,
So shining and bright were the beads of perspiration of my remorse

As soon as Iqbal finishes his recitation, the skies burst with applause. Arshad Gorgani shakes his head in astonishment at the poetic majesty and spiritual depth of this young man's composition. 'Iqbal! Such a beautiful verse at such a young age!' he heaps praises on him. Emboldened by this ovation, Iqbal becomes a regular participant in this mushaira and Lahore's poetry lovers begin to take note of this promising young poet.

It is in one of these mushairas that Muhammad Deen Fauq who has arrived in Lahore from Ghadtal, Sialkot, meets Iqbal. He too is a poet. Both of them become close friends, a friendship that will last for the rest of their lives. More than for his poetry, Fauq will go on to make a name for himself as a historian and journalist.

In another mushaira, Iqbal recites his poem '*Himala*', his tribute to the Himalayas as India's protector. This marks the beginning of the patriotic phase of Iqbal's poetry.

The opening stanza goes like this:

Aye Himala! Aye faseel-e kishwar-e Hindustan
Choomta hai teri peshani ko jhuk kar asmaan
Tujh me kuch paida nahin derina rozi ke nishaan
Tu jawan hai gardish-e sham o sehar ke darmiyan

O Himalayas! O rampart of the realm of India!
Bowing down, the sky kisses your forehead
Your condition does not show any signs of old age
You are young in the midst of day and night's alternation[7]

'*Himala*' becomes Iqbal's first contribution to *Makhzan*, a literary journal founded by his friend Shaikh Abdul Qadir. Many more will follow in the later years. Qadir can see that this poem has a new style—its thoughts are Western, but the composition is Persian sautéed with the sauce of patriotism. Initially, Iqbal is reluctant to part with this poem, thinking that it still needed some technical tweaking, but on Qadir's insistence, he finally parts with it.

This poem contributes to Iqbal's increasing fame as a nationalistic poet. More patriotic poems follow '*Himala*' including '*Tarana-e Hindi*' ('*Saare jahan se achcha Hindustaan hamara*'), and '*Hindustani Bachchon Ka Qaumi Geet*'.

God has gifted Iqbal with a sonorous voice. Iqbal's increasing fame for singing his compositions in mushairas partly results from his beautiful voice and his sensible ear for music. Iqbal's style of singing his poems becomes so popular that many others emulate him to achieve popularity for themselves. Arshad Gorgani once said:

Nazm-e Iqbal ne har ek ko gawaiyya kar diya

So wedded is Iqbal to musicality that he purchases a sitar for himself and takes lessons to learn to play the instrument. He practices the instrument regularly and cultivates the habit of sitar appreciation, a passion that will continue until 1905 when he leaves for Europe.[8]

Iqbal's poetic performances, however, are reserved for Lahore's audiences only. Whenever he visits his family in his hometown Sialkot, he keeps a safe distance from any literary soirees or mushairas.

As far as the quality of his poetry at this stage is concerned, his compositions during his student days (1893–1899) seem to be in the style of his ustad, Daagh Dehalvi, but slowly he emerges out of his shadows to find his own voice.

During this phase, he draws his intellectual nourishment from a variety of sources including Hegel, Goethe, Mirza Ghalib, Abdul Qadir Bedil, and William Wordsworth. While Hegel and Goethe guide him to reach out to the 'internal reality of things', Bedil and Ghalib teach him how to keep his oriental soul alive despite having absorbed the values of Western poetry. Wordsworth occupies a special place for him as he saves him from 'atheism' ('*dehriyat*') during his student days. He finds the thoughts of Wordsworth similar to Ibn Arabi's existential teachings. At this stage of mental development, it is Arabi's Doctrine of Absolute Unity (*Wahdatul Wajood*) that brings him out of a confused mental and spiritual state.

Many of Iqbal's early poems are inspired by Western poets. For example, '*Ek Pahad Aur Gilahari*' is influenced by Emerson's writing, '*Hamdardi*' is sourced from William Cooper, and '*Payam-e Subaha*' from Henry Longfellow.

British rule and education gives rise to new values in Urdu literature. The Aligarh Movement has been espousing such values and writers such as Hali, Shibli, and Azad have already adopted this new style. Slowly, Iqbal emerges out of Daagh's shadow, and begins to be influenced by Maulana Altaf Hussain Hali who started writing nationalist or *milli* poetry. Iqbal takes nationalist poetry to new heights, culminating in his masterpieces, *Shikwa* and *Jawab-e Shikwa*. His poems like '*Sir Syed Ki Loh-e Turbat*', '*Shayar*', and

'*Bilal*' demonstrate this change of direction. He says in '*Sir Syed Ki Loh-e Turbat*':

Mudda'a tera agar duniya me hai taleem-e deen
Tark-e duniya qaum ko apni na sikhlana nahin
Wana karna firqa bandi ke liye apni zabaan
Chhup ke hai baitha hua hangama-e mehshar yahan

If your aim in this world is to spread religious education,
Don't teach your nation rejection of the world.
Do not open your mouth to create fissures among your people,
Lies in silent ambush the trouble of the Last Days.

In closure, he says:

Sone walon ko jaga do sher ke ejaz se
Khirman-e baatil jala do shola-e awaz se

Awaken the sleepy ones with the magic of your verse
Set ablaze the harvest of the wicked with the heat of your sounds

By now, Iqbal is at the prime of his youth. A full-bodied handsome man of an athletic build, he keeps his dense brown moustaches trimmed from below and sports a pair of spectacles. However, psychologically, he finds himself to be a bundle of contradictions. The man is a mystery to himself, his mind a laboratory of various thoughts, ideologies and feelings—a living example of a life of contradictions. In his poem '*Zuhd Aur Rindi*' ('Piety and Inebriation'), Iqbal lays bare his own contradictory nature:

Majmua-e azdad hai Iqbal nahin hai
Dil daftar-e hikmat hai, tabiyat khafqani
Rindi se bhi agaah, shariyat se bhi waqif
Poocho jo tasawwuf ki to Mansur ka saani

Main khud bhi nahin apni haqiqat ka shanasa
Gehra hai mere behr-e khayalat ka paani

Not Iqbal, but a heterogeneous creature,
His mind crammed with learning, with impulse his nature,
Acquainted with vice, Aware of admonishments too
In divinity, doubtless, as deep as Mansur;
For me also my nature remains still enravelled,
The sea of my thoughts is too deep and untravelled[9]

As Iqbal's popularity rises and the number of his fans and admirers swells, he gets involved in various literary associations of Lahore, including the Association of Kashmiri Muslims in Lahore and Anjuman Himayat-e Islam. Even though by now he starts to get published in literary magazines such as *Zabaan, Dehli, Shor-e Mehshar,* his fame is limited to those who attend the mushairas in Lahore in which he performs. It would be wrong to assume that Iqbal is a poet of mushairas. As his student days get over, he too slowly moves away from such soirees.

6

A Patriotic Poet

Islam appeared as a protest against idolatry. And what is patriotism but a subtle form of idolatry; a deification of a material object. The patriotic songs of various nations will bear me out in my calling. Islam could not tolerate idolatry in any form. It is our eternal mission to protest against idolatory in all its forms. What was to be demolished by Islam could not be made the very principle of its structure as a political community. The fact that the Prophet prospered and died in a place not his birthplace is perhaps a mystic hint to the same effect.

—Iqbal, *Stray Reflections*

The summer of 1899 brings a fresh air of change in Iqbal's life. He has finished writing his M.A. exam and now he is ready to start his working life. His academic record is sterling and he hopes to land a good job by virtue of it.

When an opportunity to teach at Oriental College, Lahore, comes his way, he accepts it, even though it is only a temporary position. On May 13, he is appointed as the Macleod Arabic Reader at a monthly salary of 72 rupees and 1 anna.

Even though Iqbal takes up teaching as his first job, he wants to eventually get an administrative job or become a lawyer. Teaching, in that sense, is just a stop-gap arrangement as he is still figuring out the contours of his professional life and the immense possibilities that lie in front of his talented self.

Iqbal serves his post in the college for four years until 1903. Within those four years, he takes an unpaid leave for six months from January 1, 1901, to teach English in Government College, Lahore as an assistant professor.

In the same year, he also writes the competitive exam for the post of extra-assistant commissioner. He succeeds in the written test but the medical board declares him unfit for the job because of a weak right eye. This is where the leech episode assumes significance.[1]

The news of this rejection on the grounds of health is a major disappointment—it is something Iqbal was not prepared for. He wonders how a little incident in his childhood has extracted a heavy price from him and now he has to forgo his dream of becoming an administrative or judiciary officer.

Meanwhile, he has developed good relations with the Canadian principal of the Oriental College, Mr Stratten. He appreciates Iqbal's brilliance and they often discuss the possibility of Iqbal pursuing higher education in Canada or the United States. From these discussions a desire takes birth in Iqbal's bosom to go abroad to drink from the ocean of knowledge. He tries to find out about the admission process in the US but nothing materializes at this point.

Stratten unfortunately passes away in Gulmarg in 1902—a sudden death caused by a heart attack. His death saddens Iqbal. But by now he knows that change is an immutable part of life and no one but God can stop the forward flow of time. After Stratten's death, as an unbidden consolation Iqbal's favourite teacher T.W. Arnold takes charge as a temporary principal of Oriental College. Iqbal is already very close to Arnold and once he is back in Oriental College, he convinces Iqbal to go to England for higher education.[2]

In Lahore, Iqbal lives alone in a house in Bhati Darwaza. His wife and children move between Sialkot and Gujarat, spending time with both his parents and in-laws. Though Iqbal is not very demanding about his food, he needs a servant to cook for him and run his errands. Opposite his rented house lives Moulvi Hakim Ali, the principal of Islamia College. He has a servant, Ali Bakhsh. Bakhsh is hardly fourteen years old, a village bumpkin from Moza Atal Garh of district Hoshiarpur, not trained in the ways of city life. Iqbal offers him a job as a helper.

Bakhsh joins Iqbal's household as a servant and will continue to work for him for nearly forty years, serving him for as long as he will live. While Iqbal toils in college and reads and writes at home, Bakhsh does the cooking for him and frees him from the mundane tasks of life. Iqbal eats whatever Bakhsh rustles up for him. It does not mean that Iqbal does not like good food—he insists on having at least two or three different kinds of dishes on his dastarkhwan . However, he is not a big eater. Usually he eats once a day and at night he drinks salted tea. In the morning he leaves for college without eating breakfast and has lunch upon his return. Plain rice does not suit his stomach so he prefers rotis . If he is fond of anything it is pulav.

His daily routine consists of getting up early in the morning and performing his namaz and reciting the Quran loudly in a mellifluous voice. Everytime he recites the Quran, his soulful recitations move Ali Bakhsh to tears. After the prayers, Iqbal does some light exercises including sit-ups. Then he leaves for college to teach.

After finishing his stint in Oriental College, Iqbal gets appointed as an assistant professor of English in Government College, Lahore, in 1903. The subjects that Iqbal teaches at Oriental College are history and philosophy. His job description includes, among other things, the teaching of economics to the students of the bachelor of Oriental Learning (B.O.L.) in Urdu, and translating works of English and Arabic into Urdu.[3]

This is also the time when he embarks upon his life-long journey of writing books. Interestingly, none of the books he writes or translates in this phase of his life are on or about poetry. He does most of the reading and writing at home, after college duty is over.

His bedroom has a huge desk that overflows with books and research material. He likes this arrangement and prohibits Ali Bakhsh from organizing his books.

Once, when an earthquake rocks Lahore, Iqbal is lying on his bed, reading a book. Ali Bakhsh, in fear, begins to run around the house. Even when the floor of his house begins to shake, Iqbal continues reading unperturbed, his head buried in the pages of the book. Looking at an anxious Ali Bakhsh, Iqbal raises his head and says, 'Ali Bakhsh! Don't just scurry around! Go on and stand on the stairs!' After saying this, he goes back to his book.

In four years, he publishes four books, most of them translations: *Nazarya-e Tauheed-e Mutalaq* presented by Shaikh Abdul Kareem Aljili (in English)—a research paper on Aljili's essay on the perfect man;[4] a translation of William Stubbs' *Early History of England* (from Henry II to Richard III); another translation of Walker's *Political Economy*;[5] and a treatise on economics, *Ilmul Iqtisaad.*[6]

Through Aljili's essay, Iqbal introduces a classical text, *Al Insan al-Kamil-Ibn-e* [The Perfect Human Being], to modern readers. The mystic philosopher Abdul Karim Aljili (1365–1408) had also written commentaries of Ibn-e Arabi's work. Aljili was compared with modern thinkers like Hegel.[7]

Ilmul Iqtisad is his first published work in Urdu. The Steam Press, which was run by *Paisa Akhbar*, Lahore, published the book in 1904.[8] The book is dedicated not to Arnold or Stratten but to W. Bell who was the director of the Department of Education, Punjab. He was also Iqbal's teacher of philosophy before Arnold came over to teach at the Government College, Lahore.

Iqbal claims that his book *Ilmul Iqtisad* is the first authentic book on economics in Urdu.[9] He declares in the preface of the book that it is not a translation and has been written in a textbook style. Iqbal uses the available literature of the day to convey the essentials of the subject. He makes use of the personal libraries of Professor Lala Jaiaram and classmate Fazal Hussain for the purpose of writing this book.

The book's preface 'dwells on the nature and method of economics, poverty, significance of the study of economics for India, importance of education, the reasons for writing the book, the extent of originality, terminological issues and the difficulties of translation in Urdu, and the acknowledgment of personal debts.'[10]

This is also the time when Iqbal's nationalistic poems get broadcast and his views on nationalism and national life are formed. While he visits his elder brother Shaikh Ata Muhammad in the north-western hill station of Abbottabad, a local literary circle requests Iqbal to deliver a lecture. He develops the contents of this lecture into an essay in Urdu titled, 'National Life' ('*Qaumi Zindagi*'). The essay is published in two installments in *Makhzan* in October 1904 and January 1905.[11]

In 1904–1905, Indian nationalism is still evolving. The British government announces its decision to partition the Hindu-majority province of Bengal in two. The Indian National Congress, established in 1885, opposes this move, further strengthening the spirit of Indian nationalism.

In the same issue of *Makhzan* which carries the first installment of his essay, Iqbal publishes the patriotic poem, 'Our Homeland' ('*Hamara Desh*') in Urdu.[12] In this poem, Iqbal chants, '*Saray jahan se achha Hindustan hamara*' ('Our India is better than the entire world.').[13] In a similar patriotic vein Iqbal composes other patriotic poems such as '*Naya Shivala*' ('The New Temple'), asking the Muslim nation to unite with Indian Hindus. It is in this poem that he says, '*Khak-e watan ka mujh ko har zarra devta hai*' ('Each dust particle of my motherland is God to me'):

Sach keh doon aye Brahmin gar tu bura na mane
Tere sanam-kadon ke b'ut ho gaye purane
Sooni padi huyi hai muddat se dil ki basti
Aa ek naya shivala hum phir se yan bana de'n
Shakti bhi shanti bhi bhakton ke geet me hai
Dharti ke waasiyon ki mukti preet me hai

I'll tell you truth, oh Brahmin, if I may make so bold!
These idols in your temples—these idols have grown old,
Too long has lain deserted the heart's warm habitation—
Come, build here in our homeland an altar's new foundation,
Firm strength and calm peace shall blend in the hymns the
        votary sings—
For from love comes salvation to all earth's living things.

During this time, Iqbal is very close to his friends like Abdul Qadir,
Babu Meera Bakhsh, Faqir Iftekharuddin, and the son of his teacher
Mir Hasan, Syed Taqui Shah. Sometimes, when he is in a mood to
write, he invites his friend Abdul Qadir and dictates poems to him.
While doing this, he becomes totally oblivious to time. Sometimes, he
begins composing a poem at night and only finishes by early morning.
    Iqbal tells Abdul Qadir that the study of Hindu philosphy has
brought much peace to his heart and he has finally understood the
meaning of the Hindi word, *shanti*. Because of this understanding,
Iqbal tells his friend there is no room for prejudice against any religion.
'I have respect for all religions,' he says.[14]
    During this time, Iqbal also composes a long poem *Aftaab* (*The
Sun*), which is a translation of the Gayatri Mantra, one of the holy
prayers of the ancient Hindu scripture the Rig Veda:

Ae aftab! Rooh-o-rawan-e-jahan hai tu
Shiraza band-e-daftar-e-kaun-o-makan hai tu
Baees hai tu wujood-o-adam ki namood ka
Hai sabz tere dam se chaman hast-o-bood ka

O Sun! The world's essence and motivator you are
The organizer of the book of the world you are
The splendor of existence has been created by you
The verdure of the garden of existence depends on you[15]

* * *

At Government College, Iqbal's tenure is until September 30, 1903, but it is extended for six months. After this period ends, he is given another extension to teach philosophy. His salary goes up from two hundred to two hundred and fifty rupees a month.

It is from this position that Iqbal will take unpaid leave for three years to leave for Europe on October 1, 1905.

By the summer of 1904, Iqbal has made up his mind to go to England for higher studies and to become a bar-at-law. Though the seeds of Iqbal's desire to leave for higher studies abroad were first sown in Iqbal's heart by Stratten and Arnold,[16] the most obvious push came from one of his friends who moved to London a year ago. In 1904, his friend Shaikh Abdul Qadir leaves for England and Iqbal tells him that he will write to his brother Shaikh Ata Muhammad and ask him to arrange funds for his education in London. He also promises Abdul Qadir that he will come to England within a year.[17]

Once the decision is made, it is time to raise money for the expedition. Iqbal has saved up some money over the years but it is not enough to fund the entire cost of his undertaking in Europe. Fortunately, his brother Shaikh Ata Muhammad chips in with the rest of the money.[18]

With the money arranged, preparations soon begin for the journey. Iqbal used to wear simple traditional garments at home such as a *tehmand* and vest but this kind of dressing will not do in Europe. Therefore, he has some Western suits stitched before he leaves for England.[19]

Before departing, he spends his summer holidays with his parents and family members in Sialkot. He also consults with his teacher Mir Hasan regarding the research that he is to undertake in England.

Before departing for England, an emergency in the family arises when his brother Ata Muhammad is implicated in a criminal case. At this time, Ata Muhammad is posted as a military engineer in Baluchistan. Iqbal is perturbed by this. He is sure that his brother's adversaries have framed him. He, along with Ali Bakhsh, leaves for

Baluchistan to rescue his beloved brother from this legal tangle. On
the way, he writes one of his famous poems, 'Parinde Ki Faryad' ('A
Bird's Prayer'). In its last line, he prays:

> *Azad mujh ko karde oh qaid karne wale*
> *Main bezabaan hoon qaidi, tu chhod kar dua le*

> O the one who confines me make me free!
> A silent prisoner I am, earn my blessings free.[20]

After learning the facts of the case, Iqbal puts together this
information in a document and sends it directly to the viceory of
India, Lord Curzon. Meanwhile, he composes an ode to Nizamuddin
Aulia, to intercede on behalf of Ata Muhammad and help him get
out of this entanglement unscathed. The poem is called 'Barg-e Gul'
('The Petals of a Flower'). Iqbal's beseeching bears fruit and due to
Lord Curzon's intervention, the charge against Ata Muhammad is
withdrawn.

Finally, it is time to start his long journey to Europe—first from
Sialkot to Lahore, then from Lahore to Delhi, and finally from
Lahore to Bombay where he is to take a ship to England.

Bidding farewell to his parents and family, Iqbal first reaches
Lahore and then on the night of September 1, 1905, he leaves
for Delhi. His friends Nairang and Shaikh Muhammad Ikram
accompany him to Delhi for a final goodbye.

When the train reaches Delhi on the morning of September 2,
1905, Iqbal's friends Khawaja Hasan Nizami[21] and Munshi Nazar
Muhammad receive him and his companions at the railway station.
After getting off the train, Iqbal moves to Nazar's house to rest for a
while. Later, he and his friends leave for the dargah of Nizamuddin
Aulia. On the way, he says *fatiha* prayers on Humayun's tomb and
visits the grave of the Mughal prince Dara Shikoh.

At the dargah of Nizamuddin Aulia, Iqbal sits down by the grave
of the saint and reads out his poem 'Iltejay-e Musafir' in complete

solitude. He has requested all his friends to stay out in the verandah. Later on, facing the *mazaar*, he reads aloud the same poem at the insistence of his friends:

Chaman ko chod ke nikla hun misl-e nukhat-e gul
Huwa hai sabr ka manzoor imtihaan mujh ko
Chali hai le ke watan ke nigar-khane se
Sharaab-e ilm ki lazzat kushan kushan mujh ko
Maqam hum safron se ho iss qadar agay
Ke samajhe manzil-e maqsood karwaan mujh ko
Meri zuban se kisi ka dil na dukhe
Kisi se shikwah na ho zair-e asman mujh ko

Leaving the garden I have come out like the rose of your fragrance
I am determined to go through the test of perseverance
I have started with zeal from the homeland's tavern
The pleasure of the wine of knowledge is speeding me up
May I be so far ahead of the fellow travellers
That I may be regarded as the destination by the caravan
May my pen not hurt anybody's feelings
May I have complaint against none under the sun[22]

After paying a visit to the dargah, Iqbal stays at Khwaja Hasan Nizami's house. Before returning to the city, Iqbal also visits the grave of the great Urdu poet Mirza Ghalib which lies in a desolate corner of the graveyard. Iqbal sits down there lost in a spiritual reverie while his friends stand around him, encircling the grave.

In the sun-bleached afternoon, the air is oppressive in Delhi but no one is feeling the sting of the heat. Under a windless blue sky, a qawwal breaks into a melodious ghazal, transporting the party into a rapturous state:

Dil se teri nigaah jigar tak utar gayi
Dono ko ek ada me razamand kar gayi

Your hearty gaze penetrated my soul,
with a single nod an agreement it stole

Emotionally moved, Iqbal kisses the grave of the great poet before
leaving for the city of Delhi. He spends his night at Munshi Nazar
Muhammad's residence. On the morning of September 3, he gets
on the train for Bombay, taking leave of Mir Nairang, Shaikh
Muhammad Ikram, and his other friends in Delhi.

7

Bombay

The weak lose themselves in God; the strong discover Him in themselves.

—Iqbal, *Stray Reflections*

On September 4 Iqbal reaches Bombay by train—the first outpost in his long journey to the West. The city lies on the west coast of India and it has a deep natural harbour. Iqbal is aware of the port city's history and how it has evolved over three centuries from a collection of seven small, swampy islands into a giant metropolis.

The physical metamorphosis of the islands began only after the Portuguese takeover from the Muslim rulers of Gujarat in 1534. In 1661, the islands were gifted by the Portuguese to King Charles II of England as part of his marriage dowry when he married Catherine of Braganza. The British East India Company, which leased the islands from the Crown, foresaw the potential of the harbour and built a castle and fort to develop it as a trading port. Later on, through a number of reclamation projects, the Company welded the seven islands together to provide space for the constantly growing population.

By the middle of the nineteenth century several industries were set up, textile mills being the most important. People flocked to Bombay seeking jobs in the railways, the docks, and the mills.

A weird stroke of fate helps in Bombay's enrichment. In 1861 when the American Civil war begins, it results in a blockade of the ports of the American south. Because of this quirk, the Lancashire mills in England are unable to procure raw cotton from the United States. Instead, the mills are forced to purchase cotton from the markets of Bombay during the five-year period of the war, bringing, according to one estimate, over eighty one million pounds into the city. This leads to 'not only a phenomenal commercial boom but also a mania for speculation in the shares of companies that were primarily established to undertake extravagant schemes of reclamation.'[1]

Unfortunately, after the war ends in 1865, Bombay's commercial boom ends and several companies go bankrupt. Sir Bartle Frere, governor of Bombay from 1862 to 1867, decides to restructure the town by demolishing the fort walls. The fort ramparts, gates, and moat are completely removed and a new city emerges with an array of imposing Gothic buildings. By the end of the nineteenth century, Bombay evolves as the *Urbs Prima in Indis*, the leading city of India and the country's most important commercial, financial, trading, and industrial centre and port. When an unfortunate plague epidemic hits the city in the 1890s, it forces the administration to make improvements in the city. New areas and townships are developed. As the distances within the city grows, the transport system is modernized and in 1901, Jamsetji Tata becomes the first Indian to own a car.[2]

It is at this stage of Bombay's history that Iqbal encounters the city. [3]

Even though Iqbal is just passing through Bombay, he has three days to himself to explore the famous city. When Iqbal arrives at the Bombay railway station, he notices how one can buy tickets for all hotels in the city right at the station. However, he follows Thomas Cook's advice and settles for the English Hotel. This hotel is considered most suitable for Indian students going to England for higher studies.

The manager of this hotel is an old Parsi gentleman whose

countenance drips with so much piety that he reminds Iqbal of one
of Iran's old prophets. Iqbal observes that the art of business has
taught this man a humility that is rarely found even in the ulema
who regularly say their prayers and sit in the company of spiritually
evolved souls.[4]

A Greek gentleman also comes to stay in the same hotel. He can
speak a little bit of English. Iqbal and he strike up a conversation.
The Greek tells Iqbal that he used to do trading in China but the
Chinese don't buy his goods anymore. On hearing this, Iqbal's
thoughts veer towards nationalistic sentiments. He thinks that
the Chinese 'opium-eaters are cleverer than us Indians as they are
protective of their own industry.' 'Bravo Opium eaters! Bravo!' he jots
down in his diary, admiring the gutsy Chinese. 'Wake up from your
slumber. You have just started to rub your eyes and that has made
other nations worried about themselves.' Then he says that India will
not be helping China in this awakening and in re-establishing its
pre-eminence as a great power because Indians don't know how to
cooperate with others. 'The fragrance of love and affection has left
our land,' he ponders bitterly. 'For us a *pucca* Mussalman is someone
who is thirsty of Hindu blood and a *pucca* Hindu is someone who
is a sworn enemy of Muslims. We are book worms and thoughts
emanating from Western brains are our food. I wish the waves from
the Bay of Bengal had drowned us.'

One night when Iqbal is having dinner in the dining hall, two
gentlemen walk into the hall and take their seats opposite him. They
are having a conversation in French. After finishing the meal, one of
them takes out a Turkish cap from under his chair, an act that betrays
that this fellow is a Turk. Iqbal, who has not met anyone Turkish
before, is overjoyed to see a man from the land of the Ottoman
Empire. A desire to meet him consumes our young poet.

The very next day, Iqbal strikes up a conversation with him and
finds out that this young man is affiliated with the subversive Young
Turks.[5] He is a strong opponent of the autocratic Ottoman sultan,
Abdul Hameed.[6]

During the conversation, Iqbal discovers that this man is a poet too, just like him. He requests him to recite some of his poetry. 'I am a disciple of Kamal Bey,' the man says. Kamal Bey is Turkey's most famous poet at the time. He recites some couplets of Kamal Bey and Iqbal finds all of them to be excellent. However, when the man recites his own poetry, all of them are critical of the sultan.

The two poets decide to explore Bombay together. They visit the Islamia Madrasa of Bombay and Iqbal enjoys watching kids playing cricket in the school ground.

Within the limited time that Iqbal stays in Bombay, he finds it to be a strange city. Wide markets, paved concrete roads everywhere, skyscrapers so tall they baffle the ordinary visitor. In the markets, the motor traffic is so heavy that it is difficult to walk about.

'In this city, Parsis are not more than 80 to 90 thousand but it seems they own this city,' Iqbal observes. He admires the talent of this community and notes that their wealth and greatness is beyond any estimate. However, he is not sure if Parsis have a bright future because he finds them extremely materialistic. He thinks that Parsis are consumed by the idea of earning wealth and are not able to look at anything but from an economic perspective.

He also laments the fact that the wealthy Parsis are so poor in culture—they neither have a language nor a literature. On top of that, he is surprised at their attitude of looking down upon the Farsi language, to the extent of hating it because of its perceived Arab connection. Iqbal knows that the fact is otherwise, that there is hardly any Arab influence on Persian; rather, the literature is steeped in Zoroastrian colour which is the secret of the beauty of its literature.[7]

Iqbal sees many Parsi school-going kids roaming around in the markets. He finds them to be fine examples of smartness but is sad to notice that eighty per cent of them wear spectacles, hiding the beauty of their eyes.

'Bombay seems to be in a very good state educationally,' Iqbal notes in his diary. In the hotel where he is staying, the barber knows of all the big events in India's history. He reads a Gujarati newspaper everyday and is fully aware of the Russo-Japanese War.[8] He also mentions Dadabhai Naoroji[9] with utmost respect. Below the hotel, Iqbal further notes, there are many Muslim shopkeepers and they too read Gujarati newspapers everyday.

Iqbal stays in Bombay for three days, then departs for London. This will be a long journey for Iqbal, his first sea voyage. He has no idea how he will react to the heaving sea over the next two weeks on board. However, he is not afraid; his heart and mind are full of excitement at the prospect of drinking from the taverns of knowledge in Europe.

A Journey to the West

Civilization is a thought of the powerful man.
—Iqbal, *Stray Reflections*

From the docks of Bombay, the ocean stretches far into the horizon. In the harbour, ships and fishing boats bob in the water and the sun shines on brightly, giving a silvery hue to the gloomy waters.

It is about 2 o'clock in the afternoon of September 7 when Iqbal walks towards the French steamship that will take him on his maiden journey to England. Accompanying him is one of his friends, advocate Lala Dhanpat Ram and one of Dhanpat Ram's friends who incidentally happens to be in Bombay. They have come to see him off.

Iqbal is all of twenty seven when he steps on a ship for the first time in his life. He walks across the gangplank, cautious and yet jubilant for his heart is full of excitement by the prospect of this voyage.

Iqbal locates his cabin and after examining his room, he rushes out to the deck of the ship, not wanting to miss the rites of departure. Passengers and sailors throng the deck, observing the crowd in the harbour. Iqbal sees a stream of people rushing across the waterfront, and it seems they have brought along the city's din and bustle with them to the docks.

At about 3 p.m., the ship blows its horn. Iqbal finds a spot on the deck from where he can witness the ship's parting from land. He waves at his friends in the dock with his pocket handkerchief, following the other passengers. He stands there for a while, soaking in the sights and sounds of the land he is leaving for three years.

As the ship anchors off the port, the city's noises recede and the faces of people on the dock become distant, and the yells of porters and sailors become soft whispers in his ears. From across the span of water that stands between him and the city, between the ship and shore, Bombay's skyline slowly shrinks behind the veil of waves.

Iqbal's heart swoons with joy and excitement for what is to follow in the next few days. He is in awe of the French liner that he is on board now—his vessel to a new future, bringing him to Europe, to the shore of knowledge, and passing through the lands of his spiritual ancestors.

Iqbal takes a tour of the liner. It is a fine ship, sophisticated and full of finesse. He spots some black workers from Egypt milling around. These men are Muslims and they speak Arabic and even for a stranger it is hard to miss their warm camaraderie. At the same time, the polite French officers, with their refined etiquette, are as cultured as the folks in Lucknow. The French love for food and cuisine is reflected in the excellent dining arrangements in the ship.

There are not more than sixty passengers on this vessel. Iqbal busies himself by observing the routines of his co-travellers. The entire day they sit on chairs on the deck from dawn to dusk and only at night they retire to their respective cabins. Some read books, some indulge in conversations while others while away their time by pacing about on the deck.

Iqbal follows a similar routine. He likes to spend most of his time on the deck and feels uncomfortable in his cabin because of the heavy movement of the ship.

One of the peculiarities of the ship is that passengers are not allowed to use matchsticks on board. They have to light up their cigarettes at a brass fire pan that hangs by the wall of a room on the deck. Passengers light up their cigarettes or cigars using smoldering pieces of wood from the fire pan.

As the ship enters the Indian Ocean, the waters become a bit rough and their high waves toss the ship up and down.The waves are so high that they scare Iqbal.

'The voyage through the ocean impresses the individual with God's unlimited power,' Iqbal writes in his diary.'No other experience generates a similar impression. Apart from the spiritual and cultural benefits of the pilgrimage to Mecca, a deep ethical enrichment takes place when you encounter the expanse of the high seas with their awe-inspiring tidal waves, which compel even a very self-centred and arrogant individual to recognize his own powerlessness.'[1]

The next day Iqbal notes that all his friends on board have become seasick, but luckily he has escaped their fate. He is tempted to admire his own strong constitution.

One of Iqbal's co-passengers on the ship is the deputy commissioner of Quetta who is visiting England on a leave of eighteen months. As they begin chatting, Iqbal finds him very well-informed. The discussion moves into India's political space. The hot topic of this time is Lord Curzon's announcement of the partition of Bengal in July 1905. The partition is to take effect in October, just a few months away. The partition is to separate the largely Muslim eastern areas of the province from the largely Hindu western areas.

The deputy commissioner knows Arabic and Persian and at one point, they start discussing Sir William Muir's books, *The Mohammedan Controversy* (1897)[2] and *A Life of Mahomet and History of Islam to the Era of the Hegira* (published in four volumes between 1858 and 1861 by Smith, Elder, & Co).[3]

The commissioner underlines Muir's biases and remarks, 'I wish [Muir] were a little less prejudiced.'

When the discussion turns to poetry, the government official extols the merits of Omar Khayyam's poetry. 'Europeans have not yet studied the rubaiyat of Sahabi Najafi,' Iqbal informs him.'If they had, they would have forgotten Omar Khayyam long ago.'[4]

After this long discussion, Iqbal retires to his cabin. He puts on a safety belt to avoid falling off his bed.

* * *

On the morning of September 12, Iqbal wakes up very early and leaves his room for some fresh air. Sweepers are cleaning up the decks. Bright lights have become dim and the sun appears to be rising from a spring of water. The ocean reminds Iqbal of the Ravi river near Sialkot.

To the young poet, the sight of a sunrise is a command for Quranic recital—'This striking scene of sunrise inspires a sensitive soul to contemplate the majesty of the Almighty. This is the same sun that I have seen rising and setting in the plains many times . . . in fact those who have declared worshipping the sun their religion, they have a worthy excuse to do so,' he wrote.

When Iqbal is told of the approaching coastline and the ship is about to reach Aden, the news stirs a spiritual fervour in his heart. This happens at the mere possibility of sighting the holy lands from a distance. In a surge of emotion, Iqbal is inspired:

'O Sacred land of Arabia, I congratulate you. You were a stony and arid land, neglected by the architects and builders of the world. But an orphan boy spelled such a magic in your soul that the foundations of the civilization of modern age were laid down in your territory. Thousands of sacred individuals walked through your deserts. The shadows of your lush palm trees sheltered numerous saints and kings (like Solomon). How I wish that the particles of my body could mix in the grains of your sand, and then wander about in your spaces. Perhaps this wandering about in your land would enlighten my dark days. How I wish to be lost in your deserts, and then be free from the attachments of life, I would burn under the scorching sun, and being impervious to the blisters on my feet would reach the sacred land, where Bilal once chanted the adhan [call to prayers], which was filled with the love of faith.'[5]

The ship finally reaches the port of Aden but unfortunately it is quarantined in the shore and the ship has to anchor outside the dock.[6] This prevents Iqbal from venturing out and taking a tour of Aden. It is a splendidly sunny day and the weather is extremely hot. Iqbal takes a look outside and he is blinded by the glare and dazzle.

After a few hours, the ship moves out of Aden and, passing through the Red Sea, enters the Suez Canal.

In Suez, a large number of Muslim merchants come on board and the deck becomes picturesque as it transforms into a bazaar. Some merchants sell fruits, some hawk post cards, and some the old statues from Egypt. Among these is a sorcerer who has a young domestic fowl in his hands and by some unknown trick he converts one chick into two.

Iqbal wants to buy cigarettes from a young Egyptian shopkeeper and casually he mentions to the young man that he is a Muslim. 'Really?' the shopkeeper says, finding it difficult to believe him, given his outfit and appearance. He is suited and dons an English hat.

'Why do you wear a hat?' the shopkeeper further enquires of him.

'What's wrong with wearing a hat?' Iqbal retorts. 'Does Islam scoot away if a person wears a hat?'

'If a Muslim is clean-shaven, then he should at least wear a Turkish cap,' the shopkeeper argues simple-mindedly. 'Otherwise what will be the symbol of Islam on him? How will one know that the fellow is a Muslim?'

Iqbal recites some *ayats* from the Quran for the Egyptian's benefit, to convince him of his faith, and hearing the verses the Egyptian shopkeeper turns extremely happy. He kisses Iqbal's hands in excitement. Like a trophy, he takes him around to meet all the other merchants on board and they stand around him, chanting 'Masha Allah!' 'Masha Allah!' in appreciation. When they come to know of his purpose of travel, they offer their prayers for his success. At this reception and appreciation, Iqbal feels that for a moment, these merchants have risen from the mean status of trading to climb to the heights of Islamic brotherhood.

Iqbal notices a troop of beautiful, young Egyptian men arriving to tour the vessel. Their faces seem familiar to him. Where has he seen these faces? Aligarh, yes, Aligarh! These young and pretty faces remind him of a delegation from the Aligarh College in India. They stand in a corner of the ship and gossip loudly. Iqbal goes over to them and conducts a long conversation. Among them is a young man who speaks Arabic with great felicity and eloquence. Hearing this, Iqbal feels as though the boy were reading out an essay by Hariri.[7] Finally, this group of young men depart from the ship and slowly the ship moves into the Suez Canal.

Iqbal is quite impressed by the Suez Canal which was built by a French engineer, Ferdinand de Lesseps. He knows that it is one of the wonders of the world.[8] Admiring the canal, he notes: 'Even Mahatma Buddha hadn't had such a great influence on the spiritual life of the world that the Western mind has had on contemporary trade and business. When the canal is fine, hundreds of people work on it and they take care of the sand that blows in from both sides of the canal.'

Then comes a sight that takes not only Iqbal but many other passengers on the deck by surprise. Iqbal knows that workers who operate on the sides of the canal are sometimes quite mischievous. The ship is passing slowly along and a few of the young English girls are on the deck enjoying the view, when suddenly one of the workers begins to dance. This mad fellow is stark naked. The scandalized girls sprint back to their rooms.

As the ship moves further into the canal, it is soon passed by an Egyptian ship full of soldiers. They sport Turkish caps and sing songs in Arabic loudly and harmoniously. This scene provides some unexpected entertainment to our young poet.

The French vessel was yet to reach Port Saeed when news arrives that an explosive-laden ship has blown up and sunk. Soon Iqbal witnesses proof of this accident—he spots parts of the broken ship floating in the waters of the canal.

At Port Saeed, Muslim traders put up their merchandise on the deck of the ship for sale. Iqbal rents a boat and goes out to tour the port along with a Parsi fellow passenger. They hire a tour guide and visit a madrasa, several mosques, the residence of the Islamic governor, and the statue of the creator of the Suez Canal, Ferdinand de Lesseps. Impressively, the Muslim guide knows many languages, and after the tour is complete, Iqbal tips him and returns to the ship.

Upon his return, a very different scene greets Iqbal—three Italian women and two men are playing violins and people are dancing to their tune. Among the three women is a girl of heart-stopping beauty, barely thirteen or fourteen years old. Her sight tugs at Iqbal's heartstrings but the fascination is short-lived: 'When she started begging for gratification, with a little dish in her hand, I became disenchanted with her,' he records in his travel diary. 'A beautiful woman should not only be attractive, she should be indifferent, and not expect a reward for her performance or for her looks.'[9] Beauty without self-respect is worse than ugliness, he thinks.

From here the ship sails for the Mediterranean. As they enter the Mediterranean, the view of the sea changes to a serene beauty, the weather turns pleasant and the air becomes so exhilarating that it could cheer up even a dead man. Iqbal feels the poet in him coming alive when he sees the Italian shore, responding to this great confluence of location and weather.

Hare raho watan-e Mazzini ke maidano
Jahaz par se tumhein hum salam karte hain

Stay evergreen, O the pastures of the land of Mazzini!
I salute you from on board my ship

On the twenty third of September, the ship anchors at the historical French port of Marseilles. Iqbal takes a sigh of relief as the journey has been without an incident. The main voyage is over and from here Iqbal is to take a train to board a liner which will bring him to Dover and finally to London.

Iqbal has eight to ten hours to kill. He goes about the historic port city to discover its wonders. He notices how the Notre Dam church of Marseilles has been built at a higher ground. Looking at the magnificent structure, he concludes that the influence of religion and faith is the catalyst behind all knowledge and arts.

On the way to Dover, Iqbal catches sight of the French countryside and admires its beauty. The finely tended farms manifest the fine taste of the French people.

The next day, on the evening of September 24, 1905, Iqbal reaches London via Dover.

In London, his friend Shaikh Abdul Qadir is waiting for him. He recognizes Iqbal from a distance (even though Iqbal is in a suite and a hat) and runs over to him to embrace his old friend.

PART TWO

1905–1908

Europe

Iqbal in England: London and Cambridge

Philosophy is a set of abstractions shivering in the cold night
of human reason. The poet comes and warms them up into
objectivity.

—Iqbal, *Stray Thoughts*

Iqbal's stay in Europe is to last for three years.

When Iqbal reaches England at the turn of a new century, it is a
period of crisis for Britain. The country faces 'increasing competition
from its rivals overseas. Germany and the United States are catching
up with Britain and challenging its dominance. The century begins
with war against Dutch settlers in South Africa. At home, a new
breed of capitalists who control large enterprises are making great
fortunes. Despite the wealth and material progress, in terms of
equality, Edwardian society is no better than Victorian Britain.'[1]

Although at this point of time London is the centre of the empire
and an extremely wealthy city, working-class poverty and misery
remain widespread. Most working-class people live in slum-like
dwellings. Jack London, the American writer, who wrote *The People
of the Abyss* after living as a slum dweller in the East End, is shocked
by the physique and small stature of the people he encounters in the
capital of the British empire.[2]

Some of the major constitutional and political issues of the day are the reform of the House of Lords, Irish Home Rule, and voting rights for women. Trade unions are on the rise, as is industrial militancy. All these developments, however, come to a sudden halt when the Great War begins in 1914.

It is also a very interesting time for the politics of gender. Demands for women's equality were a topic of the day. Women were beginning to get involved in radical politics and demand a status equal to men. Most middle- and upper-class women were denied a proper education until late in the nineteenth century. Their educational situation improved when Cambridge created women's colleges and London University allowed women to sit degrees.[3]

Ideas of 'free love' are permeating British society, at least among the privileged middle classes. Around this time, the Norwegian playwright Henrik Ibsen is writing plays like *A Doll's House* which expresses controversial views about 'women's role and the stifling nature of the family'. *Ann Veronica* by H.G.Wells shows a heroine who comes to London to escape the constraints of her background, rebelling against conventional society. Among the writers of the age, Oscar Wilde is at the height of his success and fame.

When Iqbal arrives in London, the city already has a population of six million and the infrastructure of its public transport is firmly in place.[4]

In the early twentieth century, London is *the* place to be. Among its six million people, there is 'a large and growing population of Irish Catholics, Germans, Czechs, and Italians' who have come looking for work; while Ukrainians, Poles and Russians have come fleeing persecution.[5] Many Russian émigrés flock to London to escape the Tsarist repression. Vladimir Lenin and his wife Nadezhda Krupskaya come to London in 1902. Leon Trotsky escaped from Siberia in 1902 and came to London following Lenin. Much earlier, in 1888, Gandhi had come to London to become a Barrister; as had Jinnah in 1892.[6] And as does Iqbal in 1905.

Among these foreigners in London, there are about one thousand Indians. Two of the most influential Indians in London are Dadabhai

Naoroji and Abdul Karim. While Naoroji, initially an agent of a trading company, had set up a forum to represent Indians in the United Kingdom; Karim, a Muslim from Agra, worked in Queen Victoria's staff.

On September 25, 1905, Iqbal arrives in Cambridge from London.[7] Prof. Arnold has already made arrangements for his admission in Trinity College. At twenty seven, he enrolls in Trinity College as an Advanced Student. In his application to the college, he had stated that he would like to 'make a contribution to knowledge in the West, of some branch of Muhammaden philosophy. I would propose as a subject of research "The Genesis and Development of Metaphysical Concepts in Persia" or some contribution to the knowledge of Arabic philosophy.'[8] Iqbal takes residence in 17, Portugal Place and his academic life in Cambridge starts for Michaelmas term in October.

For his research, Iqbal needs some Quranic evidence on *tasawwuf* and he writes to Khwaja Hasan Nizami on October 8, 1905. He needs help finding *ayats* in the Quran that demonstrate a connection between Islam and mysticism.

While doing research for his dissertation, Iqbal delves deeply into the study of both Eastern and Western philosophy.[9] His dissertation first examines the thoughts and belief systems of the ancient Persian sages Zoroaster, Mani, and Mazdak; and then goes on to Islamic scholars, such as Ibn Maskawaih and Ibn Sina (Avicenna). He also examines the works of Greek philosophers like Plato, Aristotle, and Plotinus on Perso-Islamic thinkers.[10]

Once enrolled in Cambridge, the atmosphere of free knowledge-gathering and scholarship enthuses Iqbal. He is fascinated by the kind of scholarship and knowledge available at Cambridge. He loves the freedom to attend any lecture he desires. Given his interest in philosophy, he takes permission from the university and starts attending the philosophy classes of professors such as McTaggart (who lectured on Kant and Hegel), A.N. Whitehead, W.R. Sorely, and Professor James Ward at Cambridge.' A charming Iqbal befriends all these scholars and philosophers, especially McTaggart who is like a sufi-hearted person. Iqbal not only listens to his lectures but also discusses with him issues of mysticism. He also comes in close contact with the giants of Orientalism such as Professor E.G. Browne and R.A. Nicholson. Years later, in 1920, the latter will translate into English Iqbal's Persian *masnavi*, *Asrar-i Khudi* (*Secrets of the Self*), which will introduce Iqbal to Europe.[11] Interestingly, at this time, Ludwig Wittgenstein, Bertrand Russell, and George Moore are influential scholars in Cambridge but it is not known if Iqbal ever encountered them.

During his stay in Cambridge, Iqbal also eagerly attends lectures in economics. He presents an essay to the Department of Philosophy and Ethics on March 7, 1907 and receives the degree of B.A. from Cambridge University on June 13, 1907.

At Cambridge, Iqbal's devotion to his studies is so deep that he nearly gives up writing poetry. 'Nations that have work to do, do not have the time to indulge in literary pursuits,' he writes to his friend Abdul Qadir, the editor of *Makhzan* and publisher of his early poetry. This purposefulness on Iqbal's part indicates that he is no more just a poet but has taken up a mission to awaken the members of his nation—Indians and Muslims.

When Iqbal's mentor, Prof. Arnold, learns about Iqbal's dissatisfaction with poetry, he intervenes and persuades Iqbal to continue writing poetry as a service to the nation. Because of his research work, Iqbal has no time to contribute to newspapers back in India. However, he composes a poem now and then and his friend Abdul Qadir publishes it in *Makhzan*.[12]

When he resumes writing poetry, it comes to acquire a new colour and a new tone and tenor, forged in the oven of his European experience. By March 1907, he is already predicting the demise of the West:

Tumhari tehzeeb apne khanjar se aap hi khudkushi karegi
Jo shaakhe nazuk pe aashiyaan banega napaidaar hoga

Your civilization will commit suicide by using your own dagger,
A nest that is built on a slender bough cannot have much
   permanence!

Iqbal's doctorate programme in Europe takes about three years. Professor Arnold is so pleased with his thesis that he advises him to submit a German translation to a German university. Following the advice, he has his research topic registered in Munich University. Not only do they allow him to present his essay in English but also exempt him from staying on the campus of the university. [13]

Before and after Iqbal, many students from India come to England to become barristers. Gandhi, Jinnah, and Nehru are the most remarkable examples. The prestige and lucrativeness of the legal profession in India attacts Iqbal to England's law colleges. The incident wherein his brother Ata Muhammad was framed by his adversaries in Baluchistan reminds Iqbal of the importance of legal knowledge too. 'Not only the degree will help me start out on a new profession that pays far more than teaching, it will also help me understand Islamic jurisprudence in a better way,' Iqbal thinks as he decides to enroll himself for the bar-at-law.

For the barrister's exam, one has to register with one of the four Inns of Court in London. However, to qualify as a barrister, a candidate is not required to stay in London or attend law classes. The Inns are not residential campuses. The requirement is to pass two examinations, the first to be taken after keeping four terms and the second after nine terms. The terms are held in January, April, June, and November. The exam has two parts, each comprising six papers. For the first part, one can write the six papers separately. However, for the second part of the exam, one has to write the six papers in one go.

In each term, the enrolled candidate has to attend a minimum of six dinners and a total of seventy-two dinners. This practice apparently allows apprentice lawyers to meet and speak with their colleagues and superiors.[14]

On November 6, 1905, Iqbal joins the Lincoln's Inn to qualify for the Bar. For this, he will have to go to London from Cambridge and start completing the terms. Each time Iqbal visits London for this purpose, he meets with his friend Abdul Qadir during the lectures and dinners.[15] Both of them are from Lahore and both of them share a keen interest in Indian politics and Urdu literature and journalism. It was Abdul Qadir who had persuaded Iqbal in Lahore to allow him to publish his early poems in his journal, *Makhzan*.

Iqbal is not very sociable, so rarely makes new friends in London and sticks to his old friends from Lahore. He is slightly lazy too, so he does not like to go out much. However, he loves to take the subway in London whenever he goes out to meet a friend or return from one of the dinners at the Lincoln's Inn. He loves to observe people changing trains when the guard shouts, 'All Change!' at each terminal.

Once he is travelling on the subway when he overhears a few fellow British passengers discuss Buddhism. Iqbal figures out that they are arguing about the essence of the Buddhist faith. Seeing that Iqbal is probably Asian, they turn to him for a definition of the Oriental religion. 'What is Buddhism?' one of them asks him. 'I'll tell you,' Iqbal says and falls silent. The passengers, who are holding newspapers in their hands, look at Iqbal expectantly. 'What is Buddhism?' they enquire of him again after a few minutes. 'Sure, I'll tell you,' Iqbal replies and goes back into his silence. A few more anxiety-filled minutes pass. The passengers consider Iqbal with curiosity. 'Perhaps you are thinking about the answer,' one of the passengers says. 'Yes.' Iqbal gives them a brief smile and maintains his silence. By now the station has arrived. The guard shouts, 'All Change!' The passengers make their way to the carriage door. 'This is what Buddhism is,' finally Iqbal tells his fellow travellers, indicating the significance of silence.

* * *

Though Iqbal's food habits are simple, one of the challenges of his stay in England is the arrangement of halal meat. Again, his mentor Arnold comes to his aid in this matter. He helps find him accommodation in a Jewish household.[16]

Iqbal moves into the house of a 50-year-old Jewish landlady. She treats him very kindly and Iqbal is impressed by her family's merits. For example, the family members perform their prayers on time, and provide Iqbal with whatever he needs (provided he pays for it), making life convenient for the young scholar. Whenever he is home and it is time to pray, Iqbal happily joins them. He tells them that because Moses is his prophet too, despite being a Muslim, he can follow him. After sometime, he finds out that the family has been making a profit on all the consumables they provide him by taking a cut. This revelation embitters his heart towards them.[17]

Interestingly, this is also the time when Iqbal gets to exchange information on the cultural and religious habits of Muslims with his English landlady. For example, Iqbal's landlady does not understand why he always carries his lota into the toilet. Iqbal explains to her that in Islam, one is not considered clean if one uses only paper or soil after answering the call of nature. For a Muslim it is mandatory that he wash himself with water. They begin to discuss principles of hygiene and Iqbal explains to her the rules of bathing and cleanliness according to Islam.

Iqbal starts work on his research topic, 'The Evolution of Metaphysics in Iran', as soon as he arrives in England. The work is complete by 1907. It is then presented to the Ludwig-Maximilians-Universitaet, Munich. His nominal supervisor in Munich is Professor Fritz Hommel but he dedicates his book to Professor T.W. Arnold. His nominal supervisor at Cambridge was noted neo-Hegelian philosopher J.M.E. McTaggart.

He receives the degree of Doctor of Philosophy on November 4, 1907.[18]

Arnold, who is a professor of Arabic at the University of London recommends Iqbal's thesis in these words: 'So far as I am aware this is the first attempt that has been made to trace the continuous development of ancient Iranian speculations as they have survived in

Muhammaden philosophy and so bring out the distinctively Persian character of many phases of Muslim thought.'

* * *

During the long holidays, while other students either visit their families or travel around Europe, Iqbal stays back and works on his research. Most probably, he does not have the resources to travel around Europe and so he stays put and focuses on his work.

In Cambridge, Iqbal is friends with Syed Ali Bilgrami[19]of Hyderabad. Bilgrami teaches Marathi in Cambridge and is well-known for his translations of *Arab Civilisation* and *Indian Civilisation*. In Cambridge, his house is the centre of activities for all students from the subcontinent. During holidays, Iqbal loves to spend his time with the Bilgramis. Sometimes, he goes with one of his English friends to their house and spends a few days with them.

An interesting incident takes place during one of the holidays. Once he visits a friend's house in a remote village in Scotland. After a few days he comes to know about a missionary who has come from India. The missionary is to give a lecture on the growth of Christianity in India in a nearby school. Iqbal and his host attend the missionary's lecture. When they arrive at the venue, Iqbal finds that a large number of women and men have gathered to listen to the missionary.

The missionary starts by saying that although thirty crore people live in India not one of them is fit to be called a human being. 'In terms of habit and characteristics and their living and dwelling standards, they are sub-par humans and only better than animals,' he says. 'After years of struggle, we have introduced these animal-like people to civilization but the work is vast and important. Please support our mission with your large-hearted donations so that we can achieve as much success as possible in this great humanitarian mission of ours.'

After saying this, the missionary shows pictures of Indians on the screen through a magic lantern. Iqbal recognizes the awful pictures that are of the semi-naked people belonging to the tribes of Bheel, Gond, Dravid, and the tribes living in Orissa's jungles.

When the lecture ends, Iqbal seeks permission from the president of the assembly to allow him to address the audience, which the president happily does. Iqbal rises from his seat and walks up to the podium. He speaks for nearly twenty-five minutes during which he tells the audience that he is an Indian, made of the soil of the same land that the reverend was referring to. 'Please look at my constitution, colour, appearance, and behaviour,' he dares the audience. 'I am speaking in your language as fluently as the missionary just did. I have been educated in India. Now I am at Cambridge for higher education. By looking at my appearance and by listening to me, you can draw your own conclusions regarding the veracity of this missionary's description of my people. The truth is that India is one of the most civilized nations of the Orient which has raised the lamp of knowledge and culture for centuries. Even though we have been politically enslaved by the British, we have our own literature, our own culture, and our own national traditions that are no less spectacular than the traditions of the Western people. The honorable missionary has shown you these misleading pictures of Indians only to provoke you to empty your pockets generously.'

As soon as Iqbal is done speaking, the people assembled in the gathering express their agreement with him and the poor missionary, now stonewalled, has to return empty handed from the meeting.

As mentioned earlier during his stay in Cambridge, Iqbal focuses on his studies; his poetry is given the back seat. In 1906, when the Swadeshi Movement[20] begins in India in response to the Partition of Bengal in 1905, Iqbal writes an opinion piece on this movement. This piece of political writing is published in *Zamana* from Kanpur in April, 1906. In this piece he emphasizes the unity of peoples of India and argues that achieving political rights is predicated on uniting the interests of a nation's people:

Religion has come to the world to create peace and not to
instigate war. If [the Swadeshi] movement generates a unity of
interest between Hindus and Muslims and slowly gets stronger
and stronger then that will be a great achievement for India. If
this actually happens, India's fortunes will be reawakened and the
name of my long-standing nation will be written in bold letters
in the history of nations.

Iqbal stays in Cambridge until June 1907 while working on his
research.

10

Atiya Begum

Love is a playful child. She makes our individuality and then
quietly whispers in our ears—'Renounce it'
—Iqbal, *Stray Thoughts*

Ten years after Iqbal is born in Sialkot in undivided India, a girl
named Atiya is born thousands of miles away in Istanbul.[1] Just as
Iqbal's father ran a business in Sialkot, Atiya's father Hasan Ali Fyzee
(1827–1903) ran a business in that Turkish metropolis.

After a few years, the Fyzee family moves from Turkey to India
for better business prospects.

In 1906, one year after Iqbal arrives in Europe, Atiya receives a
scholarship to pursue higher studies in England. And that's where
these two great souls meet—in London.[2]

The day they meet for the first time is April Fools' Day—1 April,
1907. By that time Iqbal has spent nearly a year and a half in England
and Atiya nearly a year.

They meet at a party in Miss Beck's place in London. Miss Beck
is the sister of Professor Theodore Beck (1859–1899), who was once
the principal of M.A.O. College, Aligarh. A legendry academic, he
was appointed to that position at the ripe young age of twenty four.

The occasion for Atiya's meeting with Iqbal is provided by Miss
Beck, who is the secretary of the National Indian Association in

England, and as such, she attracts Indian students and visitors who gather at her house to meet other Indian students.[3]

The meeting is not incidental. Miss Beck has primed Atiya for Iqbal. She had sent him a special invite to come to the gathering on April 1, asking her 'to meet a very clever man by the name of Muhammad Iqbal, who was specially coming from Cambridge' to see her. The invitation had amused Atiya. She has not even heard of him. At the same time, it does not rouse much curiosity in her because she was used to getting such invitations from various Indians in London. Not wanting to disobey Miss Beck, given her dedication to the welfare of Indian students in London and 'the motherly care' that she bestowed upon them,[4] she decides to meet Iqbal.

The party is on when she reaches Miss Beck's place. Soon, Iqbal too arrives at the scene. The tall, young mustachioed Punjabi man looks dashing in his suit that evening. His 'deep-set eyes hide his feelings and mood, making him appear confident and invulnerable.'

Miss Beck introduces Iqbal to Atiya. They start talking at the dinner table. Though she finds the surroundings of Miss Beck's place 'prosaic and uninspiring', she finds her conversations with Iqbal exhilarating.

As they carry on their discussion, she realizes the depth of Iqbal's scholarship and the sharpness of his wit. While Iqbal is talking, she studies him like a subject. What she finds out about him impresses her even more: a scholar of Persian, Arabic, and Sanskrit; 'a ready wit, and ever alert in taking advantage of one's weak point, and hurling cynical remarks at his audience.'

While she admires Iqbal's scholarship and wit, Iqbal takes to her directness and straightforwardness as a person. The two are barely able to contain their liking for each other.

Atiya is curious to know why he particularly wanted to see her. When she enquires about this, he says: 'You have become very famous in India and London through your travel diary and for this reason I was anxious to meet you.'[5]

'Wow! Is that right?' Atiya thinks, overjoyed with the compliment that the young scholar had just paid her. However, she is a bit skeptical. Is Iqbal being sarcastic?

'I am not prepared to believe that you took the trouble to come all the way from Cambridge just to pay me this compliment, but apart from this jest, what is the real idea behind this meeting?' she looks into his eyes.

That's blunt, Iqbal thinks, but he does not let go of his composure. Eventually, he tells her the truth, embellished by his poetic sensibility. 'I have come to invite you to Cambridge on behalf of Mr and Mrs Syed Ali Bilgrami as their guest, and my mission is to bring your acceptance without fail,' he says, sounding ambassadorial. 'If you refuse you will bring the stigma of failure on me, which I have never accepted, and if you accept the invitation, you will be honouring the hosts.'

As the conversation rolls on, she gets to know the young poet better. She further observes that Iqbal makes himself agreeable or disagreeable depending on his mood. Give him company and he will be vivacious and witty—'never at a loss for wit or compliment'. But most of the time, Iqbal behaves and speaks like a cynic.

When they talk about Hafiz,[6] Atiya quotes many of his appropriate verses. Iqbal too is an admirer of this great Persian poet. 'When I am in the mood for Hafiz,' he quips, 'his spirit enters my soul, and my personality merges with the poet's and I myself become Hafiz.'

Iqbal is in the mood to have a discussion. He further opens up. 'I admire another great Persian poet, Baba Fughani,' he says. Fughani is not known in India. 'You must read him at all costs,' he exhorts. 'Very few of his books are to be found in India, but they must be read as they reveal a different vision of the truth.'

The conversation rambles on and they lose track of time. It is late in the evening and Atiya has to return to her residence. Before departing, she accepts Iqbal's invitation to visit the

Bilgramis in Cambridge. A date is fixed. It is to be the twenty second of April.

* * *

A few days pass. An invitation arrives from Iqbal inviting Atiya for supper. Iqbal has chosen a fashionable restaurant in London named Frascatis to host Atiya. He wants her to meet some German scholars with whom he has been working.

At the restaurant, the decor is thoughtful and the dinner arrangement delicate. 'This is so nicely done,' she remarks in appreciation.

'I am two personalities in one,' Iqbal replies, appreciating the praise. 'The outer is practical and businesslike and the inner self is the dreamer, philosopher, and mystic.'

The dinner is delicious but the intellectual discussion that follows with the German philosophers is even more interesting. That is the real treat. As usual the discussion hovers around deeper matters of philosophy that scintillate her mind.

After the dinner date, now it is Atiya's turn to return the courtesy. She arranges a little tea party for Iqbal on April 15.

For the party, she invites some of her scholarly friends. Miss Sylvester and Miss Levy are well-known in London as language and philosophy students. M. Mandel and Herr Metztroth are famous musicians. They all join the party to make it unforgettable. When Iqbal arrives at her place, it turns into a chirpy party with food, conversation, poetry, and music. 'When Iqbal composed a humorous poem these ladies capped the verses in a similar manner, and the air crackled with intellectual fireworks from start to finish.'

As the evening drags on, a lively Iqbal is on a roll with his amusing verses. Atiya is so fascinated by his lines that she wants to note them down. When she starts scribbling her notes, he stops her. 'These expressions are meant only for this particular occasion, and their mission has ended the moment they are uttered,' he gently reprimands her. She respects Iqbal's wish and stops writing.

Atiya's musician friends play some classical music. The party goes on for three hours and becomes a memorable event for all of them.

One week later, on April 21, 1907,[7] Atiya leaves for Cambridge to keep her promise to visit the Bilgramis. It is to be a day-long trip. Accompanying her are Iqbal and his friend Shaikh Abdul Qadir.

At twelve noon the party reaches the residence of the Bilgramis. Iqbal plays a ceremonious courtier when he introduces Atiya to Syed Ali Bilgrami, who receives her graciously. 'If ever I faced the prospect of courting a failure in life, it was with Miss Fyzee, who, out of sheer consideration for you, saved me by not declining your invitation,' he says. He follows that ceremonious sentence by quoting a couplet of his own in Persian.

As usual, there are other guests at the Bilgramis' parlour that day. They all indulge themselves in conversations that Atiya finds brilliant and learned.

Atiya observes that Iqbal has a peculiar habit—sometimes during a conversation, he looks dull and tired, but that is not to be mistaken as a sign of withdrawal. He would rather be watching and waiting for any remark that can be responded to with a quick repartee. Once someone gives him this kind of an opportunity, he pounces on his prey with such a 'lightening rapidity' that it stuns his opponent for a moment.

He is like William Gladstone, Atiya thinks. The British prime minister is well-known for adopting a similar tactic in the House of Parliament.

In the evening Atiya returns to London.

For more than a month, they do not meet again. However, an opportunity to meet appears courtesy of Professor Arnold.

Arnold invites her to Cambridge for a picnic. Again it is a gathering of scholars but this time the location is scenic. The picnic has been arranged under a tree by the banks of a river.

When the conversations ramble on in the spirit of relaxed picnicing, Arnold tries to give them some direction. He asks everyone to offer an opinion on life and death. This is a grave topic and when the arguments become hazy, Arnold turns to Iqbal to ask him his opinion on the topic. Iqbal has been silent until now, patiently listening to all the remarks being made. A cynical smile emerges on his face. 'Life is the beginning of death, and death the beginning of life,' he puts it coolly.

This suitably brings the discussion to an end.

Another week passes by. On June 9, 1907, Iqbal and Atiya meet again at Arnold's place. Professor Arnold starts talking about a rare Arabic manuscript in Germany. It has been recently discovered and needs a scholar to decipher it. Instead of going to Germany himself, he opines that Iqbal go in his place. 'Iqbal, I am going to send you there and you are the right man for the job,' he says.

Iqbal tries to excuse himself from this assignment. 'I am only a novice, Sir,' he pleads. 'You are the expert for this job.'

'Don't worry, Iqbal,' Prof. Arnold says, 'In this case the student will surpass his teacher.'

Iqbal acquiesces but adopts a slightly cynical tone which is his trademark style, 'If this is your conclusion, Sir, I accept my teacher's idea, and obey his commands.'

The next day Iqbal goes to Atiya's place with some German and Arabic books on philosophy. This time a German professor accompanies him. He reads out from those books and starts a discussion with Atiya. He is referring to Hafiz as a point of reference, comparing his thoughts with those of European philosophers. Atiya is already aware of Iqbal's fascination with Hafiz from their first meeting. Now that Iqbal is arguing and comparing notes with others, Atiya is convinced that Iqbal believes in Hafiz more than any other Persian poet. He keeps on comparing the ideas and ideals of Hafiz with other philosophers. The discussion goes on for three hours. It is not a futile discussion but a method Iqbal adopts to sharpen his arguments. He acknowledges at one point that 'by reading and discussing in this manner my ideas expand and convictions become firm.'

On June 23, 1907, Iqbal is invited by Atiya for a party at her place. The guests include both Indian and English notables. Atiya's friends play some entertaining music which puts Iqbal in a good mood. He composes some extempore verses that are clever and witty 'referring to almost every important guest present by making exaggerated remarks about their peculiarities', sending the attendees into roars of laughter.

* * *

A few days later, a German woman named Miss Sholey invites Atiya to an Indian dinner on June 27. It is not everyday that you get to have an Indian dinner in London, Atiya thinks. She gladly accepts the offer. When she goes over to her place, she finds Iqbal present and discovers that he is staying at Sholey's and had requested her to invite Atiya.

Atiya enjoys the meal which has a 'real Indian touch and flavour'. Over dinner, Iqbal tells her that he can cook nearly any Indian dish.

Dinner with Atiya is not all Iqbal wants from her. He wants to go over his thesis with her. Atiya sees no problem in this and Iqbal reads out his thesis in its entirety. Very clearly, his thesis demonstrates a vast and deep amount of research.

After Iqbal finishes reading, he invites her to make comments on his work. Iqbal listens to her carefully and makes notes for improvement.

As soon as they are done with their discussion, some of Iqbal's friends walk in. A quick plan is chalked out and together they all march out to attend the annual party of the Imperial Institute. Iqbal is not very excited about attending this event but he accompanies his friends reluctantly. He does not want to be a spoil sport.

Some members of the British royal family are also in attendance at the Institute, however, Iqbal looks bored.

'What a delightful waste of time,' he keeps muttering throughout the evening.

'What?' Atiya quips, 'Not a very original observation!'

* * *

Barely two days have passed when Iqbal and Atiya bump into each other again. This time, the meeting happens at the house of Lady Elliotts, a society hostess. She has thrown a party, and frankly speaking, she does not expect Iqbal to be there. But he is in attendance and they both begin chatting.

While they are having a conversation, Miss Sarojini Das[8] rushes in, 'dressed in the richest garments, outrageously bejewelled, and incongruously decked.' Atiya sizes her up, remembering 'this specimen of humanity' who had travelled with her to England and 'regarded herself as a paragon of all that is desirable'. Excited to see Iqbal, she ignores Atiya and everyone else and 'bubbling with copious sentiments' she takes Iqbal's hand. 'I only came to see you,' she gushes. 'This shock is so sudden that I shall be surprised if I am able to leave this room alive,' Iqbal replies.

This was original, Atiya thought.

* * *

By July 4, 1907, Iqbal tells Atiya that he has finished writing the history of the world, a topic he undertook for his German examination. When he reads out the manuscript to her, she makes some comments on a few historical facts. 'Each person has his own particular angle with which he approaches facts, and I see the history of the world in this particular light,' he says.

Atiya can hardly help but be impressed with Iqbal's depth of knowledge and his remarkable memory, both of which could be gauged from the facts he had collected for his work. Miss Sholey offers her a delicious Indian lunch again, prepared under Iqbal's guidance.

Seeing her interest in philosophy, Iqbal proposes that Atiya and he hold two-hour long reading sessions on the thirteenth, fourteenth, and fifteenth of July. Iqbal and Atiya, along with Prof. Herr Schaccent, who had completed his doctorate in Germany, read and discuss poetry and higher philosophy on the assigned dates.

During the discussions, Atiya observes that Iqbal had a very high regard for German knowledge. 'If you wish to increase your understanding in any branch of learning, German should be your goal,' he tells her.

Iqbal also reveals to her one of his key methods of knowledge gathering: 'By discussing with others, a new world opens, and it is with this method, that I acquired all that I know,' he declares to her.

The following day Iqbal presents her his original manuscript of *Political Economy* and also the thesis that secures him his degree.[9]

Iqbal leaves for Heidelberg in July 1907. He moves to Heidelberg to learn German for the oral examinations of his dissertation in Munich University.

By the end of July 1907, news reaches Atiya through a student named Parmeshwar Lal that Iqbal's patriotic songs published in *Makhzan* have become so popular that they are being sung in the whole of northern India: 'houses, streets, alleys resounded with Iqbal's national songs, which created a feeling of nationalism unknown in India before.'

A delighted Atiya wants to share this good news with Iqbal but by now he is already in Germany.

On August16, Atiya goes over to Wimbledon at the invitation of Prof. Arnold. She tells him that she is thinking of going back to India after wrapping up her work in London. Arnold pleads with her that she should spend a little time in Germany, especially Heidelberg, and that the experience there could broaden her intellectual horizons. She decides to visit Germany with her brother Dr Fyzee, who is conversant in German and is desirous of visiting Germany a second time.

When Iqbal comes to know of her visit to Heidelberg, he starts collecting books for her to read. He duly informs her about this in a letter on August 6, 1907. Atiya, in turn, messages Iqbal that she will be visiting him in Germany on August 19, because by then, her responsibilities in London would be over.

11

Heidelberg, Germany

No nation was so fortunate as the Germans. They gave birth to
Heine at the time when Goethe was singing in full-throated ease.
Two uninterrupted springs!

—Iqbal, *Stray Thoughts*

Heidelberg is a small, university town, in south-west Germany,
situated in the lap of rolling green hills and valleys. It lies on
the River Neckar in a steep valley in the Odenwald, flanked by
Königsstuhl and the Gaisberg mountains on one side, and the
Heiligenberg mountain on the other. The River Neckar leads to
the River Rhine approximately twenty-two kilometres north-west
in Mannheim.

In 1905, the town's population is around fifty thousand. A former
residence of the Electorate of the Palatinate, Heidelberg is the
location of Heidelberg University. The university is located on top of
a hill, giving it an idyllic setting. The town's romantic and picturesque
cityscape, including Heidelberg Castle and the baroque style Old
Town, attracts tourists. It is a peaceful place full of almond and fig
orchards, numerous gardens and a variety of fauna.

Iqbal stays in a boarding house for students by the Neckar—the
Pension Scherer (Iqbal also used to call it the Heidelberg School).
The hostel has over a hundred students and professors. The seventy

year old Frau Prof. Herren, a clever woman and a great musician, manages the hostel.

Atiya leaves London for Heidelberg on August 19, 1907, with a group of Indian students. Accompanying her is her brother, Dr Fyzee. The group reaches Heidelberg at 5 o'clock the next day.

Gathered at the station are a bunch of people, the most prominent among them Herr Prof. Iqbal. That is how he is known in Germany.

He has mastered the German language in three months and hence has developed a reputation for himself.

Atiya immediately feels at home being in the company of so many Indians and Germans, who shower her with a warm welcome. In such company, one's stiffness melts away quickly. Then there is no room for formalities. Among the ladies in the group are Frau Prof. Wegenast and Frau Prof. Seneschal. Both are quite young and good looking. Wegenast is not more than twenty seven. Both teach Iqbal the German language and literature.

The party arrives at the well-laid out University garden. There is coffee and cake, and other delicious refreshments for the guests.

Iqbal's newly acquired humility in Heidelberg strikes Atiya. Is it the same Iqbal whom she had known in London, the man with an 'egoistic cynicism'?

Iqbal tells her how delightful his sojourn in Germany is. Besides the academic work, as a student Iqbal has to learn boating, classical music, singing, gardening, hiking, and climbing. Iqbal shows great interest in all these activities. His only failures are, if you will, a bad singing voice and lack of punctuality. But his tutors tolerate these minor deficiencies of the Indian poet scholar.

In the university students and teachers live alike and it is difficult to distinguish between them until it is time for class.

During classes, when Frau Wegenast and Fraulein Seneschal, start discussing German, Greek, and French philosophy, Iqbal gets totally absorbed in their discussions. Whatever is taught and discussed, Iqbal pays great attention to it. He gets so absorbed in the process that it seems like 'he is coming out of a dream when the class is dismissed'.

When Fraulein Seneschal catches Iqbal giving a wrong answer, he bites his fingers like a school boy, as if saying, 'Oops! Why didn't I think of that!'

Iqbal the cynic has been lost and a new Iqbal has taken birth in Germany, Atiya figures out.

After the class, the group walks up a hill nearby, climbing one thousand steps, to reach the Schloss on top of this hill. As a game, every member of the group is asked to relate the history of this hilltop. Iqbal's version is correct. 'You get the finest view of the Necker valley from here,' he tells the group.

They reach the summit of the hill while singing operatic songs. Iqbal joins them in the singing but he is obviously off key, and out of tune.

On August 22, 1907, a picnic excursion is planned, combining study and recreation. At the appointed time, Atiya and a group of picnickers go from room to room to collect the rest of the team mates. Iqbal's residence is at the end of their route and he is supposed to wait for the team in front of his lodge. When they reach there, they find no trace of Iqbal. One of them goes into his room to find him. He is aghast at what he sees. Iqbal has gone into trance since the night before and he refuses to come out of it. Frau Senechal and Fraulein Wegenast jump out of their clothes seeing Iqbal lost in a reverie, like a lifeless statue, staring vacantly at an open book.

The whole group is dazed, and no one knows what has happened to Iqbal. Did he freeze overnight? Will he come back to consciousness?

Atiya is both impressed as well as amused at the situation. She strolls to the table where Iqbal is lost in his meditation. 'Iqbal!' She calls out to him a couple of times but there is no response. She shakes him up with the help of Frau Professor. Slowly, he comes to himself, and asks why he has been disturbed. She gently reprimands him. 'Iqbal, you are in Germany, not in India where these idiosyncrasies can be understood,' she says.

Iqbal then becomes fully conscious and joins the party for the excursion.

On the way, Fraulein Wegenast starts singing a song—a song Atiya had taught her the night before: *'Gajra bechanwali nadan yeh tera nakhra.'*

All the team mates join in the singing, creating the effect of a choral symphony. They collect wild flowers to weave into a wreath. The wreath is placed round Iqbal's head, and the assembly choruses, 'We crown you the king of the unknown'.

Over the next few days, more picnics and excursions follow, and Iqbal is at his brilliant best in the company of bright teachers like Emma and Seneschal. When they visit Munich on August 28, 1907, Iqbal falls in love with the city. He calls it the 'Isle of Bliss, bathed in the sea of imagination'.

Teaching and instruction take place amid this apparent frivolity. On one occasion, Atiya sees Iqbal perform, a bit awkwardly though, a folk dance at the famous Schloss Neckerbeinstein.

When Atiya is to return to England, her friends throw her a party and everyone prepares a dish for her. Iqbal's dish is Indian. Before her departure a song is sung in her farewell, led by Iqbal.

Atiya returns to India and does not meet Iqbal until 1908 when she briefly visits England accompanying her sister and brother-in-law, their Highness Nawab Sidi Ahmed Khan and Rafiya Sultan Nazli Begum of Janjira. Iqbal leaves her a poem in her sister's autograph book.

The year she returns to India her mother falls very sick. But Iqbal and she maintain a regular correspondence. Iqbal considers her such a close friend that in many future letters he will bare his heart to her. But will he ever confess his love to her? Will he ever propose to her?

He sends her this poem titled *'Wasl'* ('Union') from Munich:

Justuju jis gul ki tadpati thi aye bulbul mujhe
Khubi-e qismat se aakhir mil gaya woh gul mujhe
Qaid me aya toh haasil mujh ko azaadi huyi
Dil ke lut jaane se mere ghar ki abaadi huyi

The flower I was restlessly in search of, hark O nightingale!
Fortunately now I hold that flower in my hands
I've found freedom in my captivity
And found my homeland when my heart was plundered[1]

Atiya is attractive, intelligent, and a modern Muslim woman. She comes from a rich family of businessmen. Even if he wants to take his relationship with Atiya any further, provided that she reciprocates, Iqbal faces many barriers: he is already married, he faces an uncertain future in India, and he is totally dependent on his brother Ata Muhammad for his financial needs. His relationship with his wife is already estranged and bringing a modern woman like Atiya into a traditional family like Iqbal's would have created an unsavoury situation in Sialkot.

At the same time, Iqbal also enjoys the affections of his German tutor and friend, Emma Wegenast in Heidelberg. So, perhaps there is no urgency to dive into matrimonial union with Atiya. After all, she is just a close friend and, at best, an intellectual companion—a relationship not very uncommon to have in the corridors of European academia.

When Iqbal returns to India, the emotional emptiness of his life will make him confess to Atiya her debt to him:

> You are not conscious of what good you have done me—this is true and better so. You could not have been conscious of it. I am conscious of it, but cannot give an expression to it. Let us drop the subject. It would be futile on my part to describe the indescribable, and then you say you are not open to conviction.[2]

What Iqbal feels for Atiya is an unspeakable truth, but that truth will never leave his lips. It will remain buried in his heart with the stony silence of a solemn mystic.

12

Emma Wegenast

A woman of superb beauty with a complete absence of self-consciousness is to me the most charming thing on God's earth.

—Iqbal, *Stray Thoughts*

The three and a half months that Iqbal spends in Germany will leave an indelible mark on his heart and soul. He will form a deep bond of affection for his German tutor Emma Wegenast, a beautiful, sincere, and serious-minded girl of twenty seven who teaches him the works of Goethe, Heine, and other German poets. He will be so moved by this European country that he will say, in his future letters, 'My body is here, my thoughts are in Germany'; or that 'it is impossible for me to forget your beautiful country where I have learned so much. My stay in Heidelberg is nothing now but a beautiful dream. How I'd wish I could repeat it!'; and 'I am very fond of Germany. It has had a great influence on my ideals and I shall never forget my stay in that country.'

He would even go on to say that Germany is a kind of second home to his spirit. 'I learned much and I thought much in that country. The home of Goethe has found a permanent place in my soul.'[1]

What was it that created so much love for Germany in Iqbal's heart?

Even before coming to Europe, Iqbal was acquainted with Kant, Spinoza, Schopenhaur, and Hegel, *et al.* 'What was unique here was that for the first time he was living in a country without feeling the oppressive yoke of colonial subjugation.'[2]

Iqbal admires Europe's vitality. He finds active and dynamic people on the continent who believe in creating their own destinities. They are confident and restless, ready to change whatever they do not like. This spurs Iqbal to sing of action and satirize passivity, asking his people to 'glow with the sunbeams of desire', and to learn from the wave, which is always on the roll, restless, in movement.

In Europe, Iqbal comes to admire the philosophies of Nietzsche and Bergson. Nietzsche's idea of the Superman, of self-creation and self-assertion and Bergson's *Elan Vital* inspire him to develop his own philosophy of *khudi*, inspired by Quranic teachings, the Prophet's Traditions, and Arab and Persian literature. 'The Western people,' he writes, 'are distinguished in the world for their power of action; and for this reason, a study of their literature and philosophy is the best guide to an understanding of the significance of life.'[3]

Besides the intellectual stimulation that Iqbal receives in Germany, one cannot discount the fact that without the company and friendship of the pretty and brilliant Emma, who was only two years younger than him, it is doubtful whether Iqbal would have loved Germany as much. She became his window to German art, culture, and philosophy, and their friendship brought the fragrance of love into his life in the idyllic setting of Heidelberg.[4]

* * *

Emma was born on August 26, 1879, in Heilbronn in Germany—a small town nearly eighty kilometres away from Heidelberg, situated by the side of the Neckar. She had an elder sister, Sophie Wegenast who lived to the ripe old age of a hundred and two years. She passed away in 1978. She had a brother too but Iqbal never got to meet Emma's siblings.[5]

After finishing her primary schooling in her hometown, Emma moved to Heidelberg where she developed a special interest in philosophy and literature. She studied at the university in Heidelberg and, after her graduation, she became attached to the *Pension Scherer*.[6] She, and several other young women, taught German to international students staying in a student hostel on the Neckar River.

This is where Iqbal and Emma meet for the first time.

Iqbal came to Heidelberg specifically to learn the German language. He wanted to speak German well enough to successfully pass the oral examination for his doctoral dissertation at Munich University.

When Iqbal reaches Heidelberg in 1907, he stays at the hostel. He seeks out Emma, most probably, at the instruction of Atiya's brother who had already learnt German from her.

She is the fourth child of a small business owner from Heilbronn. At five feet and seven inches, she is an inch taller than Iqbal. She has 'black hair, blue eyes', and is 'good looking and elegant without being self-conscious'.[7]

She helps him to learn the German language. She introduces him to Goethe and other German poets. Iqbal finds her to be an honest and good-hearted person and their shared love for German literature and language brings them closer.

The period of around six months that he spends in Germany—most of which was in Emma's company—'witnessed the composing of some of his most moving love poems'.[8]

In early October 1907, Iqbal moves to Munich. He writes three letters to her from there. In one of the letters, he complains about her tearing one of his letters. He says she was being cruel to him by doing this.[9]

During the nine months that Iqbal stays in London after meeting Emma, he sends her several letters, which are full of passionate exhortations about their friendship.[10] On December 2, 1907, he informs her in a letter that Professor Arnold has gone to Egypt and he has become a temporary professor of Arabic at London University.

He is responsible for two lectures in a week. He says that he can't write too much on paper but she can imagine what is in his soul. He expresses his desire to see her again, to talk to her again, and wrings his hands in despair for not being able to do so, for being far away from each other. Once a person has become your friend, it is not possible for him to live without you, he writes. Then he seeks her forgiveness for giving vent to his emotions in a letter. He understands that she does not like such direct expressions of sentimentality.

Iqbal requests Emma to send him her photos. On January 29, 1908, he receives two pictures of her. The next day, he writes to her, thanking her for sending him the photos. Both the pictures are very beautiful, he says, and they will adorn his study table forever. But please don't believe even for a moment, he assures her, that your pictures will remain on paper alone. No, they are imprinted on his heart and they will live on in his bosom till the end of days, he says, like an ardent lover. He expresses his doubt if he will be able to see her again but says that for him she has become a real life force, that he will never be able to forget her and that he will always remember her kindness towards him.

Emma faces hardships in her life after Iqbal leaves Germany. It is not known what these hardships were. Iqbal writes to her on January 21, 1908: 'After going through many storms you have achieved your independence.'[11]

Nearly a month later, he informs her that he will return to India in early July and he desires to meet her. He will try his best to come to Heidelberg for a few days but will it be possible for her to meet him in Paris? He tells her that her photo is on his table and keeps on reminding him of those beautiful moments that they had spent together.

For almost three months there is no communication between them. Iqbal burns with desire to hear from Emma. When he can't hold it any longer, he writes to her on June 3, 1908, telling her how sad he is for not having heard from her for such a long time. 'My body is here, my thoughts are in Germany,' he confesses. Then he informs her of his plan to return to India. Please send me a few lines before I head back to my country, he implores her. With a heavy heart he also tells her that it might not be possible for him to travel through Germany before his return to India.

He sends her his picture on June 10, 1908, and informs her that he is departing for India on July 2. He will write to her from India, he promises.

In his last letter from London, dated June 27, he again regrets that he is not able to travel through Germany, despite his desire to do so. He is returning to India on July 3 via Paris where he has an engagement. He desires to receive a letter from her before he departs from England. No matter what, he says, countries and oceans cannot keep them apart and an uncanny relationship will live on between them. Like a magnetic force, his thoughts will always sprint towards her. Please keep writing to me and keep remembering me, he requests her. He reminds her that she has a true friend in Iqbal and even though he is at a distance, it does not matter because when hearts are fused together, distances become meaningless.

They continue to correspond with each other even after Iqbal returns to India. Sometimes, they exchange gifts and Iqbal often sends her some of his poems. With Emma's help, several of Iqbal's translated poems will get published in Heidelberg's newspapers.

Iqbal writes twenty-seven letters to Emma between 1907 and 1933—seventeen in German and ten in English.[12]

While Iqbal moves to India and busies himself with his career, Emma stays on in Heilbronn until 1914. During this time, she visits Heidelberg off and on. Her father passes away in 1913 and when the Second World War gets underway, she permanently moves to Heidelberg. Iqbal will send his last seven letters to her between 1931 and 1933.

Emma serves as a Red Cross nurse during the First World War, and then as a technical assistant at the University Pharmacy from 1920 to 1928 in Heidelberg. She keeps working, off and on, until

1947. She retires at the age of sixy-eight due to bad health. After retirement, she becomes a pensioner. Her life ends at the age of eighty-five on October 16, 1964.

She never marries.

13

Return to India

Self-Control in individuals builds families; in communities, it builds empires.

—Iqbal, *Stray Thoughts*

Iqbal's oral examination in German for his research dissertation takes place on November 4, 1907, in Munich University. It is conducted by a board presided over by Professor Dr Friedrich Hommel.

The thesis is submitted with the approval of Professor Dr Hommel, Iqbal's supervisor or 'doctor-father' as they are called in Germany, to the Faculty of Philosophy of the Ludwig Maximilians University at Munich.

Since the university does not have a specialist to evaluate research on Persian metaphysics, a special provision is made by treating Arabic philology as Iqbal's principal subject, and English philology and philosophy as subsidiaries. He is awarded first grade in the principal subject, and second and third respectively in the two subsidiaries. The doctorate is awarded Cum Laude, i.e. 'With Great Praise' in November 1907.

He reaches London on November 5, 1907, and starts preparing for the final exams of the bar-at-law. The finals take place in May 1908 and he stays on in London until July. The results come out on the first of July and soon after he leaves for India.

During his last days in London, Iqbal starts a series of lectures on Islam and culture covering topics such as Islamic mysticism, the influence of Islam on European civilization, Islamic democracy, and Islam and the human mind, among others.

Iqbal teaches Arabic in London University for six months as a temporary lecturer when Prof. Arnold is on leave.

During the nine months that Iqbal spends in London, he has been an active participant in the organizational activities of Muslim students. He establishes a semi-political organization there which is known as the Pan Islamic Society. The society's general secretary is Sir Abdullah Saharwardi, and Mirza Jalauddin and Sir Sultan Ahmed are its joint secretaries.

In May 1908, the British Committee of All India Muslim League is inaugurated. Syed Amir Ali is selected as the president of the committee and Iqbal is appointed a member of the Common Assembly.

Even though Iqbal does not write much poetry during his days in London, he is won over by his friend Abdul Qadir and his mentor Arnold. He adopts Persian as the language of his poetic expression. The move to Persian occurs during a small party where Iqbal is invited as a guest. When asked if he has composed poems in Persian, he acknowledges that he has not done so, except for maybe a few couplets.

That night, so moved he is by the questions, that he starts composing shers in Persian lying on his bed. In the morning, when Abdul Qadir meets him, he recites to him two fresh ghazals in Persian, which he remembers by heart. This exercise convinces Iqbal that he is capable of writing poetry in Persian and from then, he composes poems in Persian. Urdu becomes his second choice.

During his European sojourn, Iqbal becomes conversant not just with the great English poets but also the great French and German poets. He develops a spiritual connection with the German poet Goethe. He will pay tribute to him in one of his books in the future.[1]

Iqbal composes twenty-four poems and seven ghazals during

his time in Europe—all of these are included in the second part
of *Bang-e Dara*. Many of the poems composed during this period
contain messages—indicating that Iqbal is slowly moving into a new
phase of poetry that seeks to spur people into action. Two examples
are '*Tulba-e Aligarh Ke Naam*' ('To the Students of Aligarh') and
'*Abdul Qadir Ke Naam*' ('To Abdul Qadir').

Europe transforms Iqbal's ideas about the world. It makes him
reject territorial nationalism and begin to celebrate Islamic culture
and history. There is no single event or series of events that propel
his mind in this new direction but it's fair to say that an up-close
scrutiny of Western civilization led to this transformation. Iqbal saw
the seeds of Europe's destruction in its material culture, which he
believed lacked spirituality. Europe's achievements in science and
technology were marvelous but its focus was the body, not the heart.
Love is dead in the West because thought has become irreligious,
reckons Iqbal. Notwithstanding its progress, Europe's Achilles heel is
in its manifest materialism, he is convinced, and underpinned by the
Darwinian understanding of the survival of the fittest. This leads him
to form the belief that the West will destroy itself through excessive
materialism. In 1908, he warns the West against its impending doom:

Dayaar-e Maghrib ke rehne walon
Khuda ki basti dukaan nahin hai
Khara jise tum samajh rahe ho
Woh ab zar-e kum ayaar hoga
Tumhari tehzeeb apne khanjar se
Aap khud khudkushi karegi

O, dwellers of the cities of the West,
God's world is not a shop,
And that which you regard as true coin,
Will prove to be only a counterfeit.
Your civilization will commit suicide
With its own sword.[2]

It is in Europe that Iqbal begins to see racial discrimination and territorial nationalism as the biggest enemies of Islam. While Western imperialism exploits the world, the Islamic world faces imminent dissolution. Russia hastens the disintegration of the Ottoman Empire and also makes Persia its target. Iqbal locates nationalism as the root cause of Europe's excesses and the world's problems. He will wage a life-long war against this evil.

When Iqbal sees Western nations divided on the basis of race, language, or geographic boundaries, he begins to appreciate the universal message of Islam which, instead of dividing people, unites them irrespective of their race or colour or language and culture. While in Europe, the history of Islam seeps into his soul and shapes it for the rest of his life. Europe's atmosphere turns him into a real Muslim.[3]

In contrast to Europe's race towards self-annihilation, Iqbal sees Islam as a rescuer of humanity. He becomes increasingly 'convinced that the progress of Indian Muslims lay not in imitating Europe but in reforming and reviving the religious community they had been born into.'[4] In Islam, Iqbal finds a better model to combat the ills of the West—competition, heartlessness, capitalism, and nationalism.[5]

On July 3, 1908, Iqbal bids adieu to England. He takes a ship via France. When his steamer passes by the isles of Sicily, he does not see it as Mazzini's motherland but as the tomb of Islamic civilization:

> *Hai tere asaar me poshida kiski dastaan*
> *Tere sahil ki khamoshi me hai anadaz-e bayan*
> *Dard apna mujh se keh main bhi sarapa dard hoon*
> *Jis ki tu manzil tha, main us karvaan ki gard hoon*
> *Rang tasveer-e kuhan me bhar ke dikhlade mujhe*
> *Qissa ayyaam-e salaf ka keh ke tadpaade mujhe*
> *Main tera tohfa su-e Hindoostan le jaonga*
> *Khud yahan rota hoon, auron ko wahan rulwaonga*

Whose story is hidden in your ruins?
The silence of your shores harbours a unique mode of expression.
Tell me of your sorrow—I too am full of pain;
I am the dust of that caravan whose goal you were.
Paint over this picture once more and show it to me;
Make me suffer by telling the story of ancient days.
I shall carry your gift to India;
I shall make others weep as I weep here.[6]

He arrives in Bombay on July 25 and boards a train to Delhi. On many of the stops on the way, school children greet him with the singing of his famous patriotic poem, 'Saray jahan se achha Hindustan hamara ...'

He spends the whole day at Nizamuddin's dargah in Delhi. He arrives in Lahore on July 27, where friends and admirers give him a grand reception. Then he leaves for Sialkot to meet his family.

PART THREE
1908–1925

A Lawyer in Lahore

14

A Wretched Soul

Suffering is a gift from the gods to make men see the entirety of life.

—Iqbal, *Stray Thoughts*

The first thing that bothers Iqbal upon his return from England is employment. While he was in Europe, his elder brother Ata Muhammad supported him financially. Now that Ata is only years away from retirement, this arrangement cannot go on any longer. Also, Ata has his own family to take care of, and it is a fairly large family, comprising a wife and six children.

Iqbal had resigned from his academic job at Government College, Lahore in 1908 while he was still in Europe. On his return to India, while he is celebrated as a poet, he still has no source of income.

The only option for Iqbal now is to start working as a lawyer, but that too requires some basic investment. His generous brother Ata Muhammad comes to his rescue again.

In August 1908, while Iqbal is still in Sialkot, Ata Muhammad sets up a residence cum office for Iqbal in Lahore on Mohanlal Road (now Urdu Bazaar). After Iqbal arrives in Lahore, he hires a *munshi*, Kahin Chand. Ali Bakhsh, Iqbal's long-serving domestic help, also arrives to take care of the household chores.

Iqbal starts his legal practice from Lahore's lower courts. This continues for a few months but he does not enjoy working in the environment of the lower courts. The pettiness of the affairs he deals with tires him out. Moreover, Kahin Chand, instead of being a loyal aid, often squabbles over payments. This further upsets Iqbal, making the entire experience unpalatable to him.

On October 20, 1908, Iqbal has his first breakthrough. He gets enrolled as an advocate in the Chief Court of Punjab. This affords him an entry into the Bar Room of Lahore where legal luminaries such as Mian Shah Din, Sir Fazal Hussain, Sir Muhammad Shafi, Sir Shahabuddin, Sir Shadi Lal, Lala Lajpat Rai, Pandit Shiv Narain Shamim, and Mirza Jalaluddin are regular visitors. In the years to come, Iqbal will increasingly interact with these legal pundits as they assume significant roles in the politics of Punjab. Some of them will even become his close friends. But for now, all this is new for a young Iqbal.

As a lawyer, Iqbal works hard for the court cases that come his way. Not to dilute his focus from the job at hand, he stays away from poetry for a while. Once he joins the Chief Court, he also moves his office and residence to Anarkali—a bigger accommodation than what he had at Mohanlal Road. In place of Kahin Chand, Sir Muhammad Shafi's *munshi* Tahiruddin is hired. He occupies a rear section of the house and ultimately becomes Iqbal's trusted aid. Tahiruddin will remain his lifelong treasurer and will keep Iqbal's accounts throughout his life.

Also, to indulge in an old love, Iqbal brings along his pigeons from Sailkot to play with them on the rooftop of his house.

Meanwhile, academic jobs keep knocking at his door. The famous M.A.O. College in Aligarh offers him the position of professor of Philosophy. He rejects the offer. In April 1909, Government College, Lahore, offers him professorship in history. That too is given the same treatment. Iqbal wants to remain focused on his legal practice—a profession more lucrative than academia.

However, teaching continues to follow Iqbal like a loyal shadow. In May 1909, Austin White James, a temporary professor of

Philosophy at Government College, Lahore, passes away and there is an urgent need for a teacher to take his place. On the principal's recommendation, the government of Punjab requests Iqbal to accept this temporary position. Iqbal obliges on the condition that his academic work should not interfere with his legal work. He comes on board once that condition is agreed upon by the authorities. He is given early morning classes to teach in the college. After college, he goes to the courts. The government also makes a special provision for him—his court cases come up for hearing only later in the day when he is free of his teaching responsibilities. At the college, his basic pay is fixed at five hundred rupees.

With time, Iqbal the lawyer also becomes preoccupied with additional social and professional responsibilities. In 1909, he becomes a joint editor of a legal journal, *Indian Cases Law Reports*. He also becomes a member of Anjuman Islamia Punjab, an association that will prove to be a life-long affair for Iqbal.

In December 1908, when Khawaja Saleemullah Khan, the nawab of Dhaka, comes to Amritsar to preside over the All India Muhammedan Educational Conference, Iqbal meets him as part of a Kashmiri Muslim delegation. He reads out a memorandum to lobby with the government to declare Kashmiris farmers and to increase their effective representation in the armed forces. Again, a year or so later, Iqbal meets Maharaja Pratap Singh of Kashmir as part of a Kashmiri delegation. Initially, Iqbal is reluctant to go for this meeting but one of his friends drags him to it.

The meeting turns out to be amusing. The maharaja has heard of Iqbal's intellectual acumen, scholarship, and poetic prowess. '*Dakdaar Saheb*,' the Maharaja asks him, '*Suna hai aap bait banate hain?*' (I have heard that you make poetry?'). 'Sarkar! Neither me nor my ancestors have ever worked on *bait*,' Iqbal quips. 'Besides, I am not a *dakdaar* because neither I nor my elders have been postmen at any point of time.'

The maharaja is astonished to hear this from Iqbal's mouth. Raising his brows, he looks at Iqbal's friends for explanation. One of them clarifies: 'Sir, he is a poet and he composes poetry. A sher is also called a *bait* but he took *bait* for *baid*, the cane reed that is used to make furniture.' The maharaja now understands what is going on. He requests Iqbal to declaim some poetry for him. When Iqbal obliges the maharaja, he asks him to sing his poetry aloud. At this, an irritated Iqbal whispers in the ears of his friend Fauq: 'I feel like telling him—I will sing but first you will have to tie ghungroos on my friends' feet.' He finally sings aloud some of his poetry and the maharaja also shares some Persian poetry with him.[1]

By this time, a change of heart, has already taken place in Iqbal. The Iqbal, who had started out as an Indian nationalist in the footsteps of Akbar Illahabadi, who celebrated India's multiculturalism in 'Tarana-e Hind' and 'Naya Shiwala', called the god Ram 'Imam-e-Hind', and India the land of Chishti and Nanak, and sang paeans to its eternal beauty, that Iqbal is lost forever. The new Iqbal, who still respects all religions and communities, has a new mindset now (which he will refer to as 'higher communalism in his later years'). That Hindus and Muslims are two separate nations and they should develop themselves indepedently of each other. This attitude is visible when he is invited, a few months after his return from England, to participate in a Hindu-Muslim-Sikh forum at Amritsar. Iqbal spurns the invitation politely, saying:

'I've myself been of the view that religious differences should disappear from this country and even now act on this principle in my private life. But now I think that the preservation of their separate national identities is desirable for both the Hindus and Muslims. The vision of a common nationhood for India is a beautiful ideal and has a poetic appeal . . . but appears incapable of fulfillment.'

For a year or two, Iqbal is so busy juggling his academic and legal work that he can hardly spare any time for poetry. But he has still not let go of the poet in him. One evening in May 1910, he is at his residence when a friend Wajahat Hussain Jhanjhanwi comes to meet him along with Fauq. Hussain starts to recite his poetry to Iqbal and Iqbal enjoys the recitation. Meanwhile, his assistant Munshi Tahiruddin enters the room to inform Iqbal that a client has come to see him. 'Please ask him to wait,' Iqbal says, 'I will call him once I am done here.' 'My friend, first you should take care of your *pet* [stomach],' advises Fauq. 'This business can continue later; it is not that important, is it?' 'It is this business that is the food of the soul,' Iqbal corrects his friend, twirling his brown moustache. 'And as long as the soul is there, everything is there. If the client has come to see me, hearing my reputation, he will not go anywhere else.' True to his belief, Iqbal meets the client only after the poetry session finishes.[2]

On 9 April, 1909, he writes to Atiya from Lahore:

'Yes, I refused the Aligarh Chair of Philosophy and a few days ago I refused to accept the Lahore Government College Chair of History. I do not wish to enter any service. My object is to run away from this country as soon as possible. You know the reason. I have a sort of moral debt to my brother, which detains me. My life is extremely miserable. They force my wife upon me. I have written to my father that he had no right to arrange my marriage especially when I had refused to enter into an alliance of that sort. I am quite willing to support her, but I am not prepared to make my life miserable by keeping her with me. As a human being I have a right to happiness—if society or nature deny that to me, I defy both. The only cure is that I should leave this wretched country forever, or take refuge in liquor which makes suicide easier. Those dead barren leaves of books cannot yield happiness; I have got sufficient fire in my soul to burn them up and social conventions as well. A good God created all this, you say. Maybe. The facts of this life, however, tend to a different conclusion. It is intellectually easier to believe in an eternal omnipotent Devil rather than a good God ...'

In this letter, he is only unburdening his soul to a friend whom he could confide in.

Clearly, at heart, Iqbal is not happy with his circumstances—he is so torn between his academic and legal work that he barely has time to write poetry, the actual work that sustains his soul. He wants to find a reliable source of income that might free him from all unnecessary work that he has to do to survive and afford him time

for his creative work. Like his favourite German poet Goethe, who
was also a lawyer by training, Iqbal desires to find a head of state
who could become his patron, freeing him from all his worries of
earning a living.[3]

For this purpose, he decides to visit Hyderabad. Though he has not
visited the rich princely state before, his poetry has been published in
the journals of that state and he has acquaintances such as Sir Akbar
Haidari and Maharaja Kishan Prasad who can host him there. His
friend Ghulam Qadir Garami also works as the *Shair-e Khaas* with
the Nizam, Mir Mehboob Ali who heads the state of Hyderabad.

He takes a ten day leave from his college and on March 18, 1910,
he leaves for Hyderabad.

Iqbal stays at the residence of Sir Akbar Haidari who is a great
supporter of arts and literature. During his stay, he meets and dines
with the major poets of the state. When he visits the mausoleums of
Golconda's Qutubshahi rulers, he writes a poem titled, '*Goristan-e
Shahi*' ('The Royal Graveyard'). Later, it is published in *Makhzan*.

In Hyderabad, Iqbal also meets Maharaja Kishan Prasad Shaad, a
high-ranking Minister in the nizam's government and a descendent
of Raja Todarmal. A Khatri by caste, he is a scholar of Arabic, Persian,
and Urdu, and a sufi at heart. Like Iqbal, he too has been a disciple
of Daagh. He owns an estate, which gives him an annual income of
1.6 million rupees. He has three Muslim begums and three Hindu
ranis. He visits temples as well as offers prayers in mosques. Iqbal
falls in love with this unique human being and fellow poet, and
they develop a deep bond of friendship. Iqbal writes a poem in
appreciation of the maharaja with the title, 'Shukriya'. Later on, it
is published in *Makhzan*.

Iqbal leaves Hyderabad on March 23, 1910. The fact that he met
a number of eminent personalities in Hyderabad makes the trip
worthwhile but the basic purpose of finding a patron for himself
remains unfulfilled.

On his way back, he visits the mausoleum of Aurangzeb,[4] along
with his brother Ata Muhammad. On March 28, he arrives at Lahore.

By 1910, Iqbal is offered two options by the college authorities. He can either continue with his legal practice or become a full-time professor of Philosophy at the Government College. Iqbal decides in favour of the legal profession where the chances of earning a high income are better, depending on one's enterprise and luck. Even though he detaches himself from active teaching, he will continue his association with various universities throughout his life as an examiner or a question-setter to supplement his income.

By 1911, Muslims all over the world face a situation of disarray, subjugation, and humiliation at the hands of the European powers. In India itself, even though Muslims remain loyal to the British rulers, the partition of Bengal is carried out in 1911—a setback for the Muslims of Bengal. According to Maulana Shibli, a prominent Muslim voice of his period, this was a severe slap across the face of Indian Muslims.

Outside India, the Muslim world sees some disastrous changes. In 1911, Germany and Russia enter into an agreement, putting Iran under Russia's suzerainty. A year later, Russian forces bombard Mashhad, and British and Russian forces occupy Iran, destroying the movement for a constitutional government, and usurping the freedom of Iranians.

Turkey also goes through a crisis as the European powers dismember the Ottoman Empire: Austria announces that Bosnia and Herzegovina are parts of its kingdom, not Turkey's. Bulgaria also announces freedom from the Ottomans. In 1911, the Italo–Turkish war[5] starts between the Ottoman Empire and the kingdom of Italy and lasts until 1912. As a result of this conflict, Italy captures the Ottoman Tripolitania Vilayet, of which the most notable sub-provinces are Fezzan, Cyrenaica, and Tripoli itself. These territories together formed what became known as Italian Libya.

In 1912, Bulgaria, Greece, Montenegro, and Serbia achieve independence from the Ottoman Empire, as a result of the First Balkan War. The Ottoman Empire loses almost all of its European territories to the west of the River Maritsa. A major disaster in

Turkey's history, the consequences of which prove to be far-reaching: within five years, the Turkish Empire itself will collapse.[6]

Though Iqbal has been reluctant to recite poetry in public gatherings ever since his return from Europe, he is so moved by the changing fortunes of Muslims in India and abroad that he pens one of his most famous poems: *Shikwa* (*The Complaint*).[7] He presents this poem to a conference of the Anjuman-e Himayat-e Islam in Islamia College.

Safa-e dahar se baatil ko mitaya hum ne
Nau-e insaan ko ghulami se chhuraya hum ne
Tere Kaabe ko jabeenon se basaya hum ne
Tere Quran ko seenon se lagaya hum ne
Phir bhi hum se yeh gila hai ke wafadar nahin
Hum wafadar nahin, tu bhi to dildar nahin!

We who removed from this world's book the leaves which were
        with falsehood stained,
We who from a tyrant's ignorance, the imprisoned human race
        unchained,
We who with myriad sajdas filled Your Holy Kába's hallowed
        shrine,
Whose bosoms reverently held Your great and glorious Book
        Divine—
If our meed still the obloquy that we have shirked the faithful's part,
How then cans't You make claim to be the kindly faith-compelling
        heart?[8]

It is a daring poem. 'Your world presented a weird look until we arrived on the scene,' he asks God the creator on behalf of the Muslim nation. 'Why, then, the Divine Benevolence seemed to be reserved exclusively for non-Muslims today?' The poem, however, is a prayer in spirit that celebrates 'the bonding between the human soul and the Creator':

Chaak is bulbul-e tanha ki nawa se dil hoon
Jaagne wale isi bang-e dara se dil hoon
Yani phir zinda naye ahl-e wafa se dil hoon
Phir usi baada-e dereena ke pyasee dil hoon

Allow the song of this solitary nightingale to pierce through the
     hearts of the listeners!
Let the call of this marching bell awaken the hearts from deep
     slumber,
and be freshened up with a new covenant but thirsting for the same
     old wine.

The audience is spellbound when he recites the poem. They shower
flowers on him. An old man shouts, 'Illallah!' and comes to stand in
the middle of the assembly, tears streaming from his eyes. There is
not a single soul in the audience whose heart is not howling listening
to Iqbal's complaint to God. Iqbal's father is also in the audience,
his eyes moist at his son's success as a poet as well as at his poignant
message to the Muslims of the world.

After he breaks his poetic silence in public with *Shikwa*,
nothing gets in the way of his poetry, as if someone or something
had opened the sluice gates to his poetic heart. Iqbal pours forth
from the decanter of his soul, goblet after goblet of soul-stirring
poetry—'*Fatima Bint-e Abdullah*', 'Prayer', 'The Anthem of the
Muslim Nation', 'The Candle and the Poet', and 'In the Presence of
the Holy Prophet' among others.[9]

Some of the conservative ulemas, however, do not approve of his
poem. Its tone and tenor is disrespectful, they complain. In 1913,
Iqbal presents his answer to *Shikwa* by writing *Jawab-e Shikwa* (*The
Answer to the Complaint*) in the garden outside the Mochi Darwaza
in Lahore. A huge audience is in attendance; every couplet that Iqbal
recites is met with huge applause, and it is auctioned off handsomely.
The purpose of the congregation is to raise funds to support the
Turkish soldiers fighting in the Balkan Wars.

In 1913, a tragic event occurs in Kanpur. When parts of a mosque are destroyed during road work by the civil administration, a group of Muslim protestors assembles at the site and starts to rebuild the broken part of the mosque. The deputy commissioner of police arrives at the site and gives firing orders without any warning. As a result, some Muslims, including children, are killed. The incident enrages the entire Indian Muslim community. Iqbal, along with Mirza Jalaluddin, visits Kanpur in September 1913 to provide legal aid to those arrested during the incident. He also meets the collector in this regard. On his way back, he meets Akbar Allahabadi in Allahabad and Hakim Ajmal Khan in Delhi.

During this time, educated Muslims slowly lose confidence in the leadership of the All India Muslim League, which was founded during the partition of Bengal. The view that is gaining ground is that Muslims should cooperate with Hindus and too much reliance on the British government is harming Muslim interests. Muslim scholars like Maulana Shibli openly criticize the League, claiming that it represents only the interests of the rich and the wealthy. He calls for a new political awakening among Indian Muslims.

The League's old leadership slowly loses its influence and young voices begin to emerge. They begin to hold conferences along with the Indian National Congress. Iqbal notices these changes in the attitude of the League but he does not say much on this matter. Nothing matters more to him than Islamic solidarity.

Amid all this tumult and action, the truth is that he is a lonely man. He writes to Akbar Allahabadi in October 1911 that, even though Lahore is a big city, he finds himself suffering a lonely life. There is not a single person in whom he can confide.

In truth, Iqbal still misses Europe, where his heart remains. The rough and tumble of leading a practical life weighs on his soft, poetic temperament. He is torn between the struggles of securing material success and managing his unsatisfactory marital life. As such, only those beautiful memories from his European sojourn are a balm on his distressed soul. He partly maintains his sanity by regularly corresponding with Emma Wegenast.

His first letter to Emma, upon his return to India, is dispatched on September 3, 1908. He informs her that he is starting off his career in law. I have forgotten all my German, he says, but I remember only one word—Emma.

In letter after letter, Iqbal reminds her how he misses her beautiful country and how he longs to see her and meet her again. By 1909, Iqbal still dreams of returning to Europe with enough money to settle down there, and build a house for himself. He also tells her how lonely and sad he feels in India.

On September 22, 1910, he sends her a 'posteen' (brooch) of a Tibetan sheep. On May 11, 1911, he thanks her for sending him some beautiful ties.

When Wegenast's father dies, he writes to her on July 30, 1913:[10]

I am extremely sorry to hear the sad news of your father's death; and though my letter must reach you a good many days after this sad event, yet neither time nor distance can make my sympathy with you in your bereavement any the less warm. The news has pained me very much indeed, and I pray that Almighty God may be pleased to shower his choicest blessings on the venerable old man, and to give you strength to endure your sorrow . . . You remember that Goethe said in the moment of his death—'More Light! Death opens up the way to more light and carries us to those regions where we stand face to face with eternal Beauty and Truth.' I remember the time when I read Goethe's poems with you and I hope, you also remember those happy days when we were so near to each other—so much so that I spiritually share in your sorrows.

Likewise, he also disburdens his heart in letters to Atiya Faizi. The good times they had shared in Europe provided beautiful memories in a far away land, much different from the harsh realities of the day.

When 'dark and sombre moods' overtake him, he writes to Atiya in a letter on April 17, 1909:

> I do not talk much with others now; my own wretched self is a mine of miserable thoughts which emerge snake-like from the deep and dark holes of my soul. I think I shall become a snake charmer and walk about in the streets with a host of curious boys behind me. Don't think I am a pessimist. I tell you misery is most delicious; and I enjoy my misfortune and laugh at those who believe they are happy. You see how I steal my happiness.

On July 17, 1909, he writes to Atiya again:

> You are not conscious of what good you have done me—this is true and better so. You could not have been conscious of it. I am conscious of it, but cannot give an expression to it. Let us drop the subject. It would be futile on my part to describe the indescribable, and then you say you are not open to conviction.
>
> Of course, everybody is waiting patiently for the place of rest. I am anxious to go to that place because I shall like to meet the Creator and call upon Him to give me a rational explanation of my mind, which I think is not an easy task for Him to do. I am incomprehensible to myself—you should not complain. Years ago I wrote:
>
> *Iqbal bhi Iqbal se agaah nahin hai*
> *Khuchh iss me tamaskhar nahi, wallah nahin hai*
>
> Iqbal himself does not know Iqbal
> By God, this is not a joke
>
> I am sorry to hear that you were distressed to find people in north India not respecting or admiring me. I tell you that I do not care

for other people's respect—I do not mean to live by other people's breath.

Jeena woh kya jo ho nafas-e ghair par madaar
Shuhrat ki zindagi ka bharosa bhi chhod de

It is no life, if one has to live on others' breath;
Stop relying on a life of fame

I live a straightforward honest life; my heart is in perfect unison with my tongue. People respect and admire hypocrisy. If hypocrisy brings me fame, respect, and admiration, I would rather die unknown and unlamented. Let the many-headed monster of the public give their dross of respect to others who act and live in accordance with their false ideals of religion and morality. I cannot stop to respect their conventions, which suppress the innate freedom of man's mind. Byron, Goethe, and Shelly were not respected by their contemporaries—and though I am far inferior to them in poetic power I am proud that I am in their company in this respect.

15

The Three Wives

The beauties of nature can be realized only through the eyes of
a lover. Hence the importance of a true marriage.

—Iqbal, *Stray Thoughts*

While Iqbal is being celebrated as a poet in India and his reputation
as a lawyer and Muslim leader in Lahore is on the rise, his domestic
life is much less cheerful. He has never come around to accept his
first marriage with Karim Bi which took place much against his
wishes in 1893. At that time, he was sixteen and he did not have
the courage to defy the orders of his elders.

All these years, Karim Bi has not been able to spend any time
with Iqbal. If there was any chance of this relationship working out,
it was doomed by time and separation. She spent only the first two
years of her marriage with Iqbal in Sialkot while he was still doing
his F.A. Once he moved to Lahore for higher education, the gulf
separating them widened. Then Iqbal moved to Europe and after
returning to India in 1908, he set up shop in Lahore. There too,
Karim Bi had no place in his life.

In Iqbal's absence, Karim Bi would spend most of her time with
her parents or at her parents' home in Gujarat. During holidays, Iqbal
would often come to spend time with his family in Sialkot or spend
a few weeks with his in-laws. For Karim Bi, the only consolation

was her two kids—Meraj Begum and Aftab Iqbal. By the time Iqbal returns from Europe, Meraj is twelve years old and Aftab ten.

Despite his parents' wishes and the efforts of his brother, Iqbal's relationship with his wife had reached a point of no return. Only two options were left—either Iqbal could divorce her or he could give her a monthly allowance to look after the family. With his family's advice, Iqbal settled for the latter option. He will fulfill his promise till the end of their lives.

In a letter to Atiya on April 9, 1909, he pours his heart out, sharing the anguish of his soul. In the letter, he says that he does not want to do any full time work and wants to run away from this godforsaken country.

The worst consequence of the failure of his marriage is that his two children, Meraj and Aftab, are deprived of paternal love and affection. Since both the children spend their time with their mother, they are more sympathetic towards her. However, Iqbal dotes upon Meraj, and Aftab is his grandfather's favourite. Unfortunately, Meraj dies after falling sick at the age of nineteen. Aftab's relationship with his father remains strained, until he cuts all ties with his father.

* * *

By the time Iqbal returns from Europe he is thirty-one, and desirous of another marriage of his choice. As he establishes himself as a lawyer in Lahore, the possibility of another marriage arises.

In his early thirties, Iqbal is an attractive man, a famous poet, highly educated, and a barrister to boot. In other words, he is a great catch. Now a lawyer in Lahore, he carries himself very well sartorially—usually wears a dark suit, with a Turkish hat. Sometimes, he wears glasses on an eye, after the fashion of his times.

Iqbal receives many letters from educated women desirous of a match with him. However, he is too traditional to go down this route for his second marriage.

Once, in 1910, Iqbal sees a photograph of Sardar Begum with the help of his aide, Munshi Tahiruddin. The munshi knows her brother Khwaja Abdul Ghani. Both brothers and sisters were orphans and belong to a poor family in Mochi Darwaza. Both were raised by an aunt. Abdul Ghani is a carpet-seller and Sardar is a literate, homely girl, without any formal education.

Iqbal begins to like her when he sees Sardar's photo. His mother arrives from Sialkot to finalize the alliance. Soon, Iqbal marries her at his house but their rukhsati is postponed until a later date.

She is then nineteen years old. However, now comes a mysterious turn in Iqbal's matrimonial alliance with Sardar.

Soon after the nikaah, Iqbal begins to receive anonymous letters that inform him Sardar Begum is a morally corrupt girl. This new scandal puts Iqbal in a dilemma—did he choose the right girl? Has he made a mistake?

He discusses this with his family and friends. They all decide that the matter should be investigated before a decision is made to end the marriage. This will take another three years.

But Iqbal wants to move on. He has decided to divorce Sardar and look for a new wife. This time luck favours him. One of his friends Syed Bashir Haider, who is an excise inspector in Ludhiana, informs him of a possible alliance. The girl, Mukhtar Begum, belongs to a rich Kashmiri family in Ludhiana. Not much time is wasted in securing this alliance. In early 1913, Iqbal weds Mukhtar Begum and brings her to his residence in Anarkali in Lahore.

By this time, his friends find out the source of the anonymous letters regarding Sardar Begum's character. It turns out that the letters are from a disgruntled lawyer who wanted Sardar Begum to marry his own son. Because of this situation of confusion, Sardar has already suffered mentally and socially for three years. She too writes a letter to Iqbal, asking him not to believe the rumours about her. 'I am married to you now and I can't imagine another nikaah with another man. I will spend my entire life like this and will ask God for justice on the Day of Judgement.'

Iqbal is shattered after reading this letter, and after discovering how wrong he was about Sardar. He holds his head in his hand, thinking about how he took a step like this. Because of him an innocent girl had suffered.

He shares the news with Mukhtar, his new wife. Being a soft-hearted lady, she comes to tears hearing Sardar's story. Both decide to bring Sardar to their house to live with them, to right a wrong that had happened in a state of confusion.

Since Iqbal had once thought of divorcing Sardar, he has another nikaah done with her in August or September 1913. In a few weeks, both Sardar and Mukhtar begin to live as sisters at Iqbal's Anarkali residence. They are almost the same age and they both love each other more than sisters.

This marks the beginning of a happy phase in Iqbal's life. One of his unmarried sisters also lives in his Lahore house. Sometimes, even his first wife, Karim Bi, comes to stay with her estranged husband.

A tragic event occurs in the family when Iqbal's mother, Imam Bibi, dies in Sialkot on November 9, 1914. Her death comes as a major blow to him. For a while, he loses interest in the world. 'My interest in worldly matters and my urge to be successful in life was due only to her,' he says in a letter. 'Now I am just awaiting my death . . .' While he continues to work on the first part of *Secrets and Mysteries* (*Asrar-o Rumooz*), he pays homage to his mother in August 1915 in a long Urdu poem, 'In Memoriam of the Late Mother.' In prayer for his mother, he says:

Asmaan teri lahad par shabnam-afshani kare
Sabza-e nau-rusta is ghar ki nigahbani kare

May the sky shed dewdrops on your grave
May new blossoms guard over this abode

Until now, even though Iqbal has become a celebrated poet throughout India, he has not thought of seriously publishing his poetry. He used to give his poems to his editor friends like Shaikh

Abdul Qadir and Maulana Zafar Ali Khan. There was even a calligrapher named Munshi Fazal Ilahi who made some money by publishing a collection of Iqbal's poems. Only Iqbal was so far oblivious to the money he could make from his poetry. One of his friends Chaudhury Muhammad Hussain makes him aware of this possibility.

As a result, Iqbal takes the matter of publishing his poems in his own hands. He first publishes his Persian poem *Asrar-e Khudi* (*Secrets of the Self*) in 1915. The book becomes a success, finding readers among Persian speakers in Iran, Afghanistan, and parts of Turkey and Russia. When R.A. Nicholson translates it into English in 1920, Iqbal becomes known in England and the United States too. [1]

After *Asrar-e Khudi*, Iqbal publishes another Persian poem, *Rumuz-e Bekhudi* (*Mysteries of Self-Denial*) in 1918. A sequel to the former poem, it throws light on Iqbal's ideas about the development of the human Ego or Personality. Iqbal considers Power and Courage as the ideals that man needs to perfect to achieve his great destiny. In *Rumuz*, he places the service of mankind as the highest goal for the ambition of man.

16

Knighthood

Khilafat Movement and Non-Cooperation Movement 1920–1922

It is idle to seek logical truth in poetry. The ideal of imagination is beauty, not truth. Do not then try to show a poet's greatness by quoting passages from his works which, in your opinion, embody scientific truth.

—Iqbal, *Stray Thoughts*

On August 4, 1914, the First World War begins in Europe. Both Germany and Britain are vying for Turkey's support. The Turkish Empire, at this time, not only covers the Arabian lands but because of the Caliphate, it has influence over all the Muslim countries.

After much consideration, Turkey decides to ally with Germany on November 4, 1914. During the Great War, many of the British soldiers fighting for the Allies are Muslims. Since, in effect, they are fighting against their own Caliph, Britain, Russia, and France assure the Muslims that they are not fighting this war to deprive Turkey of its territories.[1]

By early 1918, it becomes clear that the Allies are going to win the war. Anticipating the consequences, Muslims fighting with the Allies appeal to the British, reminding them of their promise to not dismember the Turkish Empire. On October 31, 1918, first the Turks make a peace deal with the Allies and on November 11, the Germans surrender to the Allied forces. After this, the Muslims foresee that the Allies are not going keep their word—they are going to dismember Turkey and put an end to the Caliphate. Muslims in India feel spiritually connected with the Caliphate and they perceive its possible dissolution as an emotional blow, even a humiliation, at the hands of the Western powers.

The last year of the second decade of the twentieth century finds India in a state of discontent—the Rowlatt Act, the Jallianwala Bagh massacre, and martial law in Punjab have 'belied all the generous wartime promises of the British'. Only a few are satisfied with the Montagu-Chemsford Reforms, 'with its ill-considered scheme of diarchy.'[2]

Indian Muslims are incensed to discover that the British have tricked them into selling their loyalty during the War 'by assurances of the generous treatment of Turkey after the War—a promise British statesmen had no intention of fulfilling.'[3]

To preserve the Ottoman Caliphate, Muslims in India organize a Khilafat Conference on September 20, 1919, in Lucknow, and with this the Khilafat Movement is launched in India.

A second conference is organized in November 1919 in Delhi. The participants include Gandhiji, Motilal Nehru, Madan Mohan Malviya, and others. Gandhi presides over one of the sessions in the conference in which he declares that the Hindus of India will support the demand for Khilafat unconditionally. Originally, it was suggested that the Hindus will support the movement in lieu of a law against cow slaughter.

In his speeches Gandhi makes it clear that all along he had believed that the British have committed 'a breach of faith by making promises they had no intention of keeping.'[4]

Gandhi's simplicity and sincerity win over the hearts of Muslims, who select him to lead the movement forward. However, not all Hindu leaders in the Congress are convinced of lending their support to a Muslim religious cause. Sardar Vallabh Bhai Patel finds it ridiculous to support a movement for the Caliphate when Indians themselves are slaves of the British Empire.

Gandhi tries hard to drum up support for the Khilafat Movement among the Hindus but fails to elicit any significant response. In February 1920, he suggests to the Khilafat Committee that it should adopt a programme of non-violent non-cooperation to protest the Government's behaviour. On June 9, 1920, the Khilafat Committee at Allahabad unanimously accepts the suggestion of non-cooperation and asks Gandhi to lead the movement.[5]

The Non-Cooperation Movement programme entails the surrender of all titles and honours, boycott of government-affiliated schools and colleges, law courts, foreign cloth, as well as resignation from government service and mass civil disobedience, including the non-payment of taxes. People are also asked to maintain Hindu–Muslim unity, give up untouchability, and avoid violence of any kind.[6]

Gandhiji makes a nationwide tour with the Ali borthers (Muhammad Ali Jauhar and Shaukat Ali), addresses hundreds of meetings and meets a large number of political workers. About 90,000 students leave government schools and colleges and join more than 800 national schools and colleges.[7]

On July 8, 1921, Muhammad Ali throws a new bombshell on the government. At the All India Khilafat Conference held in Karachi, he declares that it is 'religiously unlawful for the Muslims to continue in the British Army'. He asks that this message be conveyed to every Muslim in the Army. Ali, along with other leaders, is immediately arrested. In October, forty-seven leading Congressmen, including Gandhiji, issue 'a manifesto repeating whatever Muhammad Ali had said', adding that 'every civilian and member of the armed forces should sever connections with the repressive Government.'[8]

Iqbal initially supports the Khilafat Movement as it represents his own idea of a universal Muslim brotherhood. When the movement starts, Iqbal becomes the secretary of the Punjab Khilafat Committee.

However, when the country's Hindu leadership gets involved in the movement, he withdraws his support. He feels that the Hindus are organizing themselves behind the façade of the Khilafat movement and they are using the Muslims only as a means to achieve their own ends. He resigns from his position as the secretary of the Punjab Khilafat Committee and becomes indifferent to the movement.[9]

In his resignation letter he writers: 'Apparently the members of Khilafat committees seem to be zealous Muslims but in reality they are a brotherhood of Devils.'[10]

When Muhammad Ali Johar visits Lahore during the Khilafat movement, he comes to visit Iqbal. Iqbal is in his drawing room, wearing a *dhassa*, and drawing on his hooqah. Ali is very frank with him. 'Arre Zalim!' he says, 'We read your poems and go to jail and here you are, wrapped up in a blanket, enjoying your smoke!'

'Muhammad Ali! I am the nation's qawwal,' Iqbal quips, 'If the qawwal starts to sway with the crowd and gets lost in the trance, then his qawwali will come to an end!'

In December 1919, Iqbal attends the conference of the Muslim League, Khilafat Conference and Congress in Amristsar. The Ali brothers arrive at the conference directly from jail. Iqbal pays them a tribute:

Hai Aseeri aetebar afza jo ho fitrat buland
Qatra-e neesaan hai zindan-e sadaf se arjumand

Imprisonment adds to your credibility if you are a man of great
    character
Just as the captivity of the shell turns a raindrop into a pearl

Iqbal is not in favour of Indian Muslims sending a delegation to England to demand for the continuation of the Caliphate. His argument is—Why should Muslims beg the British for their own rights?

On September 27, he sends out a few verses to Syed Suleman Nadwi for publication in *Maa'rif*:

Bahut azmaya hai ghairon ko tu ne
Magar aaj hai waqt khaish azmayi
Nahi tujh ko tareekh se aagahi kya
Khilafat ki karne laga tu gadayi
Khariden na hum jisko apne lahu se
Musalman ko hai nang woh paadshahi

. . .

You've tried others a lot,

This is the time to put your own on trial.

Don't you know history?

That you are begging for the cause of Khilafat?

What we won't buy paying with our own blood

That regal power is anathema to a Muslim

Regardless, the Khilafat Committee sends a delegation to England on January 1, 1920, under the leadership of Maulana Muhammad Ali Jauhar. As expected, the result of the discussions with the British leadership is a disappointment for the leaders.

Iqbal writes to Suleman Nadwi on October 10, 1920: 'The Indian delegation's journey to Europe will create significant results. I am told the last word is that after getting disappointed with Europe, Muslims will learn to believe in Allah's mercy and bounty and in the power of their own arms.'[11]

A large number of Indian Muslims take part in the Khilafat movement with complete zeal. The Ali brothers reach Aligarh to shut down the Muslim university. The university's vice chancellor Dr Ziauddin opposes them tooth and nail, and yet, hundreds of university students abandon the university. For their education, a new educational institute is opened named Jamia Millia. However, no pressure is exerted to shut down the Benaras Hindu University as Pandit Madan Mohan Malviya is not in favour of this.

After the Aligarh Muslim University incident, Gandhi, along with Muhammad Ali Johar and Maulana Abul Kalam Azad, visits Lahore to separate Islamia College from Punjab University. Iqbal opposes this move.

Gandhiji announces the withdrawal of the Non-Cooperation Movement on February 12, 1922, when incensed members of a Congress and Khilafat procession in Chauri Chaura in Gorakhpur attack policemen on February 5, 1922. Twenty-two policemen are done to death by an angry mob of protestors.

Even though the movement does not fulfill the promise of attaining Swaraj within a year of the programme's launch, as was originally promised by Gandhi, the movement does succeed. It establishes that the Congress has the support and sympathy of a vast section of the Indian population, and that the Congress does not just represent a 'microscopic minority', as Viceroy Dufferin had put it in 1888.

The Muslim participation remains the hallmark of this movement. Their involvement gave it a truly mass character. But unfortunately, after the failure of the Khilafat movement, the Muslims of India lose faith in making alliances with Hindus.

The greatest setback to the Muslim desire for the Caliphate comes from a man who was idolized by the Mulims themselves, and for whom they had prayed, left work and struggled—it was Turkey's patriotic leader and military head Mustafa Kamal Pasha. In one stroke of his pen, he terminated the legacy of the Caliphate. Iqbal rued the move in these words:

Chaak kar di Turk nadaan ne khilafat ki qaba
Saadgi Muslim ki dekh, auron ki ayyari bhi dekh

The imprudent Turk has torn off the cloak of the Caliphate
How a Muslim simpleton was foxed by such cunning powers!

* * *

While the tumultuous revolutions engulf the Muslim world, Iqbal's fame is in ascendance. Some of his friends, both Muslims and Sikhs, try to showcase his poetic brilliance to the West. *A Voice from the East*—a slender volume of some forty-two large pages is published by his friend Sir Nawab Zulfiqar Ali Khan in 1922 with the aim to 'unveil his charming personality to the gaze of Europe and America'. Sardar Umrao Singh Sher Gill renders into English a selection of Iqbal's Urdu verses for inclusion in the same book.

Iqbal's thinking and his worldview, however bold, does not grow in a vacuum. His voice finds an echo in the voice of leaders and thinkers such as C.R. Das and Mary Parker Follett. While Follett is the American pioneer of management sciences, Das is a Bengali visionary.

Follett, in her work, denounces Western democracy as 'old democracy' which draws its lifeblood through a dichotomy between the government and the opposition. She also discards the totalitarian models advocated by the Bolsheviks. She rather introduces the idea of a 'new democracy' based on the notion of consensus, with an aim of developing the personality of the individual. Her book, *The New State* (1918), offers a detailed elaboration of the concept, which is quite similar to the philosophy of Iqbal.

Similarly, C.R. Das presents his political ideas in his presidential address to the annual session of the Indian National Congress in Gaya on December 26, 1922. During his speech, he references excerpts from Follett's *The New State*. He proposes, from an Indian point of view, that communities should continue to evolve their own distinct characters, and yet strengthen the spiritual unity of their country; and India should actively seek the unity of the Muslim world as part of a broader vision for the unity of all of Asia.

A few days after Das has presented his ideas, Iqbal writes to a young Muslim journalist that Das has 'presented the same spiritual principle in a political manner' which Iqbal has presented in *Secrets and Mysteries*.

The British government bestows the honour of knighthood on

Iqbal on January 1, 1923.[12] As the story goes, Iqbal's knighthood may not have happened but for a London-based journalist's intervention. Once a correspondent of the *London Times* comes to Lahore and stays at the government guest house. He has heard of Iqbal and is eager to meet him. For introduction, Sir Edward Maclegon, the governor of the Punjab, invites the great poet to the government guest house. The two discuss a variety of issues, ranging from philosophy to poetry. After Iqbal leaves, the journalist is flummoxed to find that the Indian government has not honoured such a great poet. Once persuaded, Sir Edward Maclegon, who was unaware of Iqbal's scholarship and fame, sends a proposal for his knighthood. The proposal gets approved but Iqbal has one condition before he accepts it. The government must honour his teacher, Maulvi Mir Hasan, first, he argues. The Governor of the Punjab asks Iqbal if Hasan has any creative work to show. 'I am one of his great works,' says Iqbal. Finally, his condition is met and Hasan is honoured with the title of *Shams-ul-Ulama* (The Sun of Scholars) and Iqbal is knighted.

At Jehangir's tomb, a grand celebration is organized to honour Iqbal, attended by bureaucrats, nobles, and literary figures. In this august company, Sir Zulfiqar Ali Khan, instrumental in getting the knighthood for Iqbal, praises Iqbal for his contribution to society and literature. Iqbal also delivers a speech and recites some verses from his forthcoming work, *Payam-e Mashriq*.

Iqbal's knighthood is not celebrated by everyone in India. The Muslim press, for example, denounces him for accepting an honour that India's Nobel Laureate Rabindranath Tagore had relinquished in 1919 in protest of the Jallianwala Bagh massacre in Amritsar. The Muslim press label Iqbal an agent of the colonial government. Even though Iqbal repudiates all these allegations, his arguments fail to convince his critics.

Within months of being knighted, Iqbal denounces British imperialism in his harshest tone so far, in *Tule-e Islam*, (*The Dawn of Islam*). This long Urdu poem is first recited at the annual fundraising session of the Anjuman Himayat-e Islam in March 1923.

One of the most popular poems in the Urdu language, *Tule-e Islam* was inspired by the victory of the Turks over the Greek occupation armies in Smyrna six months earlier. In the poem, he references 'Thank You to Europe' by Agha Hashar Kashmiri, which was another very popular poem of its time.

> *Hazaaron saal nargis apni benoori pe roti hai*
> *Badi mushkil se hota hai chaman me dedawar paida*

> For a thousand years, the narcissus weeps over its blindness
> Until a seer is born in the garden to rid it of its sightlessness

This poem is an ode to Mustafa Kemal Pasha, also known as Ataturk, meaning 'of Turkey'. Iqbal is initially quite impressed by this hero's victory. Although, later on he will criticize Ataturk for his absolute rule:

> *Na Mustafa na Raza Shah mein numood uss ki*
> *Ke rooh-e-sharaq badan ki talash mein hai abhi*

> Ill-lodged in Ataturk or Reza Shah,
> The soul of the East is still in search of a body[13]

Nevertheless, the Turkish leader will remain a hero in Iqbal's eyes. He believes that the enemies of Islam are targeting Ataturk unfairly to malign his efforts to unite Muslims. 'The policy of isolating the Turks from the rest of the Muslim world is still in action,' he says in 1937, 'We hear now and then that the Turks are repudiating Islam. A greater lie was never told ...'

* * *

Even though Iqbal believes in a purist form of Islam, there is still room in his spiritual life for mystics and mysticism. In 1923, the same year that he is knighted, he visits the dargah of Shaikh Ahmed Sirhindi Mujaddid Alf-e Sani. There he prays for a son and also makes a tryst that if his prayer is answered, he will revisit the mausoleum with his son.

A year later, Allah blesses Iqbal with a son, Javed Iqbal. When Javed turns ten, Iqbal takes him to the shaikh of Sirhind to fulfil his promise. A young Javed enters the mazaar holding his father's fingers. Wide-eyed, he considers the awe-inspiring surroundings of the holy place with cautious steps, the cold silence of the shrine overwhelming his senses. They both sit down, facing the grave. Iqbal draws Javed closer to him. He recites a chapter from the Quran. Iqbal's baritone voice adds to the eerie darkness of the mausoleum. Nearly spooked, the young child looks at his father's face. He sees tears rolling down his cheeks. He does not know why his father is crying. They stay there for a day and then return to Lahore, but Javed will carry this image of his crying father for the rest of his life.

Iqbal's father Shaikh Noor Muhammad

Iqbal's teacher and guide Syed Mir Hasan

Allama Iqbal with his son Javed Iqbal

Iqbal's wife Sardar Begum

Javed Iqbal

Karim Bibi, Iqbal's first wife

Munira Bano, Iqbal's daughter

Allama Iqbal in Spain

Iqbal in London in 1931

Iqbal offering prayers in the Qartaba Masjid (Spain)

Iqbal in his room with his favourite hookah

Iqbal in Aligarh

Allama Iqbal reaches Allahabad to deliver his famous presidential address at the historic session of the All India Muslim League (1930)

Iqbal at a party during the Second Round Table Conference in London (1931)

Allama Iqbal with Sir Ross Masood and Syed Sulaiman Nadvi
in Afghanistan (1933)

Iqbal at a reception hosted by the National League, London, in 1932

Portraits of Iqbal

PART FOUR

1926–1938

The Years in Politics

17

A Tulip in the Wilderness

If you wish to become a public leader you ought to know how to
flirt with the Dame Public. Entertain her with platitudes and, if
necessary, with lies.

—Iqbal, *Stray Thoughts*

Iqbal is probably one of the first Muslim leaders in India who aspires
for a united nation,[1] but so far he has avoided getting embroiled in
politics. Even though he was in touch with the Pan-Islamic Society
and the British Committee of the Muslim League during his stay
in Europe, he did not join the Indian National Congress after
returning to India. 'By 1900, the concept of a Muslim nation was
visibly embedded in his poetry.'[2] This is how he foresees a change in
the fortunes of Muslims in 1907:

Suna diya gosh-e muntazir ko hijaz ki khamshi ne akhir
Jo ehad sehraiyon se bandha gya tha, phir ustuwar hoga

Nikal ke sehra se jis ne Roma ki saltanat ko ulat diya tha
Suna hai ye Qudsiyon se main ne, woh sher phir hoshyar hoga

The silence of Mecca has proclaimed to the expectant ears at last
That the compact made with the desert-dwellers will be made
    good again

The lion that had emerged out of the wilderness to upset the
   Empire of Rome
The angels have told me—that lion will awaken once more

1926 is a watershed year for Iqbal. An active observer of politics in India now turns into an active participant.

During the first few months of 1926, Iqbal continues with his legal practice and regularly attends the high court. He also composes one of his seminal works of poetry, *Zabur-i Ajam* (*Pslams of the East*). The poetry collection, containing the *'Mathnavi Gulshan-i Raz-i Jadid'* and *'Bandagi Nama'*, features some of Iqbal's finest Persian ghazals. Like in his other books, Iqbal emphasises learning from the past and preparing for the future in this book, preaching a life of action, dynamism, and love. Apart from this, for additional income, he sets and reviews the final examination papers of university students.

In the evenings, his friends visit him at home to discuss all kinds of things—from politics to religion to literature and philosophy—areas of deep interest for Iqbal. Soon, some of his supporters and visitors begin to insist that Iqbal should participate in the local elections for the Punjab Legislative Assembly. The Muslim constituency in Lahore will surely back him, they suggest.

The incumbent leader from the constituency, Mian Abdul Aziz, assures Iqbal that if Iqbal enters the fray, he will withdraw in Iqbal's favour. He publicly declares this and issues a statement to this effect in the daily *Zamindar* on July 15, 1926. Iqbal thanks Mian Aziz for this generous offer and issues a statement in response which appears in the same newspaper on July 20, 1926:

Muslims know it well that I refrained from electoral politics because other people were engaged in it. I had carved out another niche for my activities. At this point in time our national problems are calling on me to expand the circle of my activities. Perhaps, I might be able to render useful services to the cause of our nation—which consumes all of my daily efforts.[3]

After Iqbal declares his intention to stand for the elections, a consensus begins to build in his favour. The refrain is that a prominent personality like Iqbal should win the elections unopposed.

However, instead of getting elected unopposed, Iqbal faces two adversaries who throw their hats in the ring: Malik Muhammad Hussain, president of the municipal corporation of Lahore, and Malik Muhammad Din, an unknown lawyer. Hussain decides to withdraw his candidature from the contest. Iqbal suitably thanks him in *Zamindar*: 'I admire and compliment his sentiment and judgement that he did not allow the narrow exclusive prejudices of the brotherhood to determine his candidacy and that instead he has made a judgment for the unity of Muslims.'[4]

The other candidate, Malik Muhammad Din, does not take the cue and Iqbal has to fight the election against him.

Iqbal's supporters organize more than twenty public meetings in different neighbourhoods to bolster his chances of winning. His campaign volunteers and supporters work hard and take Iqbal's message of Muslim solidarity and his poetry of hope and inspiration to every nook and corner of his constituency. Justifying his electoral bid, Iqbal says on October 11, 1926, in one of his speeches: 'I used poetry as a medium of communication to offer Muslims an opportunity to understand the true meaning of life, and to urge them to follow in the footsteps of their ancestors, jettison hopelessness, cowardice, and be dedicated to an active life. I served my brethren intellectually to the best of my ability for twenty-five years. Now, I am offering them my service in a new style . . . I pledge to you that I will never place my personal interests above the national interest . . . I consider it worse than death to serve my own personal interests at the expense of national objectives.'[5]

Seeing the wind blowing in his opponent's favour, Din starts a smear campaign against Iqbal, calling him a Wahabi (while declaring himself as a dedicated sunni), and describing him as an enemy of Sufism. To taint Iqbal, Din claims that Iqbal had made unwarranted attacks on the Persian poet Hafiz in his Persian poem *Asrar-i Khudi*.

Also, at one point of time, Iqbal had supported King Ibn al-Saud of Saudi Arabia and a section of the ulema had issued a fatwa against him, declaring Iqbal an infidel, a kafir. All this material is used by Iqbal's opponent to malign him in the electoral battle. He also attacks Iqbal for being a Kashmiri; instead, he banks on Arain votes, the community he belongs to. Lastly, he circulates fourteen slanderous posters against Iqbal, that amount to a character assassination of the great poet.

Iqbal not only ignores the posters, he avoids making any personal attacks on his opponent. If his supporters use 'unbecoming language' against his opponent, he stops them from doing so. He urges Muslim voters to 'cultivate Islamic solidarity' and 'restore Islamic unity in their ranks'. He denounces the 'brotherhoods' as un-Islamic.

Even the *Zamindar* supports Iqbal's candidature: 'Is this not an unfortunate and regrettable development among Muslims that they did not let an honorable personality [like Iqbal] be elected unopposed to the lowly position of a member of the Legislative Assembly of the Punjab? When Muslims are so insensitive and unmindful of their own personality, then how can they be justified in their lamentations that sincere savants of the nation are not available and that there is a dearth of real leaders?'

Interestingly, the newspaper's editorial compares Muslim disunity to solidarity in the Hindu community:

Lala Lajpat Rai is so influential that he can have anyone elected unopposed. No one would have the courage to oppose his designated candidate. Despite their internal differences, Hindus have elected Pandit Motilal Nehru and Pandit Madan Mohan Malviya to the legislatures unopposed. The constituency of Pandit Madan Mohan Malviya contains hundreds of thousands of supporters and members of the All India National Congress and Pandit Motilal Nehru's constituency is filled with supporters of the Sangathan Movement. Such is their national solidarity that no one would dare challenge these outstanding personalities. Look at the Muslims—they cannot demonstrate their reverence to the magnificent personality of Allama Iqbal.[6]

However, not all newspapers support Iqbal. Two Kashmiri-owned newspapers, *Siyasat* and *Nishter* oppose Iqbal's campaign, labelling him a 'Wahabi, Najdi, [and] enemy of Islam' and even declaring him 'an outright liar'.

Support comes to Iqbal from various quarters, and these include well-known public personalities in Lahore. These are landowners, lawyers, businessmen, journalists, and writers. Muslim parties like the *Majlis-i Khilafat* (The Assembly of the Caliphate) also support Iqbal.

During his election campaigns, Iqbal seeks to win the support of every Muslim in his constituency. His platform is the unification of Muslims. He asks voters to 'demolish the idols of exclusive groups and brotherhoods'. When his opponent labels him a Kashmiri, he says that anyone who wants to vote for him because of his Kashmiri roots, he better cast his vote elsewhere. Urging Muslims to unite, on October 19, 1926, Iqbal says the following in his last campaign speech:

The secret of Muslims' success lies in their unity. I spent many nights over the years trying to unveil the mystery of Sayyidna Muhammad—what is it that he accomplished within the short period of thirty years that Arabs have followed and subsequently became the leaders of nations. The mystery is simply solidarity and national unity, which was on the lips of everyone. I wish this mystery would sink deep into the hearts of all Muslims...

My brethren Muslims! I tell you frankly if you want to survive, then unite ... The second most important imperative for Muslims is their obligation to cultivate a deep interest in the political developments in India . . . Today, most of the major world powers are arrayed against Islam. However, I believe in the divine enunciations presaging the ultimate success of Islamic forces.[7]

On December 26, 1926, Iqbal wins the elections by a margin of 3,177 votes. He receives 5,675 votes and Din gets 2,698 votes out of a total 8,400 votes that were cast.[8]

The legislative session of the newly elected Punjab Assembly is inaugurated on January 23, 1927. In the assembly, the Unionist Party is in the majority, led by Sir Fazl-e Hussain. Iqbal decides to join this party.

He remains a member of the Legislative Council from 1927–1930. During this time, he gets the opportunity to see the inner workings of the Unionist Party. Iqbal discovers, to his disgust, that this party is creating the rural–urban conflict engulfing the entire province. As a consequence, he gets alienated from the party and from Sir Fazl-e Hussain.

During his term as an elected representative, Iqbal makes significant proposals that fall on deaf ears. Some of the proposals he makes are to improve the economy of Punjab, grants in aid to the poor, support for the improvement of yunani and ayurvedic medicine, grants for Muslim educational institutions, medical care especially for women, compulsory elementary education, support for industrial development, and to reduce salaries for the upper crust of the bureaucracy.[9]

Despite making very useful recommendations, his voice remains 'a lone cry in the wilderness' since he does not get any support in the assembly. This is how he describes his state in the Assembly:

Man misaal-e lala-e Sehrastam
Darmiyan-e mehfil-e tanhastam

Like the tulip in the wilderness,
I stand alone in the assembly

18

On the Path of Separatism
The Politics of Electoral Representation

The fate of the world has been principally decided by minorities. The history of Europe bears ample testimony to the truth of this proposition. It seems to me that there is a psychological reason why minorities should have been a powerful factor in the history of mankind. Character is the invisible force which determines the destinies of nations, and an intense character is not possible in a majority. It is a force; the more it is distributed the weaker it becomes.

—Iqbal, *Stray Thoughts*

During the 1920s, Iqbal witnesses the emergence of two Hindu movements that have profound implications for Muslims in India. These are the Shuddhi and Sangathan movements.[1] These two are socio-political movements, derived from the ancient rites of *shuddhikaran* (purification), started by the Arya Samaj, and its founder Swami Dayanand Saraswati and his followers. In 1923, Swami Shraddhanand founded the Bhartiya Hindu Shuddhi Mahasabha (The Indian Hindu Purification Council).The Sangathan movement was started by Pandit Madan Mohan Malaviya, Lala Lajpat Rai, Swami Shraddhanand, Dr Monje, and V.D. Savarkar.

It was aimed at removing untouchability to create solidarity among
the Hindus. It also aimed to train Hindus to protect themselves in
the case of a communal conflict. [2]

North India and Punjab in the early twentieth century were the
locus of these movements, which slowly spread to other parts of
India. In simple terms, the movements aimed to reduce the number
of people converting from Hinduism to Islam and Christianity. Even
though the reconversions were supposed to take place peacefully, it
led to rioting between Hindus and Muslims.

In Rajasthan, Swami Shraddhanand was active in converting
Muslims into Hindus. When a Muslim youth murdered him in
December 1926, Hindu–Muslim riots erupted in Delhi. Six Muslims
were killed. The *Times of India* published an incendiary report about
the Deoband seminary's response to the murders that increased the
bitterness between the two communities. Anti-Muslim literature
and pamphlets were then circulated around India.[3]

To counter the two Hindu movements, the Muslims launched
two organizations—Tablighi Jamat and Tanzim. The Tablighis
built their case against the threat of Hindu revivalist movements
like Shuddhi. The Tanzim movement sought to internally purify
the Muslim community. In July 1923, the Jamat-e Tabligh-ul
Islam's central headquarters were founded in Ambala, Punjab. Syed
Ghulam Bhik Nairang was appointed its organizing secretary. To the
advantage of the British, these movements divided the population
along religious lines.[4]

Iqbal sees these movements as unfortunate developments in
India's history. 'Our mutual conflicts are most regrettable,' he says
in a public meeting in Lahore on January 22, 1927. 'We do not stop
to think and evaluate the impact of these internal conflicts on the
other Asian nations. In my perception the truthful reality is like
a sparkling diamond, which radiates many dimensions, reflecting
different colours. Everyone is entitled to select a radiance of colour
of his own choice, and see reality from his own perspective ... Islam
gave the same message of truth, which the [Hindu] *rishis* taught in

ancient times. I appeal to you in the name of truth to appreciate the realities, and not fight with each other. There are people in India who encourage mutual conflicts in order to serve their own interests. The peace of the country will be seriously disrupted by our in-fighting. Everyone will suffer.'[5]

At the same time, Iqbal writes to Ghulam Bhik Nairang in support of such counter-activities on January 24, 1927. 'In my judgment the missionary endeavours for Islam take priority over any other activity. If the Muslims' objective in India is to attain political freedoms and economic well-being, and the defence of Islam has no place in it—as is demonstrated in the policy of [nationalist] Muslims—then Muslims will never succeed in achieving their goals.'

Meanwhile, when Muhammad Ali Jinnah, the president of the All India Muslim League, publishes the Delhi Proposals[6] in March 1927, Iqbal opposes the idea of having joint electorates for Hindus and Muslims. He is not convinced that Muslims should abandon separate electorates. For example, in the Punjab, Bengal, and Sindh, Hindus were economically better off than Muslims and in case of joint electorates, the fear was that Hindus would not let Muslims be elected, especially those Muslim candidates dedicated to protecting Muslims interests.

He expresses his opinion on this matter in a public meeting on May 1, 1927: 'I have the right to say that I am the first Indian who recognized the imperative of a Hindu–Muslim alliance, and its urgent need. From the beginning I had hoped that this alliance would become stable. But the circumstances do not favour the introduction of joint electorates.'[7]

On May 3, 1927, riots break out in Lahore when an angry Sikh and Hindu mob enters Haveli Kabuli Mal, a Muslim mohalla, and attacks Muslims with sticks and small swords. The apparent provocation is that a Muslim youth had harassed a Sikh girl.

As soon as Iqbal hears of the incident, he rushes to the spot. He also visits other areas of the city, urging Muslims to keep calm. It so happens that three young Muslim men die on this day and their relatives are keen to take out a funeral procession. But Iqbal and other Muslim elders prevail upon them to delay the processions to prevent another possibility of rioting.

After the riots two more incidents take place which affect Iqbal. Two Hindus write two separate blasphemous books against the Prophet (one of the books is titled *Rangila Rasul*). When the courts let them go scot-free, they are murdered by two young Muslim men. Both murderers are given the death penalty.

Iqbal also notes instances of the police and administration's cruelty towards the Muslim public. These events rattle Iqbal's consciousness, making him feel that Muslims are a threatened minority in India. 'I wonder if you all have realized the fact that we are actually living in a state of civil war,' he says in the Punjab Legislative Assembly. 'If this communal hatred permeates the rest of the country, people living in villages will also come to logger heads. God only knows where this will eventually lead us.'[8]

* * *

In November 1927, the British Prime Minister Stanley Baldwin appoints seven members of the British Parliament to constitute the Simon Commission, headed by chairman John Simon. The commission was promised in 1919 to study constitutional reforms in India.[9]

The Indian leadership is outraged because the commission has no Indian representatives. Taking this as an insult, in December 1927, the Congress resolves to boycott the commission. The Muslim League under Jinnah also toes the same line.

Iqbal, however, differs with other Indian leaders. In a statement issued on November 9, 1927, he states that, 'the lack of confidence and trust that different Indian nationalities nourish toward each other spawned this development.'[10]

Response to the Simon Commission leads to a rupture in the Muslim League. While Jinnah and Muhammad Ali boycott the commission, Sir Muhammad Shafi, Maulana Hasrat Mohani, and Iqbal wish to cooperate with it. 'The boycott of the Simon Commission would damage the country's interests in general and Muslims' interests in particular,' Iqbal says in a press statement on November 13, 1927.

Baffled by his attitude, Maulana Muhammad Ali criticizes Iqbal in a comment in his newspaper *Hamdard*: 'This is a misfortune of the Punjab that Sir Muhammad Iqbal could not persuade loyal Sir Mohammd Shafi to his level of independent thinking. On the contrary, Iqbal lowered himself to the debased level of Sir Muhammad Shafi's loyalty to the [British Raj].'[11]

Even though he is criticized by Jinnah and other leaders of the Muslim League, Iqbal refuses to change his mind on the issue. 'It is imperative that we defend our rights, which they have refused to concede to us. Muslim leaders, who have signed Mr Jinnah's statement, hail from Hindu majority provinces, and Muslim members in those provinces are no more than proverbial "salt in the flour'. The policy cannot possibly shape or articulate policy for Muslims, who live in the Punjab or Bengal. Our unambiguous policy is based on the premise that we have been unsuccessful in winning our rights from the [Hindu] majority, and for us to waste a good opportunity to press our viewpoint, is against our national interest. Hindus must realize that we are not prepared to postpone the issue of our rights to an indefinite future settlement.'

This is the second time, after the Delhi Proposals, that the Punjab Muslim League leadership under Shafi and Iqbal disagree with Jinnah's position. This leads to the bifurcation of the League—one arm led by Jinnah and the other by Shafi.

For Iqbal, nothing is more important than securing the protection of Muslims' national rights, and he will go to any extent to achieve them.

In May 1928, the Shafi League creates a committee to draft a memorandum of proposals for the Simon Commission. Iqbal is part of this committee. Iqbal wants to include two issues among the proposals: the principle of self-determination and autonomy for the provinces. For reasons that remain unclear, Shafi leaves out the demand for self-determination for the provinces in memorandum's draft. When Iqbal learns about this, he is outraged and resigns from the Shafi League on June 24, 1928.

To placate Iqbal, Shafi decides to include the demand for self-determination for the provinces in the memorandum. Eventually, Iqbal signs the final memorandum, which is offered to the Simon Commission on November 5, 1928.

When the Commission's report comes out in 1930, Iqbal expresses his dissatisfaction with it, as do most other Indian leaders. Meanwhile, the British government has already announced the London Round Table Conference to hear the views of Indian leaders on the question of an Indian constitution. This renders the Simon Commission's efforts futile.

After the Congress rejects Jinnah's Delhi Proposals it adopts the Nehru Report,[12] and Iqbal and other Muslim leaders become convinced that even the most politically broad-minded and moderate Hindus are under the influence of the Hindu Maha Sabha. Together, they form a united front to counter the Hindu parties. They call this the All Parties Muslim Conference. They meet up in December 1928 in Delhi and Agha Khan presides over the meetings. Only Jinnah's League does not participate in the Delhi session. Iqbal takes active part in the deliberations and the Nehru Report is roundly condemned.

At the end of the session, a ten point resolution is adopted. One of the points is to adopt a separate electorate system of representation for Muslims in the legislatures.

After the conference ends on January 2, 1929, Iqbal leaves on a tour of south India, accompanied by Chaudhury Muhammad Hussain and Abdullah Chughtai. He stops in Madras, Mysore, Bangalore, and Hyderabad where he delivers lectures on the reconstruction of religious thought in Islam.

By 1930, rapprochement between the Shafi League and the Jinnah League takes effect, when Muslim nationalists such as Dr Ansari, Asaf Ali, Dr Kitchlew, and Abdul Kalam Azad exit the League because of differences of opinion.

19

A Turn in the South

Reconstructing Religious Thought in Islam

Given character and healthy imagination, it is possible to
reconstruct this world of sin and misery into a veritable paradise.
—Iqbal, *Stray Thoughts*

In 1929, Iqbal embarks on a multi-city tour of India to deliver six
'well-crafted and thoroughly researched' lectures that will come to
define his views on reviving the critical thinking tradition in Islam.
These six lectures are delivered in Madras, Hyderabad, and Aligarh—
and form part of Iqbal's famous treatise, *The Reconstruction of Religious
Thought in Islam*. Initially, Iqbal self-publishes them from Lahore in
1930 as *Six Lectures on the Reconstruction of Religious Thought in Islam*.
Later on, he delivers a seventh lecture in London in 1932. These
seven lectures become part of a collection titled *The Reconstruction
of Religious Thought in Islam*, published in 1934.

Even though the lecetures are delivered in 1929, their genesis
goes back to 1924. Around that time, Iqbal had been developing
his ideas on the doctrine of *ijtihaad* in Islam—which means 'the
right of interpreting the Quran and the Sunna or of forming a new
opinion by applying analogical deduction.'[1]

In 1924, Iqbal reads out one of his papers at Islamia College in Lahore. In the paper, he offers his thoughts on the doctrine of *ijtihaad* in Islam. He delivers these lectures to a general audience, including children. Some members of the ulema are offended by his views. They view Iqbal as a radical and object to his views. One moulvi, Abu Muhammad Didar Ali, not a very high-ranking cleric, issues a fatwa against Iqbal, declaring him a kafir, an infidel. This incident deeply hurts Iqbal. 'The professional maulvis had lost a substantial amount of influence after Sir Syed Ahmed Khan's movement,' he writes in reaction to the fatwa to Maulana Akbar Shah Khan of Najibabad. 'But their power was restored among the Indian Muslims by the Caliphate Committee's venture into issuing political fatwas. This was a great error.'

This very controversial lecture is not published. However, an announcement goes out through the press, which is taken note of by Seth Jamal Muhammad in south India.

The millionaire Seth Jamal is a successful and prominent trader who spends generously to run charitable institutions such as the Madras Muslim Association. One of the things that the association does is invite eminent Muslim scholars to Madras to deliver lectures on various aspects of Islam. In early 1925, after taking note of Iqbal's controversial essay on *ijtihaad*, he invites Iqbal to Madras on an all expenses paid trip. He gives Iqbal a flexible schedule—he is free to decide when and on what topic he wants to speak. Iqbal finds out that this is a genuine invitation. Before him, Seth Jamal had invited Muslim scholars such as Muhammad Marmaduke Pickthall and Syed Sulaiman Nadvi.

The possibility of a trip to south India piques Iqbal's curiosity. He has always wanted to visit the mausoleum of Tipu Sultan who died valiantly fighting the British. Such a visit, in Iqbal's vision, will inspire himself to write a stirring poem in the sultan's tribute. Iqbal accepts Seth Jamal's offer. The offer is attractive because it will also enable Iqbal to 'reconstruct Muslim religious philosophy in the philosophic tradition of Islam in different areas of human knowledge, and to articulate them in the light of modern age.'[2]

'By God's grace, I am content in my heart,' Iqbal writes to Syed Sulaiman Nadvi, sharing his anxieties about Muslim youth in India. 'This anguish that I reflect is caused by a feeling that the new generation of Muslims may adopt an erroneous style.'[3]

Having had a firsthand experience of Europe, philosophically, Iqbal sees Europe's 'modern civilization as an advanced and developed form of Islamic culture'. In Descartes he sees Al-Ghazali, in Dante he sees Ibn al-Arabi, in Roger Bacon and John Stuart Mill, he sees Yaqub al-Kindi, who scrutinized Aristotelian logic well before Bacon or Mill.[4]

Therefore, when the chance arises to present his thoughts on Islamic intellectual disciplines in light of modern developments, he welcomes this opportunity. This is the only way, Iqbal believes, to stop the march of Europe's intellectual imperialism. In a sense, Iqbal is also guided by a feeling of intellectual leadership on behalf of Indian Muslims—if they can't help other Muslims of the world politically or militarily, at least they can be at the forefront of the intellectual revival of Islam.

As he starts preparing for his lectures, he begins his research on a variety of topics, ranging from Islamic jurisprudence to the conduct of Muslim states and a possible creation of an inter-Islamic alliance. He also formulates his views of God, creation, and the universe, analyzing these concepts in the light of new scientific discoveries.

Iqbal finishes his research and cogitation by 1929. On January 3, he reaches Bombay along with Chaudhury Muhammad Hussain, Abdullah Chughtai, and his helper Ali Bakhsh.

At the Bombay Railway Station, Seth Ismail's son, Seth Hashim Ismail receives Iqbal and his companions. They are escorted to their residence. After dinner, Seth Hashim Ismail's wife, a modern young woman educated in Germany, requests Iqbal to inscribe one of his verses on a copy of Goethe's *Faust*.

Kala-o falsafa as loh-e dil faroshtum,
Zamir-e khwaish koshadam ba nashtar-e tahqiq

I washed away the philosophic formulations from my heart,
And I enlarged my heart with the certitude of faithful research

After inscribing this on the copy, Iqbal adds, 'Faust should have reached this ultimate point, but he failed to do so.'[5]

In Bombay, the Muslim Federation of Bombay also hosts a dinner in honour of Iqbal. From Bombay, Iqbal leaves for Madras to deliver his lectures. On January 5, 1929, he arrives at Madras Railway Station to a huge welcome by a large number of people, including the ulema of Madras. His hosts Seth Jamal, along with his son and secretary, receive Iqbal. He is driven to Hotel Bosoto, which is owned by Seth Jamal.

Iqbal delivers his first lecture on the topic of the religion of Islam and modern philosophy. The lecture is delivered at the Gokhale Hall. Both Muslims and Hindus attend the lecture. Presiding over the proceedings is the chief minister of Madras, P. Subbaroyan. 'Nomination of a non-Muslim to preside over a meeting like this has come to me as a surprise,' says Subbaroyan in his welcome speech. 'Nevertheless as an Indian and as a believer in the existence of a Common God who has created the entire world, it has given me the greatest pleasure in getting an opportunity to learn the main principles of Islam . . . That all persons are equal is the lesson that Islam has taught to India . . . It is, therefore, necessary that we, Hindus, have to learn the principles of fraternity, brotherhood, and equality from Islam. It is only if we, Hindus and Muslims, live as brothers can we gain independence.'[6]

In his first lecture, Iqbal claims that for the reconstruction of Islam it is necessary to learn from the historial experience of Europe. Referring to the Quran, he says that Quran has exhorted man to study nature and observe the reality of existing phenomenon.

On January 6, Iqbal delivers his second lecture at the Gokhale Hall. The topic is 'The Philosophic Test of the Revelations of Religious Experience'. In this lecture Iqbal conveys his views on the relationship between rationality and religion. He claims that rationality can only support religion to a certain, limited extent.

The third lecture is delivered on the following day, at the same venue. In this lecture, Iqbal focuses on the conception of God and the meaning of prayer. He defines God philosophically as 'a rationally directed creative will', which can also be described as the Ego.

After spending four days in Madras, Iqbal departs for Bangalore on January 8. At the railway station of the then Mysore state, the chief minister of Mysore himself, Sir Mirza Ismail, along with other dignitaries, welcomes Iqbal. In the evening, Iqbal repeats one of his lectures from Madras on the Mysore University campus.

His visit to the tombs of Haider Ali and his brave son Tipu Sultan in Srirangapatna turns out to be one of the most moving moments in Iqbal's life. The Hindu raja of Mysore appoints his court musicians to accompany Iqbal's entourage on the visit. At the raja's orders, drums are played at appropriate intervals as a mark of respect for Iqbal. Ali Jan sings Iqbal's own Urdu and Persian verses during the visit.

Memories of Tipu's martyrdom come floating back to Iqbal while he is at the tomb. The experience moves him to tears, showing how easily he gets emotional when encountering great Muslim figures from history. When the musicians see his emotional state, they stop their performance. Iqbal gestures for them to continue with their singing. He then composes a few verses in Persian in Tipu's honour.

On his way back to Lahore, Iqbal stops in Hyderabad to meet the nizam on January 18, 1929—a courtesy call to invite the nizam to the Punjab to preside over one of the sessions of the Anjuman Himayat-Islam.[7] On the following day, he leaves for Lahore.

After his lectures in south India receive good press, many universities request Iqbal to deliver similar lectures on their campuses. When Iqbal's friend Sir Ross Masood, head of the department of

Philosophy at Aligarh Muslim University, invites him to deliver his lectures at Aligarh, he obliges.

By November, Iqbal has developed three more lectures, so now he has six lectures on this topic. Iqbal leaves for Aligarh on November 17 and stays there until November 30. He delivers all six lectures in the famous Strachey Hall of the university.

20

A Poet's Vision for a Muslim State

The Allahabad Address and the Idea of Pakistan: 1930

> Nations are born in the hearts of poets; they prosper and die in the hands of politicians.
>
> —Iqbal, *Stray Thoughts*

The rise of Mahatma Gandhi in Indian politics had slowly eclipsed the appeal of Muhammad Ali Jinnah as a leader. The turning point in Jinnah's career came in 1920 when he became disillusioned after failing to form a Hindu–Muslim alliance.[1] He spent most of the 1920s in England practicing law but he stayed abreast with Indian politics. He would not return to active politics again until 1933.

Meanwhile, Iqbal's star was rising in the Muslim League. On July 13, 1930, the Muslim League decides to invite Iqbal to be the president of the annual assembly at Allahabad. When they contact him with the proposal, he agrees.

In the early morning of December 29, 1930, Iqbal reaches the Allahabad railway station to a grand welcome by Muslim League leaders such as Sir Muhammad Yusuf and a large gathering of citizens who have thronged the station to greet their beloved poet. Jinnah is in London along with other Muslim leaders for the first Round Table Conference with his fourteen-point programme of

Hindu–Muslim power sharing, which has already come to a dead end.

The Muslim League's session has been planned in Shaikh Rahim Bakhsh's expansive house in Yaqutganj. Shaikh Rahim is a prosperous merchant of tobacco products. Nearly five hundred attendees are present at the session. Iqbal arrives at the site of the meeting with Sir Muhammad Yusuf.

The meeting starts with the recitation of the Quran, and then Iqbal is invited to deliver his presidential address. Iqbal knows that his speech will have an international audience, far beyond the confines of this enclosed meeting place. Therefore, he has prepared his speech in English, which only a few of the attendees there will understand. He begins to deliver it in a slow and calm manner.

'The unity of an Indian nation must be sought not in the negation, but in the mutual harmony and cooperation, of the many,' Iqbal says after talking about Islam and Muslims in India. 'It is, however, painful to observe that our attempts to discover such a principle of internal harmony have so far failed. Why have they failed? Perhaps we suspect each other's intentions and inwardly aim at dominating each other . . . The principle that each group is entitled to its free development on its own lines is not inspired by any feeling of narrow communalism. There are communalisms and communalisms. A community which is inspired by feelings of ill will towards other communities is low and ignoble. I entertain the highest respect for the customs, laws, religious and social institutions of other communities. Nay, it is my duty, according to the teaching of the Quran, even to defend their places of worship, if need be. Yet I love the communal group which is the source of my life and behaviour; and which has formed me and what I am by giving me its religion, its literature, its thought, its culture, and thereby recreating its whole past as a living operative factor, in my present consciousness. Even the authors of the Nehru Report recognize the value of this higher aspect of communalism.'

'Communalism in its higher aspect, then, is indispensable to the formation of a harmonious whole in a country like India,' he argues, linking communalism to the creation of a Muslim India within

India. 'The units of Indian society are not territorial as in European countries. India is a continent of human groups belonging to different races, speaking different languages, and professing different religions. Their behaviour is not at all determined by a common race consciousness. Even the Hindus do not form a homogeneous group. The principle of European democracy cannot be applied to India without recognizing the fact of communal groups. The Muslim demand for the creation of a Muslim India within India is, therefore, perfectly justified.'

'Personally, I would go farther than the demands embodied in it. I would like to see the Punjab, North-West Frontier Province, Sind, and Baluchistan amalgamated into a single State,' he says, drawing the map of his proposed state within India.' Self-government within the British Empire, or without the British Empire, the formation of a consolidated North-West Indian Muslim State appears to me to be the final destiny of the Muslims, at least of North-West India.'

Iqbal's proposal for an autonomous state has a 'subtle diplomatic possibility'—the state could exist within the Indian federal structure or could be established as a member of the British Commonwealth. The scheme also does not mandate an exchange of population.[2]

After his speech is over, no resolution is passed in support of his proposals. Local newspapers ignore the event and no coverage is given to Iqbal's speech.[3] No one realizes that this speech will change the course of Indian history.

Soon, people begin reacting to Iqbal's Allahabad address. Portions of his speech are published in London's newspapers. The British leadership reacts to the proposals resentfully. The British Prime Minister Ramsay MacDonald is said to be indignant, and the London correspondent of Allahabad's daily the *Leader* reports that 'Iqbal's attacks on the government's conception of the federal structure of the Indian government, and the Indian leaders' support of it had spawned in both India and British political circles deep anger and resentment.'[4]

Toeing the government line, both the *Pioneer* and the *Times of*

India dubbed Iqbal a 'reactionary' and called his ideas impracticable. The Hindu press took Iqbal to task with abusive criticism. The *Tribune* alleged that since Iqbal was not invited to the London Round Table Conference, he took his revenge with these proposals. The Urdu daily *Pratap* characterized Iqbal as 'mentally disturbed', 'foolish', 'narrow minded', and 'a spreader of poison'.

The Muslim press, on the other hand, largely supports Iqbal's views. The newspapers that welcome his views are the *Muslim Outlook*, *Siyasat*, and *Humdum* of Lucknow. But the most aggressive support comes from the newspaper *Inquilab*, which publishes Iqbal's address in two installments (translated into Urdu by Ghulam Rasul Mehr). In an editorial, the paper argues that Iqbal's proposal for a north-western Muslim state is not new. Before him, Lala Lajpat Rai,[5] Bhai Premanand, and Professor G.R. Abhiyankar[6] had advanced similar views of partitioning India. Why should Iqbal be denied the right to articulate a similar vision?

'Iqbal's demand is justified in asking for the establishment of Muslim India within India,' the *Humdum* says in a supportive editorial. 'It can best be attained in amalgamating [the] Northwest Frontier Province, Sind, Punjab, and Balochistan into one state.'

While the diatribe against Iqbal continues, Iqbal firmly holds on to his views for a separate state for the Muslim majority areas of Punjab, the north-western Frontier, Sind, and Balochistan.

'The proposed Islamic state is an ultimate objective,' he writes to Sayyid Nazir Niyazi on January 11, 1931. 'The exchange of population is not needed. Some years ago Lala Lajpat Rai had advanced the view of exchange of population. In the Muslim state or states, which might emerge in the Northwest India under this scheme, Hindu minority's rights would be fully protected.'[7]

Reacting to Iqbal's speech at the London Round Table Conference, Dr. B.S. Moonje, Nagpur's president of the Hindu Maha Sabha,[8] pleads in these words: 'I appeal to my Muslim friends not to be carried away by emotions. We are all Indians; there is no difference in our flesh and blood, and bones. We are descendants of a single nation. We are prepared to offer you all the protection that you demand to protect your religion, culture, and the progress of your future generations.'[9]

Rebutting Dr. Moonje, Sir Muhammad Shafi says: 'I assure the Sub-Committee that I had the same intention when I came here yesterday morning ... First, unless I have the full text of the speech, I cannot express a definite view ... If Sir Muhammad Iqbal has stated that because of Hindus' absolute demographic majority the central government of India would be dominated by Hindus, and as a consequence in six provinces out of eight governor's ruled provinces Hindu states would be established, then (logically) in four provinces, where Muslims constitute the majority, why shouldn't four Muslim states be established.'[10]

Iqbal stays in Allahabad for two days. He walks around the streets of the city, taking in its tastes and smell. He visits the grave of Akbar Allahabadi and offers prayers for him. He returns to Lahore on December 31, 1930.

21

A Bloody Year: 1931

Preparations for the Second Round Table Conference

'Let fools fight for the forms of government,' says Alexander Pope. I cannot agree with this political philosophy. To my mind, government, whatever its form, is one of the determining forces of a people's character. Loss of political power is equally ruinous to a nation's character. Ever since their political fall the Musalmans of India have undergone a rapid ethical deterioration. Of all the Muslim communities of the world they are probably the meanest in point of character. I do not mean to deplore our former greatness in this country, for, I confess, I am almost a fatalist in regard to the various forces that ultimately decide the destinies of nations. As a political force we are perhaps no longer required; but we are, I believe, still indispensable to the world as the only testimony to the absolute Unity of God—Our value among nations, then, is purely evidential.

—Iqbal, *Stray Thoughts*

Iqbal was not invited for the first Round Table Conference in London. Muslim leaders such as Muhammad Ali, Agha Khan, Muhammad Shafi, Fazal Haq, and Jinnah had represented the Indian Muslims at the conference. However, when the first Round Table

Conference concludes on January 9, 1931, Iqbal is invited to attend the second and the third Round Table Conferences in London, and Iqbal happily accepts the invitation.[1] This, Iqbal reckons, not only gives him an opportunity to present the Muslim case vigorously before the British government but also affords him a chance to explore Europe and parts of the Middle East.

By now, Muhammad Ali, who was at the vanguard of the Khilafat movement, has died in London and is survived by his brother Shaukat Ali. The Muslim League, losing its significance, has fallen into disarray and a disheartened Jinnah has decided to stay on in England to practice law.

At this juncture, a reluctant Iqbal finds himself in a position of historical and political importance. He cannot escape the responsibilities foisted upon him by circumstance—by accepting this invitation he agrees to be one of the leaders of Indian Muslims.

In April 1931, the leaders of All India Muslim Conference meet in Delhi where Gandhi refuses to meet their political demands to safeguard Muslim interests. Gandhi's rejection is on the basis that their demands are 'not reflective of the unanimous views of the Muslims'.

Between the two Muslim groups, the All India Muslim Conference and the Muslim National Party, the disagreement is over the issue of 'joint versus separate electorates'.

Maulana Shaukat Ali convinces the nawab of Bhopal, Nawab Hamidullah Khan, to invite the leaders of these two Muslim organizations to bring about a rapprochement between them.

In a public meeting on May 3, 1931, at Mochi Gate in Lahore, Iqbal argues that even though Gandhi is justified in saying that there is no unanimity among Muslims vis a vis their political demands, the same is true of the Hindu leadership. There are three factions among the Hindus: one supports joint electorates, another supports separate electorates and there is a third front that demands social democracy.[2] 'If the range of disagreement among the Hindus was so wide, then to exploit disagreement among the Muslims was nothing short of political hypocrisy!' he says.[3]

In this address, Iqbal goes on to denounce European style nationalism that creates irreligiosity and he expresses his fear that the same sentiments might surface in India. 'All nations in India want to preserve their traits and characteristics,' he says. 'Muslims want no more than preserving their distinction and identity. Muslims do not want to rule over others, nor do they accept the rules of others over them; they do not want to be "slaves" of others.'

A week later, Iqbal travels to Bhopal for the two party meeting organized by Nawab Hamidullah Khan. Ghulam Rasul Mehr accompanies him on the trip. Negotiations between the All India Muslim Conference and the Muslim National Party fail and the disagreement over 'joint versus separate electorates' continues.

As no unanimity is reached between the Muslim leaders of India, Hindu–Muslim agreement between the Congress and the Muslim parties also falls through the cracks.

Meanwhile, a dangerous situation develops in north India when Hindu–Muslim riots break out in major cities like Benaras, Agra, Mirzapur, and Kanpur. Muslims are slaughtered mercilessly and a large number are killed in Kanpur. Shocked by this turn of events, Iqbal and other Muslim leaders issue an appeal on July 14, 1931, to generously donate money to help the riot victims of Kanpur. The appeal appears in the newspapers of north India:

'Hindus had not done to the British in the rebellion of 1857 what they did to the Muslims in Kanpur. The way sportsmen with their rifles on the ready pounce upon the wild animals in no less a manner and style the Hindus hunted down the Muslims in Kanpur. Thousands of Muslim houses were burned; craftsmen's tools were made useless. Helpless Muslims were not only slaughtered, but were burned alive. Blood has not dried in the houses and mosques where Muslims took shelter. These heart wrenching incidents remind us of the tragedy of their agony. [In addition to the loss of life], thirty mosques were totally or partially destroyed and the Quran was desecrated.'[4]

The riots stir Iqbal's soul, driving him to despair over Hindu–Muslim reconciliation. The despair is so deep that Iqbal is suspicious that the British government might try to appease the Hindus at the cost of the Muslims in the forthcoming London Round Table Conference. If that happens, what should the Muslims do?

'Any attempt on the part of Great Britain at the next Round Table Conference to take an undue advantage of [the current] communal split will ultimately prove disastrous to both countries,' Iqbal writes to Sir Francis Younghusband, a former British army officer, explorer and writer, on July 30, 1931. 'If you transfer political authority to the Hindu and keep him in power for any material benefit to Great Britain, you will drive the Indian Muslim to use the same weapon against the Swaraj or Anglo-swaraj government as Gandhi did against the British.' He quickly clarifies his position on Hindus, which is respectful. 'Please do not think that I have any prejudice against the Hindus,' he says. 'In fact, I have great admiration for the spirit of self-sacrifice and courage, which they have shown in recent years. They have produced men of eminence in every walk of life and are fast advancing along social and economic lines.'[5]

The other danger of this transfer of power to the Hindus in India, Iqbal warns, is that 'it may result in the whole of Muslim Asia being driven into the lap of Russian Communism which would serve as a coup de grace to British supremacy in the East ... Since Bolshevism plus God is almost identical with Islam, I should not be surprised if, in the course of time, either Islam would devour Russia or Russia Islam.'

* * *

In August 1931, there is an uprising in Kashmir against the repressive Dogra rulers. In July, police had opened fire on a crowd of Kashmiri protesters that led to the death of twenty-one Kashmiri Muslim protesters. More protests were held that degenerated into Hindu–Muslim riots. Kashmiri leaders like Shaikh Muhammad Abdullah and Chaudhury Ghulam Abbas were arrested and martial law was imposed in the state.

In Punjab, there is widespread outrage against the repressive rulers of Kashmir, an outrage that Iqbal shares. To support the protesting Kashmiris, Kashmir Day is celebrated on August 14, 1931. The Muslims of Lahore take out a protest march and Iqbal delivers the presidential address: 'There was a time when Muslims in India and the Punjab were not deeply interested in the affairs of Kashmir,' he says in his address. 'Even those Punjabis whose ancestors had migrated from Kashmir were not fully informed of the history of Kashmir. Now the Punjabi Muslims are fully awake due to the oppression of Kashmiri Muslims . . . Muslims have endeavoured for a long time to gain their well-deserved rights; now that they are more organized in pressing the demands for their rights; the rule of Kashmir and the Hindu newspapers have circulated mischievous new items, calling the Muslims' endeavours leading to Hindu-Muslim riots . . .'[6]

Iqbal not only helps raise donations for the riot victims of Kashmir, he also persuades some lawyers to visit the state and provide legal aid to those who are languishing in jails. However, the state of Kashmir bans the entry of these lawyers. Iqbal too is disallowed from entering Kashmir, a ban that will nag him for the rest of his life.

22

London Once More

The Second Round Table Conference: 1931

All nations accuse us of fanaticism. I admit the charge—I go
further and say that we are justified in our fanaticism. Translated
in the language of biology, fanaticism is nothing but the principle
of individuation working in the case of a group. In this sense all
forms of life are more or less fanatical and ought to be so if they
care for their collective life. And as a matter of fact all nations
are fanatical. Criticize an Englishman's religion, he is immovable;
but criticize his civilization, his country, or the behaviour of his
nation in any sphere of activity and you will bring out his innate
fanaticism. The reason is that his nationality does not depend on
religion; it has a geographical basis—his country.

—Iqbal, *Stray Thoughts*

As an invitee of the Second Round Table Conference in London,
Iqbal starts from Lahore on September 9, 1931.[1] The plan is to stop
over in New Delhi and Bombay before setting out for London.

By this time, Iqbal is not only recognized as a great poet but also
one of the leaders of Muslims in India. The viceroy's invitation for the
conference in London seals that reputation for Sir Muhammad Iqbal.

Besides attending the conference in London, Iqbal is also

scheduled to visit other places—in and outside Europe. He has received two important invitations: One, Mufti Amin al-Husseini of Jerusalem has invited him to attend the World Muslim Congress in Palestine, and two, Italy's Professor Marconi, president of the Intellectuals Association of Rome, has invited him to deliver a lecture in Rome.

Iqbal sets out for Delhi from Lahore on September 8 by train, from where he will depart for Bombay. A large number of his admirers assemble to see him off at the station in Lahore. In Delhi and Bombay, Muslim religious and political leaders, and fans, receive Iqbal with a hero's welcome.

Iqbal reaches Bombay on September 10 and stays at the Caliphate House. In the evening, he attends two receptions: First by his old friend Atiya Faizee and the second, by Sardar Salah-ud Din Saljuqui, Afghanistan's consul.

Atiya is now married to a Jewish artist who has converted to Islam. At the party, when the guests request him to recite a verse he's written, Iqbal shares this couplet with the audience:

Chuna ba-zi keh agar marg-e ma ast merg-e dawam
Khuda zay kardah-e khud sharmsar tar gardad

Spend your life so beautifully that if death is the unavoidable end,
Embarrassed should be God on his own act of terminating your life[2]

A dance and musical soiree follows at Atiya's house. Iqbal watches the performance of the artists while exchanging witticisms with Atiya, like they used to do when they were young students in London.

Iqbal is also the guest of Sardar Salah-ud Din Saljuqui, Afghanistan's consul, the same evening. It is a delightful evening for Iqbal and to give him company there is a well-known poet, Mirza Talat Yazdi, present.

Before proceeding to London from Bombay, Iqbal gives a detailed interview to a journalist of the *Bombay Chronicle*. It turns out to be a long interview in which he shares his thoughts on India's and the world's socio-political problems.

His main claim in the interview is that he is not against any community or nation in the world, that he is a man without any prejudice, and that he only wishes to 'see Islam returned to its pristine simplicity'. He also says that he holds India's multiculturalism dear, and his idea of India is a country where every community retains its culture and individuality.

With the journalist he also discusses his views on Pan-Islamism, a term coined by a French journalist.

Iqbal states that 'Pan-Islamism', as suggested by the person who fathered the term, does not exist anywhere except in his, the journalist's, own fertile imagination. Iqbal says that it is nothing but a bugbear, the Islamic version of the 'Yellow Peril' (the Western phobia about East Asian immigration, culture, and economic power)—an idea invented to generate Islamophobia in the West.

Iqbal also discards the view that Pan-Islamism is a political movement with its centre in Constantinople, a movement planning 'a kind of union of all the Muslim states against the European states'.[3]

He rather endorses the concept of Jamaluddin Afghani's[4] Pan-Islamism—a theory that had advised Afghanistan, Persia, and Turkey to unite against the aggression of Europe. 'This was purely a defensive measure, and I personally think that Jamaluddin was perfectly right in his view.'[5]

His own view on Pan-Islamism, he states, emanates from the Quran. 'In that sense,' he claims, 'it is not a political project but a social experiment. Islam does not recognize caste or race or colour ... Pan-Islamism, thus interpreted, was taught by the Prophet and will live forever. In this sense every Muslim is a Pan-Islamist and ought to be so. Indeed, the word "Pan" ought to be dropped from the phrase "Pan-Islamism", for Islamism is an expression which completely covers the meaning I have mentioned above.'[6]

* * *

Iqbal's journey to Europe is not very eventful. It is a typical sea voyage, and the only remarkable thing is that Iqbal is undertaking this journey after twenty-five years, when he first travelled to England as a student in 1905.

His routine on board the ship is very simple: wake up before sunrise, study the Quran, then clean up and have breakfast in the cabin. He is travelling in the company of fellow attendees of the conference in London. Iqbal loves to walk up to the deck and spend time there chatting up co-passengers and listening to news broadcasts. Sometimes the delegates indulge in discussions or read reports about the conference. Poetry recitations also take place which keep Iqbal's spirits afloat.

There are seven or eight Indian delegates of the conference travelling with him on the same ship. Among them, four are Muslim. These fellow travellers include Justice Suhrawardy, Shaikh Mushir Hussain Kidwai, Khan Bahadur Hafiz Hayat Hussain (the nawab of Chattari), Sayyid Ali Imam, and two young landowners from the Awadh province. Iqbal observes that all of his fellow Muslim travellers are *maghrib-zada*, Westernized. To Iqbal's pleasant surprise, two of them are *hafiz-e quran*—they have learnt the Quran by heart. They are the nawab of Chattari and Sayyid Ali Imam. About Kidwai, he observes that he is an 'enthusiastic Pan-Islamist and preaches his message enthusiastically.'[7]

Iqbal finds an interesting companion in Sayyid Ali Imam. One day, they are standing on the deck of the ship. Imam performs some mental calculations and declares, 'Brother Iqbal! Our ship is now moving exactly in front of Medina's shores.' As soon as he says this, his eyes well up with tears. 'There is the mausoleum of our prophet!'

Iqbal is moved by Imam's emotional reaction.

Imam's large memory also impresses Iqbal. That man can recite a large number of verses in Urdu, Persian, and Arabic.

During the journey, Iqbal loses all appetite for meat and survives on vegetables, fish, and egg. The meat available on the ship is usually

not halal. However, Imam's wife, Lady Ali Imam, makes sure that
the cook prepares halal meat, which is then served to Iqbal. Iqbal
eats this meat with great relish, and also continues to eat rice with
vegetables.

When the ship reaches Aden, Shaikh Abdullah, a young lawyer
from Lahore, takes Iqbal to his house in the city of Aden and offers
him a sumptuous Indian meal.

Iqbal notes how much Aden has changed from the last time he
travelled through the port city. It wasn't much of a city then. Now,
its population has swelled and made considerable progress. The city
has Arab moneylenders and Sindhi and Punjabi shopkeepers.

The ship docks at Port Said on September 30 where some
Egyptian visitors come on board to meet him. One of the visitors
is an interviewer, Hakim Muhammad Sadique Nadau, a Reuters
correspondent. During the interview, Iqbal apprises him of the
Hindu–Muslim situation in India and the lack of cooperation
between the two groups that has led to the Round Table Conferences.
'Hindus are constantly worried about the possibility of Indian
Muslims, supported by the Afghan and Baluch Muslims, invading
India and keeping it under their domination,' he says. 'But is it really
possible? If Egypt becomes completely free, would the Egyptians
hand over their country to the Turks, because the Turks are Muslim.
The non-violence policy of the National Congress is designed to
(not) face the British bayonets. The riots in Kanpur and Srinagar
demonstrate that violence is applied in their dealings with Muslims.'[8]

He also allays Egyptian misgivings that Indian Muslims are in
the way of India's freedom from the British. '[The] Egyptians suspect
that Muslims are a painful obstacle in the attaining of freedom for
India. There is not a grain of truth in this view,' he tells his Egyptian
visitors. 'I urge Egyptian journalists to visit India and thoroughly
examine the conditions. In India, Egyptian Muslims are subjected
to this propaganda that they have bid farewell to Allah, the Quran
and Islam, while we know that it is a great mischief.'[9]

Iqbal finally reaches London on September 27, 1931. The Round Table Conference will be held at Saint James' Palace. Iqbal stays close to the conference venue at Saint James' Court, Buckingham Gate.

23

London, Rome, Egypt, and Palestine

Islam appeared as a protest against idolatry. And what is patriotism but a subtle form of idolatry; a deification of a material object. The patriotic songs of various nations will bear me out in my calling patriotism a deification of a material object. Islam could not tolerate idolatry in any form. It is our eternal mission to protest against idolatory in all its forms. What was to be demolished by Islam could not be made the very principle of its structure as a political community. The fact that the Prophet prospered and died in a place not his birthplace is perhaps a mystic hint to the same effect.

—Iqbal, *Stray Thoughts*

Given Iqbal's interest in separate electorates and minority's constitutional rights, he is assigned to the sub-committee for minorities in the Second Round Table Conference. The sub-committee meets for the first time on September 28, 1931.

The members of the sub-committee, including Mahatma Gandhi, have a lot of differences amongst themselves. Hindus and Sikhs are opposed to Muslim demands. To give them time to iron out their objections in private, the meeting is postponed for the next two days.

When the sub-committee meets for the second session on September 30, Gandhi proposes to adjourn the proceedings for another week. The committee meets again on October 8. The delegates still have disagreements and Gandhi proposes postponing the sessions *sine die*.

After the failure of these meetings, Iqbal becomes disappointed. He is not an active participant in the discussions and largely remains silent during the proceedings.

Though the deliberations at the conference are largely a failure, his days and nights are filled with private meetings and receptions. Sir Samuel Hoare (secretary of state for India) and Sayyid Zia-uddin Tabatabie (former prime minister of Iran), are among some of Iqbal's prominent visitors. Numerous receptions are thrown in his honour and freedom fighters from Chechnya and Turkey as well as British and American scholars pay him a visit.

Margaret Farquharson, president of the National League,[1] invites Iqbal on October 27, 1931 to meet influential individuals in London.

Curious to see the mode of prayers of the pacifist Christians, Iqbal pays a visit to the Quakers Hall.

On November 4, Iqbal addresses the India Society at the invitation of its president, Sir Francis Younghusband. At the meeting, he discusses his poetry, including his upcoming book in Persian, *Javed Nama*, his philosophical thoughts and answers questions about the meaning and importance of his concept of *khudi*.[2]

The same evening he has dinner with Lord and Lady Irwin,[3] giving him another chance to articulate his position on provincial autonomy and separate electorates for Hindus and Muslims.

On November 18, he visits Cambridge to deliver a lecture for the International Muslim Association. At the train station, Chaudhury Rahmat Ali, Khawaja Abdur Rahim, and others receive him with a warm welcome.

'I want to address Cambridge students and offer them a few counsels,' says Iqbal in his lecture. 'Cambridge University is the fountain of knowledge, which has made major contributions in the shaping of Western civilized culture.'

'I advise the young men to protect themselves against materialism and atheism. In separating religion from politics, Europeans committed a blunder. This separation caused the loss of spiritual refinement for the Western civilization, and its orientation became materialistic atheism. I believe the human ego is the central point of the universe. This is the basic viewpoint; a majority of philosophers came to this ultimate unity. The true direction is to move from unity to plurality.

'Twenty-five years ago, I was able to detect the weakness of Western civilization, and had made some predictions about its ultimate end; although, to be frank with you, I did not completely understand its true meaning. This was the condition in 1907.

'Six years later, my predictions proved to be true to their content. The war of 1914 was caused by the blunder, which I have already alluded to, that is the separation of state from religion, and the advent of materialistic atheism. Bolshevism is spawned by the separation of religion from state. I advise young men to protect themselves against materialism.

'A few days ago I addressed a meeting of English women. I was asked to offer a wise counsel and I said to them that their first and foremost responsibility is to protect their next generation from the ravages of atheistic materialism. Religion is absolutely essential; religion is another name for intuitive knowledge, and divine grace.'[4]

One of the most important persons that Iqbal often meets in London is Jinnah. The government has not invited him for the Third Round Table Conference, considering him out of touch with Muslim politics in India.

Iqbal urges Jinnah to 'terminate his self-imposed exile in London and return home'. Iqbal knows that Jinnah posseses the best qualities to lead the Muslims of India and has the requisite organizational skills. He persuades Jinnah to 'adopt for the Muslim League a new national objective for the emergence of a separate Muslim state in north-west India.'[5]

* * *

On November 21, Iqbal leaves London for Paris. There his friend Umrao Singh Sher Gill welcomes him at the train station. Singh, an aristocrat with scholarly interests, is also a translator of Iqbal's poems.

From Paris Iqbal takes a twenty-four hour train journey to Rome. At the station, Professor Airastco, who teaches philosophy at Rome University and is associated with the Italian Royal Academy, and Dr Scarpa, Italy's consul-general in Bombay, receive Iqbal.

The next day Iqbal visits Rome University and meets the scholars there.

November 24 is reserved for a visit to the historical sights of Rome. Accompanied by Urdu journalist Ghulam Rasul Mehr, Iqbal visits the Colosseum. The Colosseum is the largest amphitheatre in the world. Its construction began under the emperor Vespasian in 70 AD, and his successor and heir Titus completed it in 80 AD. It could hold between 50,000 and 80,000 spectators. This site was used for gladiatorial contests and public spectacles. Seeing this wonder of Roman architecture, Iqbal cannot help but comment to Mehr: 'Look at the Roman emperors, who built a magnificent theatre so that fifty thousand people could enjoy the combat unto death between human beings and wild animals and compare it with the Shahi Mosque of Lahore, which can accommodate 100,000 so that they could congregate to express true sentiments of love, sincerity, and fraternal solidarity. This one comparative study lights up the fact that Islam is the well-spring of divine grace.'[6]

While visiting the Roman catacombs,[7] Iqbal again draws comparisons with Islamic practices of worship. 'Before Islam,' he says, 'the general religious trend of thought was toward secrecy, concealment, and darkness. Islam is the first religion which worships God Almighty in the light of the bright sun, and pealed religion out of concealment.'[8]

During his stay in Rome, Iqbal also meets Professor Gentelee, who calls upon the great Indian poet to discuss the role of poetry and music in nation building. The professor, a native of Italy, had translated Iqbal's poem 'Sicily' into Italian.

On November 25, Iqbal visits the former king of Afghanistan, Aman Allah Khan. He lives in Rome as a political refugee.[9]

While Iqbal is in Rome, the Italian dictator, Benito Mussolini, sends him an aid, seeking a meeting with the great poet of the East. Like Iqbal, Mussolini is also an admirer of Nietzsche. He invites Iqbal to visit him in his office on November 27, 1931.

Dr Scarpa accompanies Iqbal to Mussolini and acts as an interpreter.[10] The meeting takes place in Mussolini's office, which is like a large hall. When Iqbal enters his office, Mussolini occupies an ornate chair behind a large desk on a raised platform at the end of the hall. Mussolini is lost in reading some papers. When Iqbal comes closer to the dictator, Mussolini stands up and welcomes Iqbal by shaking his hand.[11]

Il Duce is not a tall man, but is barrel-chested and his arms are thick and heavy. Iqbal is struck by the brilliance of Mussolini's eyes. He thinks their sparkle is beyond description, comparable only to the rays of the sun.

The meeting lasts for about forty minutes. When Mussolini asks him about the Italian people, Iqbal replies, after hesitating a bit, 'Italians are very much like the Iranians. They are attractive, good-looking, lovers of art and very sensitive and intelligent. The magnificent part of their civilization and culture span many centuries but they lack blood.'

Mussolini does not believe in race as yet but he is proud of his Italian heritage. He asks Iqbal what he means by saying that Italians 'lack blood'? Iqbal explains: 'Iranians have one advantage, which is not available to the Italians. Surrounded by healthy and strong nations like the Turks, Afghans, and the Kurds, Iranian blood is constantly replenished, but Italians have no such possibility.'

Iqbal's thoughts seem to concur with Mussolini's thoughts. He had said two years earlier: '[When the] city dies, the nation— deprived of the young life-blood of new generations—is now made up of people who are old and degenerate and cannot defend itself against a younger people which launches an attack on the now unguarded frontiers . . . This will happen, and not just to cities and nations, but on an infinitely greater scale—the whole White race, the Western race can be submerged by other coloured races which are multiplying at a rate unknown in our race.'

'What should Italians do?' asks the leader.

'Look East,' Iqbal says. 'European culture is on the decline while the air of the East is still fresh. You should learn to breathe it in.'

'What do you think of our fascist movement?' Mussolini asks him.

'You have adopted for national life a dimension of discipline, which is very essential in the Islamic perspective,' the poet replies. 'If you were to adopt all of Islam you would be able to subdue all of Europe.'

Mussolini by then had established his rule in Libya and there was Libyan resistance to the Italian occupation.[12] 'How can I win the moral support of the Muslim world?' he asks.

'Invite young Muslim students in large numbers to study in Italy, and give them free education with free room and board,' Iqbal suggests.

'Any other wise counsel?' the dictator asks, leaning in.

'Do not let your cities' population exceed the specified limit,' Iqbal advices. Seeing Mussolini's perplexed mood, he explains, 'As the city population increases, its cultural and economic vitality declines, and then the cultural vitality is replaced by evil of all kinds.'

Mussolini is really interested in what Iqbal is saying. Noticing his high level of interest, Iqbal continues, 'I am not stating my personal opinion here. This is the wise counsel of my Prophet which was given thirteen hundred years ago for the city of Medina. He advised that when the population exceeded a certain limit, the excessive population should be settled in a new city.'

Mussolini jumps to his feet upon hearing this. Standing erect, he thumps the desk with his hand. 'This is indeed an extraordinary thought!' he proclaims.[13]

After Iqbal emerges from the meeting with Mussolini, he is surrounded by journalists. 'What do you think of *Il Duce*?' one of them asks him. Iqbal first hesitates a little and then he says, 'Your *Il Duce* is another Luther, but is without a Bible.'

* * *

From Rome, Iqbal travels to Alexandria via Venice. He takes the ship Victoria on November 29, 1931, and reaches Alexandria on December 1.

Welcoming him at the harbour is a phalanx of youth and dignitories: the Shabab al-Muslemin of Egypt, journalist Siddique Muhammad Nadu, Maulana Shaukat Ali, and Egyptian prince Umar Tawsoon's representatives.

In Egypt, Iqbal's days and nights are filled with meetings, followed by sightseeing trips. For example, he spends his first day meeting journalists, visiting the offices of Shabab al-Muslemin, signing the register of King Fawad at his palace, and going around Alexandria to get a glimpse of the historic port city.

In the afternoon, Iqbal takes a train to Cairo. It is a three-hour long train ride. When he reaches Cairo, he is received by many admirers including members of Shabab al-Muslemin, Al-Azhar University's Indian students and Indians settled in Egypt.

In Cairo, Iqbal stays at the Metropole hotel. But he hardly has the opportunity to relax, visitors either keep calling on him or he is invited out to meet members of the Egyptian elite.

He is often invited to Dr Abdul Hameed Saeed Bey's house where he meets Shaikh Al-Azhar and Muhammad Ali Pasha, the former minister of endowments. Lawyer and philosophy scholar Lutfi Bey Jumma also pays a visit to Iqbal. In all these meetings, Iqbal gathers the impression that Egyptians view Indian Muslims as an obstacle to India's freedom. He does his best to allay their doubts and shares with them the Indian Muslim position.

On December 2, Iqbal visits the historical monuments around Cairo: the pyramids, the gardens by the Nile, Khan Khalili Bazaar, and Qasr al-Aini, a remarkable modern hospital.

Iqbal is surprised when Egypt's well-known sufi Sayyid Muhammad Madi Abu al-A'zam visits Iqbal in his hotel along with his two sons. 'Why did you take the trouble of visiting me here?' Iqbal says. 'I would have loved to come over to your residence to meet you.'

'The Prophet of Islam Sayyidina Muhammad has stated that I would be pleased if you go to visit a man who is devoted to Islam,' the sufi remarks. 'I have only followed his instructions in coming to meet you, because I wanted to please my Lord and Master.' Hearing this Iqbal falls silent. After the guests depart, Iqbal finds himself teary eyed, thinking: 'My God! The time has come that people look upon so sinful a man like me and consider me a man devoted to Islam and want to meet me as such!'[14]

After a few days, Iqbal visits the sufi's house at his invitation. The sufi tells his disciples: 'When Muslims existed only in hundreds of thousands, the world's great powers licked their shoes. Now that they are in millions, the non-believers rule over them everywhere. The explanation of this situation is the fact that Muslims jettisoned Islam, and became alienated from its spirit.' Pointing at Iqbal, he adds: 'There in his heart lurks the love of Islam, and devotion to Sayyidina Muhammad.'[15]

During his stay in Cairo, Iqbal also meets the prime minister of Egypt, Mustafa al-Nahas Pasha, on his invitation. On December 4, he visits the Cairo Museum and attends a high tea organized by Jamiat al-Rabita al-Hindiya.

On December 5, when Iqbal leaves for Palestine, he visits Fustat, the first Islamic capital of Egypt, as well as the Al-Azhar University.

The train leaves Cairo, after making its way through Ismailia and Qantara, Iqbal and his companion Mehr take another train that takes them through Khan Yunus, the Gaza Strip and Ludh. From there, they take a final train to Jerusalem.

At the station, Iqbal is welcomed by Mufti Amin al-Husseini, who has invited him to attend the Muslim World Congress in Palestine, and Maulana Shaukat Ali. There are delegates from all over the world to attend the conference and the aim of the conference is to strengthen Islamic solidarity globally. Iqbal and Mehr stay in the Grand Hotel, close to the conference venue.

The conference's inaugural session takes place on December 6. 'We organized this session of the Congress because we want Muslims the world over to act like one soul in one body,' Mufti Amin al-Husseini says in his inaugural address. 'We do not want to commit any aggression against the religion and culture of others; no, no, we do not want to spawn hatred against others.'[16]

One of the goals of the World Congress is to encourage cooperation between Muslims and strengthen Islamic solidarity. The delegates make a pledge to God that they will protect sacred Islamic sites in Palestine even at the cost of their own lives. Iqbal attends the meetings of the Congress from December 7 to 14 and comments on various proposals such as the transfer of the Hejaz Railway Committee to a Muslim International Administrative Company and the establishment of a university of excellence in Jerusalem. Iqbal insists that the university must provide both traditional and modern education.

By 1931, the Zionist hold on Palestine is becoming strong. The relations between Arabs and Jews are strained. Jewish organizations have even opposed the holding of the World Muslim Conference in Jerusalem but the determination of the mufti has made it happen. The Committee on the Holy Land makes several proposals to include the boycott of Jewish goods, and warns the Muslim world of the dangers of Jewish immigration.

During his stay in Palestine, Iqbal visits Christian holy sites like the Mount of Olives and the graves of the Hebrew prophets Zechariah and David.

On December 14, Iqbal delivers his last address to the World Congress, applauding fraternal solidarity among Muslims and underlining the dangers to the Muslim nations:

> I want to congratulate you for the repeated display of fraternal solidarity and affection. It is our responsibility to guide our youth

to the highway of security, because Islam is under siege from two directions: one is the attack of the materialistic renunciation of faith, and the other one is the onslaught of territorial nationalism. It is our responsibility to confront both dangers.

I believe that the spirit of Islam can defeat both enemies. Territorial nationalism or patriotism are not bad phenomena; but if moderation in their pursuit is ignored, and extremism takes hold, then atheism and materialism can easily flourish.

I advise you to be Muslims to the core of your hearts. I do not worry much about the enemies of Islam as much as I worry about Muslims themselves. I recall a delightful statement of the Prophet Muhammad, who said: 'I speak from the line of the prophets, and you are in the line of ulema.'

Whenever I recall these words I hang my head in shame. Are we Muslims today in a condition that the Prophet Muhammad would be proud of us? Yes, it is possible, if only we rekindle in our hearts the light that he had inspired in us. Yes, in that situation, he would be proud of us.

Iqbal departs from the holy land of Jerusalem on December 15, 1931, along with Mehr. From Port Saeed he boards a ship for Bombay on December 18. On the ship he has some great co-passengers—Gandhi and members of the royal family of Hyderabad.

Iqbal reaches Bombay on December 28, 1931. There, Atiya Faizi again hosts a dinner party for him. From Bombay, he takes a train to Lahore on December 30, 1931.

24

Paris and Spain

In the sphere of human thought, Muhammad, Buddha, and Kant
were probably the greatest revolutionaries. In the sphere of action,
Napoleon stands unrivalled. I do not include Christ among the
world's revolutionaries, since the movement initiated by him was
soon absorbed by pre-Christian paganism. European Christianity
seems to me to be nothing more than a feeble translation of
ancient paganism in the language of Semitic theology.

—Iqbal, *Stray Thoughts*

The Third Round Table Conference is scheduled to meet in
November 1932. The British government is not particularly happy
with Iqbal's performance in the previous conference. To make
matters worse, Iqbal has criticized the conference after returning to
India. Regardless, on the recommendation of the viceroy's executive
council Sir Muhammad Zafarullah Khan, the viceroy accept's Iqbal's
nomination to be a delegate at the Third Round Table Conference.

Iqbal leaves early for the conference to spend some time in Europe.
On October 17, 1932, Iqbal starts from Lahore for Europe. In Bombay,
Iqbal is entertained by Salah-ud Din Saljuqi, the Afghan consul, and
his friend, Atiya, along with her husband, Samuel Faizi Rahamin.

On the way to England, Nobel Prize-winning physicist Dr. C.V.
Raman travels on the same ship as the Muslim delegation. One

day, during a conversation, Raman mentions fellow Indian and
Nobel Prize winner Rabindranath Tagore. 'Tagore lives in the East
but his fame has reached the West,' he says. Impressed by Tagore's
example, Syed Amjad Ali, the secretary of the Muslim delegation to
the Round Table Conference, suggests to Iqbal that he too should
travel to different countries of the world. 'This will really bring you
worldwide fame,' he claims. On hearing this suggestion, Iqbal says:

Tagore preaches rest, practices action
Iqbal practices rest, preaches action

On this trip, one of Iqbal's personal goals is to meet European
scholars like Louis Massignon and Bergson in Paris.[1] Massignon's
work on Sufism, and especially his contribution to the understanding
of Mansur Hallaj,[2] a ninth century sufi, had impressed Iqbal. Iqbal
had written to the French orientalist on February 18, 1932. He gets
to meet him on November 1, 1932, when he travels to Venice and
then to Paris. At the Paris train station, Iqbal's friend Sardar Umrao
Singh, along with his Hungarian wife and two children, Amrita, who
grows to become the famous painter Amrita Shergill, and Indira,
receive him.

Iqbal calls on the French philosopher along with his friends Syed
Amjad Ali and Sardar Umrao Singh. They meet in Massignon's book-
filled study and discuss Al-Hallaj's ideas. The room is filled with so
many books that there is hardly any space left for Iqbal's friends to sit.

'Several centuries before Iqbal, some Muslim thinkers in India
had reacted against Ibn al-Arabi's doctrine of pantheistic monism
(*Wahdat al-Wujud*),' Massignon writes, recording his meeting with
Iqbal. 'This view of the Sufis encompassing the annihilation unto
Him is structured on Hindu philosophy; however, the exponents of
Wahdat al-Shahud (Unitarian monism) started with Ali Hamadani
and extended to Sarhindi and Shah Wali Allah of Delhi. Iqbal
confessed to me in Paris that he did not adhere to the philosophy
of *Wahdat al-Wujud* but that of *Wahdat al-Shahud*.'[3]

Iqbal's meeting with Henri Bergson[4] takes place a little later—in the first week of January 1933. Iqbal's friend Sardar Umrao Singh sets up this meeting for him. He acts as the interpreter during the meeting. Iqbal was a forceful exponent of Bergson's concept of time which was similar to his own views. Later on he had discarded his thesis after Professor McTaggart criticized it.

When Iqbal goes to visit the famous French philosopher, he is 'weak and old and confined to a wheelchair' and has stopped socializing and receiving visitors. However, he does spare some time for Iqbal. He not only welcomes Iqbal but also has a chat with him for about two hours. They discuss Berkeley and also talk about Bergson's theory of creative evolution.[5]

'For Bergson, the notion of life mixes together two opposite senses, which must be differentiated and only then lead into a genuine unity. On the one hand, it is clear from Bergson's earlier works that life is the absolute temporal movement informed by duration and retained in memory. But, on the other hand, he has shown that life also consists in the practical necessities imposed on our body and accounting for our habitual mode of knowing in spatial terms.'[6]

While they are having this discussion, Iqbal sites a tradition of the Prophet Muhammad, 'Do not abuse time; God says, I am time.'

Bergson is astonished to hear this and asks Iqbal to confirm the authenticity of this hadith.

* * *

One of Iqbal's long-cherished dreams is to visit Spain and this dream comes true in January 1933 when Iqbal enters Spain as a tourist.

Iqbal's sojourn in Spain is three weeks long and it begins on January 5 when he enters Madrid. In this entire trip, he is accompanied by a young, slim English girl who acts as Iqbal's interpreter and secretary.

Who is she? How did Iqbal hire her? There is widespread speculation about this but no one is sure how she became Iqbal's travel companion in Spain. According to Chaudhury Khakan Hussain, Iqbal had received a cheque of six thousand rupees in London from the nawab of Bhopal. The money was to enable him to travel to Britain. With that money, he hires a British secretary.

Did she come from Britain or did Iqbal meet her in Spain? Was she really a secretary or a member of the British Intelligence Service?

The Spanish press takes her to be Iqbal's daughter. During the three weeks that she spends accompanying Iqbal to various sites in Spain, instead of serving as a private secretary, she begins to serve Iqbal as a devotee. When Iqbal asks her to explain the change in her behaviour, she says that she had an epiphany about his divine personality.[7]

Iqbal's first stop in Spain is Madrid and then he immediately leaves for the south of the country to visit Andalusia. In Madrid, Spain's minister of education receives him. Arrangements are made for Iqbal to visit the legendary mosque of Cordoba.

Cordoba's period of glory began in the eighth century after the Moorish conquest. In the year 711, the town was one of the first to fall to the Moorish conquerors, led by Tariq-ibn Zayid, after his great victory at the Battle of Guadalete. It led to the foundation of some three hundred mosques and innumerable palaces and public buildings 'to rival the splendours of Constantinople, Damascus, and Baghdad'. When Abd-al Rahman I was deposed as caliph of Damascus in 756 he set up his court at Cordoba and laid the foundations for the most glorious period of the city's history. He began building the Great Mosque in 786, on the site of a Roman temple of Janus which had been converted into a church by the Visigoths. He had the intention of creating a structure that outshone the mosque of Damascus. Work on it continued over the two succeeding centuries. In the thirteenth century, under Saint Ferdinand III, Cordoba's Great Mosque was turned into a cathedral and new defensive structures, particularly the Alcázar de los Reyes Cristianos and the Torre Fortaleza de la Calahorra, were erected in its place.[8]

Visiting this great mosque, which reminds him of the glory of

Islam's past, is a spiritual experience for Iqbal. He becomes the first Muslim to offer prayers in the mosque-converted church in more than four hundred years in January 1933.

Sitting in the mosque, Iqbal writes his famous poem '*Dua*' ('Prayer'):

Hai yehi meri namaz hai yehi mera wuzu
Meri nawaon me hai mere jigar ka lahu

This is my prayer, and this is how I perform my ablutions
My invocations are dipped in the blood of my heart

'I am grateful to God that he let me live long enough to see this mosque, which is better than all the mosques in the world,' he writes to his son Javed on a postcard. 'May God enlighten your eyes with the splendour of this mosque.'

During his European soujorn, Iqbal receives a letter from his son Javed. Javed has asked his father to bring a gramophone for him. He does not take him a gramophone; instead, he composes a message for his son through a poem, '*Javed ke Naam*':

Dayar-e ishq mein apna maqam paida kar
Naya zamana naye subah-o shaam paida kar
Mera tareeqa amiri nahi faqiri hai
Khudi na bech gharibi me naam paida kar

Stake your claim in love's empire,
Build time anew, create a new dawn, a new eve!
My way is the way of the hermit, not that of the rich man
Sell not your Ego, shine in your tattered state.

25

The Last Days

Islam is not a religion in the ancient sense of the word. It is an attitude—an attitude, that is to say, of Freedom and even of defiance to the Universe. It is really a protest against the entire outlook of the ancient world. Briefly, it is the discovery of Man.

—Iqbal, *Stray Thoughts*

On January 10, 1934, while Iqbal offers the congregational prayer of Eid in the Badshahi Mosque, Lahore, he catches a cold. Initially, his doctor suspects it is a case of influenza. But the sickness resists the doctor's medicines.

When Iqbal loses his voice, the doctors realize that his 'cold' is a serious disease. Could there be a greater catastrophe for a poet who is known for his elegant recital of poetry and his soul-stirring speeches? Later, he also develops cataract in his eyes that makes reading and writing extremely difficult for him. This, coupled with heart and kidney ailments gradually make him bed-ridden.

By 1938, Iqbal is sixty-two years old and financially, he is in dire straits.

Over the decades, his law practice has not yielded him a fortune— he has just been earning enough to keep his neck above water. By choice, he has been giving his poetry and his political engagements preference over his legal practice. The result is that he is only a moderately successful lawyer, and as he becomes deeply engaged in the political arena, his legal practice suffers further. His earnings have been dwindling, so much so that by 1935 he hardly earns anything at all as a lawyer.

Driven by his financial needs as well as responding to his Indian fans who demand of him poetry in Urdu, Iqbal publishes a collection of Urdu poems, *Bal-e Jibril* (*The Wings of Gabriel*) in 1935 and *Zarb-e Kalim* (*The Stroke of the Rod of Moses*) in 1936. Both the books stress a message of action.

At this stage, he has only two sources of income: royalty from the sale of his poetic works, and examiner's fees for the final examination papers of undergraduate and graduate students of Punjab University.[1]

To live through this crisis, Iqbal writes to his friend Syed Ross Masood, the grandson of Sir Syed Ahmed Khan, who has recently been appointed the minister of education in Bhopal state. Bhopal's ruler, Nawab Hamidullah Khan, has a reputation for 'his devotion to the cause of Muslim Renaissance' and excellence in personal courtesy. Through Masood's agency, Iqbal requests the nawab of Bhopal to grant him a monthly stipend of five hundred rupees for life. In May 1935, by Masood's intervention, the nawab approves his grant, besides making arrangements for electrotherapy in the state's hospital.[2] Iqbal welcomes the news with a sigh of relief. At least, now he does not have to worry about earning an income.

Meanwhile, the health of his third wife Sardar Begum has been deteriorating. A frugal lady, all her life she has had this wish of owning a house of her own. For most part of their life, Iqbal and his family have lived in rented houses in Lahore. She worries what will happen to their son Javed and daughter Munirah after they are gone? Won't they even own a house of their own?

Iqbal appreciates her wish but is not able to secure enough funds to purchase a piece of land in the city and build a house on it. Where will funds to build a house come from, he has no idea. The astute Sardar has been saving a little from the family's modest budget for years. Her money has accumulated and also there are some savings in a bank account under Javed's name. Together with these funds, some cash is also generated by selling off her bridal jewellery. With these funds, the Iqbal family is now able to purchase a plot of land on Mayo Road.[3] Construction of a house on that plot finishes in 1935.

Now, Iqbal and Sardar Begum have a house to their name in Lahore. Looking at his wife's worsening condition, Iqbal decides to transfer the ownership of the house to their son Javed. With this in mind, Iqbal approaches Sardar two days before her death. She agrees to the transaction. Iqbal reserves for his exclusive use two rooms in the mansion and deposits a monthly rental to Javed's account in the bank.[4]

Sardar is so ill that she has to be taken to their new house on a stretcher in an ambulance. Three days later, she passes away at the young age of forty. At this time, Javed is ten and a half years old whereas Munirah Bano is only four and a half years old.

The death of his wife is a huge personal blow to Iqbal. He mourns her passing but he knows that he is not going to get over it completely, ever. He believes that her spirit is in touch with him. Consequently, he stops dyeing his hair. Besides political concerns, and even though he has two children to look after, he entertains no thoughts of remarrying.[5]

Iqbal is not known to be a expressive father but after Sardar's death, he tries his best to show his love to Javed and Munirah. Munirah is very close to him and often she sleeps on the same bed. Both children are supposed to see their father every morning before leaving for school. When they come into the room to see him, he plants a kiss on their forehead.[6]

As the days pass, it becomes clear to Iqbal that it is not easy for him to take care of the needs of two little children. Initially, female relatives come in to help the family but he needs a more stable arrangement. What most unnerves Iqbal about Javed and Munirah is that they fight with each other. Iqbal decides to hire a help. He writes to his friend and well-wisher Professor Rashid Ahmed Siddiqui in Aligarh to find help for him. Siddiqui says that he knows

the younger sister of a professor's wife, Doris Landweer,[7] who will
be suitable for this job. Iqbal agrees to hire Doris as a governess and
she moves to Lahore in 1936 to bring order to the house and take
care of Javed and Munirah.

It does not take much time for Doris to observe how much Iqbal
loves his two children. He does not eat his lunch until they come
back from school. While eating lunch, he asks them about their day
in school. Being a heart patient, he avoids eating dinner but this in
turn has made him feeble. Doris insists that he must eat something
before going to bed. She starts making soup for him every night.

Doris does not like the school that Munirah attends so Iqbal
entrusts her with the task of enrolling Munirah in a school of her
choice. She chooses a missionary school for her and Iqbal does not
object to his daughter going to a school where the Bible is taught
and students have to participate in religious ceremonies.[8]

* * *

In the last years of his life, despite his ill health and financial
difficulties, Iqbal remains politically active and creatively productive.

When a cataract does not allow him to read and write on his
own, he receives help from young volunteers available at his disposal.
He sees his works getting published. Among the published works
are an Oxford University Press edition of the *Reconstruction*, four
new books of poetry[9] and a series of articles and press statements.[10]

To seek treatment for his throat, Iqbal visits Bhopal a few times as
a guest of Sir Ross Masood. Bhopal has facilities for electric therapy
that can help ease Iqbal's throat problems. Javed usually accompanies
him on these visits. Iqbal thinks that when he is away from home,
Javed and Munirah will quarrel, so taking him along will lessen the
chances of their quarrelling.

In Bhopal, Iqbal enjoys social gatherings at the nawab's residence.
Dinners usually take place at the residence of Sir Ross Masood, where
Ross and his wife Ummat al-Masud play generous hosts.

The electric treatment is not very effective. His friends propose that Iqbal seek treatment in Vienna, which is the centre for advanced medical treatment. Given his lack of resources, Iqbal has to reject this suggestion. 'The trip to Vienna and the treatment there will cost me a lot of money,' he says. 'The heavy expense will deprive my young children the economic support they will need after my demise.'

Forebodings of his end drive Iqbal to draft a will on August 13, 1935. He designates four individuals as the trustees of his estate, and assigns them the guardianship of his minor children. These four individuals are: Khawaja Abdul Ghani (his brother-in-law), Shaikh Ijaz Ahmad (his nephew), Munshi Tahiruddin (his former law clerk), and Chaudhury Muhammad Hussain (his friend in Lahore).[11]

In 1936, a very interesting visitor comes knocking at the doors of Javed Manzil to meet Iqbal. It is Jinnah.[12] Before Jinnah's arrival, Iqbal prepares his 12-year-old son Javed to receive 'a great personality'. In Iqbal's presence when Jinnah asks Javed what he wishes to become when he grows up, a shy Javed hesitates in responding. Iqbal then intervenes to answer Jinnah's rhetorical question: 'He is waiting for you to tell him what he should do,' Iqbal says.

The result of this meeting is that Iqbal joins the Central Parliamentary Board of the All India Muslim League in 1936 at the personal request of Jinnah. Later, he also becomes the president of its provincial branch in Punjab and plays an important role in organizing the Muslim community as a party with a 'progressive programme'.

By 1938, Iqbal has achieved a level of satisfaction with the political labours of his life. He is publicly adored and in Jinnah he has found a leader of the Muslims in India who will make sure that their interests are safeguarded.

In the same year, on January 10, Muslims in India celebrate Iqbal Day. The Inter-collegiate Muslim Brotherhood organizes celebrations in the great poet's honour. Magazines and journals publish special issues celebrating Iqbal as a poet and a political leader.

In light of these celebrations, a glad-hearted Iqbal says, 'These

Iqbal Day celebrations have given me profound satisfaction to realize that the land where I sowed my [intellectual] seeds is not a barren land.'[13]

Seeing the surge of affection for Iqbal, Sir Sikandar Hayat Khan makes an appeal to raise funds for him. Sir Akbar Hydary, the prime minister of Hyderabad, sends Iqbal a cheque of one thousand rupees from the ruler's special state fund. The cheque comes with a note that 'this fund was administered by him, and was in the form of personal entertainment for use at Iqbal's discretion.'[14]

Hydary's impudent note outrages Iqbal's sense of honour. He returns the cheque with four verses, expressing his indignation. The last two lines of the verses are:

> The personal dignity of this mystic could not accept
> This which appeared to be the mandatory charity of his majesty[15]

This bitter note soils his relationship with Sir Hydary but Iqbal has never cared about being polite when the truth needs to be told.

26

A Politician and a Patriot

True political life begins not with the claiming of rights, but with
the doing of duties.

—Iqbal, *Stray Thoughts*

Lying down in his bedroom in Javed Manzil, Iqbal receives important
visitors including Muhammad Ali Jinnah, Lord Lothian, Tej
Bahadur Sapru, and Jawaharlal Nehru.

In January 1938, Lord Lothian comes to visit Iqbal at Javed
Manzil. He is an admirer of Iqbal and he highly appreciates Iqbal's
proposed solution to the Hindu–Muslim conflict in India. Lothian
also helps obtain an invitation for Iqbal to deliver the Rhodes Lecture
at Oxford University. Iqbal selects the topic of time and space but
does not live long enough to deliver the lectures. Lord Lothian also
has Iqbal's lectures published by Oxford University Press.

On 24 January, Pandit Jawaharlal Nehru comes to meet him.
Nehru is visiting Lahore as a witness for Dr Muhammad Alam, a
local barrister who has filed a defamation suit against the daily *Civil
and Military Gazette*.

Though Iqbal and Nehru differ in terms of their political stance,
Kashmir is their common ancestral home.

The meeting is arranged through Dr Chakravarty and Nehru
calls on Iqbal at 8 p.m. in Javed Manzil.[1]

Accompanying Nehru are his hosts in Lahore—Mr and Mrs Iftikhar-ud Din. Javed and Mian Muhammad Shafi receive Iqbal's visitors at the entrance of the house. Nehru, known for his love for children, affectionately puts his arm around Javed and they enter Iqbal's room together.

Iqbal is supine on his bed. He welcomes Nehru and his team. As a mark of respect to an ailing Iqbal, Nehru decides to sit on the floor.

Nehru finds Iqbal in a nostalgic mood—wandering from subject to subject—and he listens in, talking little himself. He admires Iqbal and his poetry and it pleases him greatly to feel that the great poet likes him too.[2]

Nehru, at this point of time, is seen as a leader of the left-wing in the Congress. He is impressed with the progress made in Russia under socialism and he casts 'socialism as penance for whatever ailed India.'[3]

When Iqbal asks Nehru how many congressmen agreed with him on socialism? 'Half a dozen,' Nehru answers. 'How could you expect me to advise ten crore Indian Muslims to trust the Congress when you could not carry even half a dozen congressmen on your socialistic plank?' Iqbal says.[4]

When the discussion arrives at the topic of Hindu–Muslim conflict, Iqbal makes some broad points. He predicts that west Asia, the core of the Asian continent, will strategically rise in importance and if the Hindus of the Indian subcontinent do not treat Muslims with equity, and manage to alienate them, then India risks spoiling its relations with the Muslim states of the Middle East. Iqbal underscores the point that maintaining friendly relations with the Muslims of India is to the political advantage of the Hindus.[5]

Nehru, on the other hand, insists that if Muslims join the Congress unconditionally, the struggle for freedom would be strenghthened.

Iqbal says, with a strong emphasis, that the struggle for the freedom of India could be successfully conducted if the minorities trusted the majority, and the issue of minority rights was settled in advance.[6]

Nehru remains silent on this and refrains from making any further comments.

Iqbal tries to convince Nehru that no viable alternative to Hindu–Muslim settlement exists and the Muslims are more deeply opposed to British imperialism than even the Hindus. At this juncture, Mian Iftikhar-ud-Din, butts in.[7] Addressing Iqbal, he says, 'Whatever you say is factually true, that Muslims aspire to achieve the freedom of the Homeland like the Hindus, and are like the Hindus, enemies of British imperialism. So why don't you say the truth publicly—Muslims listen to you, who bothers about Jinnah's views?'[8]

Hearing this, Iqbal is beside himself with anger. 'Mian Sahib!' he argues, sitting upright and looking into Mian's eyes, 'Probably you would agree that Muslim unity is urgently needed ... A semblance of unity has been created under Jinnah's leadership. Since Hindus do not like the process of Muslim unity as a nation, then should it be shattered to please them? Please forgive me, I am not prepared to accept it.'[9]

With this, the discussion comes to a cold end. A little before Nehru departs, Iqbal asks him rhetorically, 'What is there in common between Jinnah and you? He is a politician, you are a patriot.'[10]

27

The Time of This Faqir Has Come

If you wish to be heard in the noise of this world, let your soul be dominated by a single idea. It is the man with a single idea who creates political and social revolutions, establishes empires and gives law to the world.

—Iqbal, *Stray Thoughts*

Iqbal, who has been calling himself a *qalandar*[1] for sometime now in his poetry, has this desire not to live longer than the last prophet, Muhammad. The founder of Islam had passed away at the age of sixty-three.

By March 1938, Iqbal's health is in critical condition—he has an excruciating pain in his back and shoulders; his heart and kidney do not function properly and asthmatic attacks have significantly weakened his body. Not a fan of modern medicines, he has discontinued using them. Once, he has a fit of asthma and he falls off his bed. This further worsens his already critical condition.

Under these harrowing circumstances, he has visions of Rumi and Ghalib in his room. He engages in discussions with these great immortal poets. His son Javed sees him having this dialogue on two occasions. Once he asks his attendant Ali Bakhsh to step out of the room and bring back Maula Rumi.

He is pronounced critically ill on the evening of April 20. His doctors are not sure if he will make it through the night.

At night, his charpoy is in the round room of Javed Manzil. His house is overcrowded by his fans and abuzz with their foreboding whispers.

Javed enters his father's room at around nine in the evening. Iqbal is conscious enough to notice his entry but can't see his 13-year-old son because of his cataract. 'Who is that?' he asks in a whisper. 'I am Javed,' his son replies.

'*Javed ban kar dikhao to jaanen*,' Iqbal teases him, with a chuckle.[2]

Chowdhury Muhammad Hussain, sitting near Iqbal, can't help but smile at Iqbal's wit. Iqbal looks towards his friend and says, 'Chowdhury Saheb, you must make him read the last dua at the end of *Javed Nama, Khataab ba Javed*.'[3]

Hussain nods. Javed tiptoes out of the room.

That night the house is full of visitors and many doctors, their faces creased with anxiety. They stand in groups of twos and threes in corners of the mansion. They speak in hushed tones and conspiratorial whispers.

The whisper is unmistakably palpable—tonight is going to be hard on Iqbal. Everyone knows this except for the great poet himself, and his children, including Javed.

Iqbal, however, has a very strong intuition. He figures out that his men are in a state of extreme anxiety. He has the premonition that tonight he might depart from this world. To ease those around him up, he is chatty and buoyant.

Not suspecting much, Javed retires to his room.

* * *

A little before dawn, Iqbal feels a congestion in the chest. He asks for the doctor but his attendants advise him that, 'it would be better if the physician was not disturbed just yet, since he had stayed up the whole night and had left shortly.'

'It will be too late otherwise', says Iqbal, moaning in pain, and reciting a Persian quatrain to Hasan Akhtar, one of Iqbal's young admirers:

The departed melody may or may not come,
The breeze from Hijaz may or may not come.
The days of this faqir have come to an end,
Another wise one may or may not come![4]

Seeing Iqbal in such a state, the attendants rush out to fetch the doctor, but the angel of death arrives first. Giving him company is his caretaker Ali Bakhsh who holds him down. Bakhsh wants to give him painkillers but he refuses to take them, because they contain sedatives, and he does not want to 'miss out on the unique experience of death'. He points to his chest and says, 'It's here,' and passes away with almost a sigh.[5]

Bakhsh sees his master's breathing come to a halt and his body getting cold.[6] Tears well up in his eyes. He rushes to Javed's room and wakes him up. 'Go and see what has happened to your Abba-jaan,' he says painfully, choking on his tears.

Javed sits up startled, sleep having vanished from his eyes. He can hear sobs and moans throughout the house. He gets out of his bed to check on his father, merely thinking that his condition might have worsened. He walks across and finds Munirah, his sister, crying in the adjacent room, the palms of her hands pressed over her face.

She sees him moving towards their father's room. She takes hold of his arm and walks with him with halting steps. Both stop walking right in front of the door of their father's room.

Javed peers inside the room from the doorstep. There is no one inside. The windows are open and Iqbal is asleep on the bed, his eyes closed, his face turned towards the qibla;[7] his moustache has become completely white while the sideburns still have the black dye that Javed had insisted his father to apply a few days ago. A long, white *chadar* covers his body until his neck.

Munirah's legs keep shaking violently, and he can hear her muffled crying. She holds on to his arm with great strength. Javed is not able to bring himself to tears. He is afraid that if he breaks down, Iqbal will get up and scold him: 'You should not cry like this. Remember that you are a man and men never cry.'

A young Javed's soul is scarred with pain but his eyes are dry. 'Life is the beginning of death and death the beginning of life.'[8] He realizes that his father has set off on a journey into a new life and he has no reason to be upset over his departure. He hugs Munirah and brings her back to her room, gently stroking her head to calm her down.[9]

EPILOGUE

A Jewel in the Dust

Only one unity is dependable, and that unity is the brotherhood
of man, which is above race, nationality, colour, or language ...
So long as men do not demonstrate by their actions that they
believe that the whole world is the family of God ... the beautiful
ideals of liberty, equality, and fraternity will never materialise.
        —Iqbal on New Year's day in 1938, All India Radio, Lahore

The twenty-first century began much like the twentieth, perhaps
only a little more dramatically. In the aftermath of the First World
War, the Ottoman Empire was dismembered and the institution
of the Caliphate was discontinued by Mustafa Kamal Pasha. As oil
was discovered in the Middle East, the Arab lands were divided and
dissected into smaller nation states, under the thumb of European,
and later American, powers.

The uncertainty of the fate of Muslims in India and the continual
fragmentation of the Muslim lands immensely saddened Iqbal in
his lifetime, inspiring him to compose poems to awaken the Muslim
masses from their slothful and lethargic slumber under colonial
subjugation.

If Iqbal were alive today, he would have seen the same story of
Muslim weakness, humiliation, and hopelessness repeating itself
in far worse conditions in this century. In the last century, the last

Muslim empire lost its power and territory as the Ottomans were forced out of Eastern Europe and the Middle East. In this century, the loss is more bloody and gory, more vivid and immediate, when the news of death of millions of Muslims reaches our homes and offices through television, the Internet and smartphones with a relentless regularity. Not just lives, millions of Muslims have lost their freedom and their future as they have been cast into war zones as helpless victims.

The circle of violence started, as most of us can clearly recall, with the 9/11/2001 attacks on the Twin Towers in the United States. Interestingly, the attackers, the Al Qaeda, was itself a creation of the American government to fight the communist threat of Soviet Russia in Afghanistan.

In response to the 9/11/2001 attacks, U.S. President George Bush started his 'War on Terror', which resulted in the invasions of both Afghanistan and Iraq. In the same vein as this watershed event, Muslims in Palestine, Bosnia, Chechnya, Xinjiang, Kashmir, Iraq, Syria, Afghanistan, Pakistan, and Myanmar have been going through repeated cycles of violence.

The issues of Palestine,[1] Kashmir, and Xinjiang[2] had, in fact, already raised their ugly heads in Iqbal's lifetime.

Even though Islam today is increasingly being equated with terrorism, the fact remains that most of the victims of terrorism, Islamic or non-Islamic, are Muslims. Nearly 200,000 Muslims were slaughtered in Bosnia by Serbian Christians and 22,000 Muslim females aged 9–82 were raped by Christian militiamen. More than a million Iraqi children died as a result of U.S. imposed sanctions during the time of Saddam Hussain. In Palestine, Kashmir, and Gujarat, thousands of Muslims have been killed or condemned to live in the filth of refugee camps. If you take the number of Muslims killed by U.S. actions in the last thirty years alone, the number is close to 300,000.[3]

In addition to this violence is the rising tide of Islamophobia in Europe[4] and other parts of the world. As a result, Muslims today feel psychologically hemmed in, insecure and unwelcome in most non-Muslim states. This Islamophobic attitude amongst non-Muslims stems from what they see and hear about the so called Islamic terrorists—a handful (maybe a few thousand) of misguided Muslims or mercenaries who have hijacked Islam, turning every Muslim into a terror suspect.

How would Iqbal have reacted to this and events like the Arab Spring? He would have pointed Muslims to his message in *Shikwa*, *Jawab-e Shikwa*, and *Javed Nama*. He would have asked them: why are you still divided? Why are you fighting amongst yourselves? What happened to your brotherhood and solidarity?[5] What went wrong with your spirit of enquiry? Have you worked on and applied the principles of khudi on yourselves? Didn't I warn you that nations that do not care to improve their social and economic conditions are bound to be obliterated?

> *Afrad ke hathon mein hai aqwam ki taqdeer*
> *Har fard hai millat ke muqaddar kasitara*

> Fortunes of Nations are shaped by the hands of its citizens
> Each one is a star to guide the destiny of the community

Closer home, Iqbal's dream of a separate state for Muslims in the north-western provinces was realized. But unfortunately, that dream has turned into a nightmare. Today, Iqbal's Pakistan is on the verge of collapse, ridden with violence, terrorism, corruption, and mismanagement. Where is Pakistan's *ijtihaad*, which Iqbal had hoped for, let alone the intellectual leadership of the Muslim world that it was supposed to produce? How would Pakistan account for the violence it perpetrated against fellow Muslims in East Pakistan?

Not only Pakistan, India too continues to fail Iqbal's expectations. Today, an unfortunate situation prevails that demonstrates, rather than belies, Iqbal's apprehensions vis a vis Muslims in India.[6] More than eighty years after Iqbal first raised his demand for a Muslim state within India, the situation has not changed much for Muslims in India. Rather, it has become worse, at least in the Hindi belt. 'The Hindu–Muslim politics in north India has resulted in developing an identity reactionary to colonialism and two-nation theories. It is rooted in alienation and distrust, "on rejecting and being rejected". The paradigm of "the other" has denied basic citizenship rights to the community.'[7]

The question for Indians is then—how have we allowed the status of Muslims to not only deteriorate in a Hindu majority India—more or less justifying the Two Nation Theory?[8]

As far as India is concerned, going forward, the onus of proving Iqbal right or wrong lies with the majority community. If Muslims are allowed to prosper in India as equal citizens in a peaceful and non-violent environment, with their cultural identity intact, then Iqbal will be proved wrong.

Iqbal's message of Muslim brotherhood and solidarity, however, is not about world domination by Muslims, as some might erroneously infer from Iqbal's poetry and exhortations. His son, retired judge Javed Iqbal reportedly said in an address in Maryland: 'As for sovereignty and international order, the situation as it exists must be accepted,' he said. 'We should accept diversity and national sovereignity, for a world order cannot impose unity. We must strive for an orderly world, not a world order.'[9]As far as Iqbal's vision is concerned, Dr Iqbal's suggestion that a genuine response to Iqbal would be the development of economic structures through which the realization of his vision can be facilitated is very plausible.[10]

That being said, it must be remembered that Iqbal was not only a poet of Islam or that his message is only for Muslims. His message is universal. In today's environment, especially for those living in the West, Iqbal's message against the excesses of capitalism still holds true.

Dayaar-e Maghrib ke rehne walon
Khuda ki basti dukaan nahin hai

Khara jise tum samajh rahe ho
Woh ab zar-e kum meyar hoga
Tumhari tehzeeb apne khanjar se
Aap khud khudkushi karegi

O, dwellers of the cities of the West,
This habitation of God is not a shop,
And that which you regard as true coin,
Will prove to be only a counterfeit.
Your civilization will commit suicide
With its own sword.

After the Occupy Wall Street Movement in the US,[11] Thomas Piketty has brought a very clear message to us, that the inequality in wealth has been steadily rising under capitalism.[12]

'Undoubtedly when the power of capital transgresses the limits of moderation, it becomes a kind of curse for the world,' Iqbal once wrote in a letter, 'the fact remains that Western capitalism and Russian Bolshevism result from a bitter struggle being waged between the haves and have-nots. However, as I have mentioned above, the way of moderation is the only correct and appropriate way which the Quran has recommended to us.'[13]

Iqbal's message is eternal, perhaps more appropriate now than ever. Only we have to ask ourselves if we are ready for it. What we must primarily keep in mind is Iqbal's optimism, a never dying hope that includes both the East and the West in its scope:

Mashriq se ho bezaar na maghrib se hazar kar
Fitrat ka ishara hai ke har shab ko sehar kar

Neither give up on the East nor turn away from the West,
Nature teaches us to turn every night into a dawn.

However, if you want to ignore all of that, and take home only one message from Iqbal, then this is it:

Agar khwahi hayat andar khatar zee

Dost thou want life? Then live dangerously

Here, taking a leaf out of Nietzsche's philosophy of development, Iqbal asks us to inure ourselves to hardships, for life is a state of war.[14]

A Note on Iqbal's Publications

Iqbal's first foray into authorship results in translations of text-book like works: *Nazarya-e Tauheed-e Mutalaq* by Shaikh Abdul Kareem Aljili (in English)—a research paper on Aljili's essay on the perfect man;[1] William Stubb's *Early History of England* (from Henry II to Richard III); Walker's *Political Economy*, and a volume on economics, *Ilmul Iqtisaad*. All these were written while he was teaching in Lahore, and before he left for Europe for higher studies.

Iqbal's first poem in Persian was *Asrar-e Khudi* (*Secrets of the Self*) which came out in 1915. The book found readers in Iran, Afghanistan, and parts of Turkey and Russia, wherever Persian was spoken or read. When R.A. Nicholson translated it into English in 1920, Iqbal became known in England and America too. Later on, the poem was translated into German and Italian too.[2] However, Nicholson's translation brought Iqbal 'a rather tardy recognition in the form of a knighthood in 1922.'[3] Many believe had Iqbal found a more publicly famous champion just as Tagore had found in W.B. Yeats and Ezra Pound, he would have been better known in the West and could have possibly won the Nobel Prize too.

After *Asrar-e Khudi*, Iqbal wrote another Persian poem, *Rumuz-e Bekhudi* (*Mysteries of Self-Denial*). A sequel to the former poem, it 'lays stress on the development of the human Ego or Personality and holds Power and Courage as the ideals to be followed by Man to accomplish his great destiny.' In *Rumuz*, the poet places the service of mankind as the highest goal for the ambition of man.

Rumuz was followed by *Payam-e Mashriq* (*Message of the East*), a collection of odes and poems in reaction to Goethe's *Westostlicher Divan*. Then Iqbal published *Zabur-e Ajam* (*Psalms of the East*) and *Javed Nama* (*The Book of Eternity*) in 1932. The last was a work styled after Dante's *Divine Comedy*—'an allegorical representation of a flight to the Upper World by the soul of the poet, in the company of the soul of the great mystic Jalaluddin Rumi.'

Meanwhile, his Indian fans demanded of him poetry in Urdu. Responding to this call, he published a collection of Urdu poems, *Bal-e Jibril* (*The Wings of Gabriel*) in 1935 and *Zarb-e Kalim* (*The Stroke of the Rod of Moses*) in 1936. Both books stress that man must lead a life of action.

His last Persian book was *Pas Chih Bayad Kard Al Aqwam-e Sharq?* (*What Then Should We Do, O Nations of the East?*) in which he recorded his 'protest against the aggressive pressure of Western nations on Oriental People'.

The last book that Iqbal readied but could not see published in his lifetime was *Armughan-e Hijaz* (*A Present of the Hijaz*), containing his quatrains and miscellaneous piece of poetry. The book was published posthumously.

In 1928, Iqbal delivered six lectures on Islam and philosophy in various cities of India—Madras, Mysore, Hyderabad, and Aligarh. These lectures were published in a collection, *Six Lectures on the Reconstruction of Religious Thought in Islam*.

Sir Muhammad Iqbal's 1930 Presidential Address to the Twenty-fifth Session of the All-India Muslim League[4]

Allahabad, 29 December, 1930

Gentlemen, I am deeply grateful to you for the honour you have conferred upon me in inviting me to preside over the deliberations of the All-India Muslim League at one of the most critical moments in the history of Muslim political thought and activity in India. I have no doubt that in this great assembly there are men whose political experience is far more extensive than mine, and for whose knowledge of affairs I have the highest respect. It will, therefore, be presumptuous on my part to claim to guide an assembly of such men in the political decisions which they are called upon to make today. I lead no party; I follow no leader. I have given the best part of my life to a careful study of Islam, its law and polity, its culture, its history, and its literature. This constant contact with the spirit of Islam, as it unfolds itself in time, has, I think, given me a kind of insight into its significance as a world fact. It is in the light of this insight, whatever its value, that, while assuming that the Muslims of India are determined to remain true to the spirit of Islam, I propose not to guide you in your decisions, but to attempt the humbler task of bringing clearly to your consciousness the main principle which, in my opinion, should determine the general character of these decisions.

Islam and Nationalism

It cannot be denied that Islam, regarded as an ethical ideal plus a certain kind of polity—by which expression I mean a social structure regulated by a legal system and animated by a specific ethical ideal—has been the chief formative factor in the life-history of the Muslims of India. It has furnished those basic emotions and loyalties which gradually unify scattered individuals and groups, and finally transform them into a well-defined people, possessing a moral consciousness of their own. Indeed it is not an exaggeration to say that India is perhaps the only country in the world where Islam, as a people-building force, has worked at its best. In India, as elsewhere, the structure of Islam as a society is almost entirely due to the working of Islam as a culture inspired by a specific ethical ideal. What I mean to say is that Muslim society, with its remarkable homogeneity and inner unity, has grown to be what it is, under the pressure of the laws and institutions associated with the culture of Islam.

The ideas set free by European political thinking, however, are now rapidly changing the outlook of the present generation of Muslims both in India and outside India. Our younger men, inspired by these ideas, are anxious to see them as living forces in their own countries, without any critical appreciation of the facts which have determined their evolution in Europe. In Europe, Christianity was understood to be a purely monastic order which gradually developed into a vast church organisation. The protest of Luther was directed against this church organisation, not against any system of polity of a secular nature, for the obvious reason that there was no such polity associated with Christianity. And Luther was perfectly justified in rising in revolt against this organisation; though, I think, he did not realise that in the peculiar conditions which obtained in Europe, his revolt would eventually mean the complete displacement of [the] universal ethics of Jesus by the growth of a plurality of national and hence narrower systems of ethics.

Thus the upshot of the intellectual movement initiated by such men as Rousseau and Luther was the break-up of the one into [the] mutually ill-adjusted many, the transformation of a human into a national outlook, requiring a more realistic foundation, such as the notion of country, and finding expression through varying systems of polity evolved on national lines, i.e. on lines which recognise territory as the only principle of political solidarity. If you begin with the conception of religion as complete other-worldliness, then what has happened to Christianity in Europe is perfectly natural. The universal ethics of Jesus is displaced by national systems of ethics and polity. The conclusion to which Europe is consequently driven is that religion is a private affair of the individual and has nothing to do with what is called man's temporal life.

Islam does not bifurcate the unity of man into an irreconcilable duality of spirit and matter. In Islam God and the universe, spirit and matter, Church and State, are organic to each other. Man is not the citizen of a profane world to be renounced in the interest of a world of spirit situated elsewhere. To Islam, matter is spirit realising itself in space and time. Europe uncritically accepted the duality of spirit and matter, probably from Manichaean thought. Her best thinkers are realising this initial mistake today, but her statesmen are indirectly forcing the world to accept it as an unquestionable dogma. It is, then, this mistaken separation of spiritual and temporal which has largely influenced European religious and political thought and has resulted practically in the total exclusion of Christianity from the life of European States. The result is a set of mutually ill-adjusted States dominated by interests not human but national. And these mutually ill-adjusted States, after trampling over the moral and religious convictions of Christianity, are today feeling the need of a federated Europe, i.e. the need of a unity which the Christian church organisation originally gave them, but which, instead of reconstructing it in the light of Christ's vision of human brotherhood, they considered fit to destroy under the inspiration of Luther.

A Luther in the world of Islam, however, is an impossible phenomenon; for here there is no church organisation similar to that of Christianity in the Middle Ages, inviting a destroyer. In the world of Islam we have a universal polity whose fundamentals are believed to have been revealed but whose structure, owing to our [legal theorists'] want of contact with the modern world, today stands in need of renewed power by fresh adjustments. I do not know what will be the final fate of the national idea in the world of Islam. Whether Islam will assimilate and transform it, as it has before assimilated and transformed many ideas expressive of a different spirit, or allow a radical transformation of its own structure by the force of this idea, is hard to predict. Professor Wensinck of Leiden [Holland] wrote to me the other day: 'It seems to me that Islam is entering upon a crisis through which Christianity has been passing for more than a century. The great difficulty is how to save the foundations of religion when many antiquated notions have to be given up. It seems to me scarcely possible to state what the outcome will be for Christianity, still less what it will be for Islam.' At the present moment the national idea is racialising the outlook of Muslims, and thus materially counteracting the humanizing work of Islam. And the growth of racial consciousness may mean the growth of standards different [from] and even opposed to the standards of Islam.

I hope you will pardon me for this apparently academic discussion. To address this session of the All-India Muslim League you have selected a man who [has] not despaired of Islam as a living force for freeing the outlook of man from its geographical limitations, who believes that religion is a power of the utmost importance in the life of individuals as well as States, and finally who believes that Islam is itself Destiny and will not suffer a destiny. Such a man cannot but look at matters from his own point of view. Do not think that the problem I am indicating is a purely theoretical one. It is a very living and practical problem calculated to affect the very fabric of Islam as a system of life and conduct. On a proper solution of it alone depends your future as a distinct cultural unit in India. Never in our history has Islam had to stand a greater trial than the one which confronts it today. It is open to a people to modify, reinterpret, or reject the foundational principles of their social structure; but it is absolutely necessary for them to see clearly what they are doing before they undertake to try a fresh experiment. Nor should the way in which I am approaching this important problem lead anybody to think that I intend to quarrel with those who happen to think differently. You are a Muslim assembly and, I suppose, anxious to remain true to the spirit and ideals of Islam. My sole desire, therefore, is to tell you frankly what I honestly believe to be the truth about the present situation. In this way alone it is possible for me to illuminate, according to my light, the avenues of your political action.

The Unity of an Indian Nation

What, then, is the problem and its implications? Is religion a private affair? Would you like to see Islam as a moral and political ideal, meeting the same fate in the world of Islam as Christianity has already met in Europe? Is it possible to retain Islam as an ethical ideal and to reject it as a polity, in favor of national polities in which [the] religious attitude is not permitted to play any part? This question becomes of special importance in India, where the Muslims happen to be a minority. The proposition that religion is a private individual experience is not surprising on the lips of a European. In Europe the conception of Christianity as a monastic order, renouncing the world of matter and fixing its gaze entirely on the world of spirit, led, by a logical process of thought, to the view embodied in this proposition. The nature of the Prophet's religious experience, as disclosed in the Quran, however, is wholly different. It is not mere experience in the sense of a purely biological event, happening inside the experience and necessitating no reactions on its social environment. It is individual experience creative of a social order. Its immediate outcome is the fundamentals of a polity with implicit legal concepts whose civic significance cannot be belittled merely because their origin is revelational.

The religious ideal of Islam, therefore, is organically related to the social order which it has created. The rejection of the one will eventually involve the rejection of the other. Therefore the construction of a polity on national lines, if it means a displacement of the Islamic principle of solidarity, is simply unthinkable to a Muslim. This is a matter which at the present moment directly concerns the Muslims of India. 'Man,' says Renan, 'is enslaved neither by his race, nor by his religion, nor by the course of rivers, nor by the direction of mountain ranges. A great aggregation of men, sane of mind and warm of heart, creates a moral consciousness which is called a nation.' Such a formation is quite possible, though it involves the long and arduous process of practically remaking men and furnishing them with a fresh emotional equipment. It might have been a fact in India if the teaching of Kabir and the Divine Faith of Akbar had seized the imagination of the masses of this country. Experience, however, shows that the various caste units and religious units in India have shown no inclination to sink their respective individualities in a larger whole. Each group is intensely jealous of its collective existence. The formation of the kind of moral consciousness which constitutes the essence of a nation in Renan's sense demands a price which the peoples of India are not prepared to pay.

The unity of an Indian nation, therefore, must be sought not in the negation, but in the mutual harmony and cooperation, of the many. True statesmanship cannot ignore facts, however unpleasant they may be. The only practical course is not to assume the existence of a state of things which does not exist, but to recognise facts as they are, and to exploit them to our greatest advantage. And it is on the discovery of Indian unity in this direction that the fate of India as well as of Asia really depends. India is Asia in miniature. Part of her people have cultural affinities with nations of the east,

and part with nations in the middle and west of Asia. If an effective
principle of cooperation is discovered in India, it will bring peace
and mutual goodwill to this ancient land which has suffered so long,
more because of her situation in historic space than because of any
inherent incapacity of her people. And it will at the same time solve
the entire political problem of Asia.

It is, however, painful to observe that our attempts to discover
such a principle of internal harmony have so far failed. Why have
they failed? Perhaps we suspect each other's intentions and inwardly
aim at dominating each other. Perhaps, in the higher interests of
mutual cooperation, we cannot afford to part with the monopolies
which circumstances have placed in our hands, and [thus we] conceal
our egoism under the cloak of nationalism, outwardly simulating a
large-hearted patriotism, but inwardly as narrow-minded as a caste
or tribe. Perhaps we are unwilling to recognise that each group has
a right to free development according to its own cultural traditions.
But whatever may be the causes of our failure, I still feel hopeful.
Events seem to be tending in the direction of some sort of internal
harmony. And as far as I have been able to read the Muslim mind,
I have no hesitation in declaring that if the principle that the
Indian Muslim is entitled to full and free development on the lines
of his own culture and tradition in his own Indian home-lands is
recognized as the basis of a permanent communal settlement, he
will be ready to stake his all for the freedom of India.

The principle that each group is entitled to its free development on
its own lines is not inspired by any feeling of narrow communalism.
There are communalisms and communalisms. A community which
is inspired by feelings of ill-will towards other communities is low
and ignoble. I entertain the highest respect for the customs, laws,
religious and social institutions of other communities. Nay, it is my
duty, according to the teaching of the Quran, even to defend their
places of worship, if need be. Yet I love the communal group which
is the source of my life and behaviour; and which has formed me
what I am by giving me its religion, its literature, its thought, its

culture, and thereby recreating its whole past as a living operative factor, in my present consciousness. Even the authors of the Nehru Report recognise the value of this higher aspect of communalism. While discussing the separation of Sind they say, 'To say from the larger viewpoint of nationalism that no communal provinces should be created, is, in a way, equivalent to saying from the still wider international viewpoint that there should be no separate nations. Both these statements have a measure of truth in them. But the staunchest internationalist recognises that without the fullest national autonomy it is extraordinarily difficult to create the international State. So also without the fullest cultural autonomy— and communalism in its better aspect is culture—it will be difficult to create a harmonious nation.'

Muslim India within India

Communalism in its higher aspect, then, is indispensable to the formation of a harmonious whole in a country like India. The units of Indian society are not territorial as in European countries. India is a continent of human groups belonging to different races, speaking different languages, and professing different religions. Their behaviour is not at all determined by a common race-consciousness. Even the Hindus do not form a homogeneous group. The principle of European democracy cannot be applied to India without recognising the fact of communal groups. The Muslim demand for the creation of a Muslim India within India is, therefore, perfectly justified. The resolution of the All-Parties Muslim Conference at Delhi is, to my mind, wholly inspired by this noble ideal of a harmonious whole which, instead of stifling the respective individualities of its component wholes, affords them chances of fully working out the possibilities that may be latent in them. And I have no doubt that this House will emphatically endorse the Muslim demands embodied in this resolution.

Personally, I would go farther than the demands embodied in it. I would like to see the Punjab, North-West Frontier Province, Sind and Baluchistan amalgamated into a single State. Self-government within the British Empire, or without the British Empire, the formation of a consolidated North-West Indian Muslim State appears to me to be the final destiny of the Muslims, at least of North-West India. The proposal was put forward before the Nehru Committee. They rejected it on the ground that, if carried into effect, it would give a very unwieldy State. This is true in so far as the area is concerned; in point of population, the State contemplated by the proposal would be much less than some of the present Indian provinces. The exclusion of Ambala Division, and perhaps of some districts where non-Muslims predominate, will make it less extensive and more Muslim in population—so that the exclusion suggested will enable this consolidated State to give a more effective protection to non-Muslim minorities within its area. The idea need not alarm the Hindus or the British. India is the greatest Muslim country in the world. The life of Islam as a cultural force in the country very largely depends on its centralisation in a specified territory. This centralisation of the most living portion of the Muslims of India, whose military and police service has, notwithstanding unfair treatment from the British, made the British rule possible in this country, will eventually solve the problem of India as well as of Asia. It will intensify their sense of responsibility and deepen their patriotic feeling.

Thus, possessing full opportunity of development within the body politic of India, the North-West Indian Muslims will prove the best defenders of India against a foreign invasion, be that invasion one of ideas or of bayonets. The Punjab with 56 percent Muslim population supplies 54 per cent of the total combatant troops in the Indian Army, and if the 19,000 Gurkhas recruited from the independent State of Nepal are excluded, the Punjab contingent amounts to 62 per cent of the whole Indian Army. This percentage does not take into account nearly 6,000 combatants supplied to the Indian Army by the North-West Frontier Province and Baluchistan. From this you can easily calculate the possibilities of North-West Indian Muslims in regard to the defence of India against foreign aggression. The Right Hon'ble Mr Srinivasa Sastri thinks that the Muslim demand for the creation of autonomous Muslim states along the north-west border is actuated by a desire 'to acquire means of exerting pressure in emergencies on the Government of India.' I may frankly tell him that the Muslim demand is not actuated by the kind of motive he imputes to us; it is actuated by a genuine desire for free development which is practically impossible under the type of unitary government contemplated by the nationalist Hindu politicians with a view to secure permanent communal dominance in the whole of India.

Nor should the Hindus fear that the creation of autonomous Muslim states will mean the introduction of a kind of religious rule in such states. I have already indicated to you the meaning of the word religion, as applied to Islam. The truth is that Islam is not a Church. It is a State conceived as a contractual organism long before Rousseau ever thought of such a thing, and animated by an ethical ideal which regards man not as an earth-rooted creature, defined by this or that portion of the earth, but as a spiritual being understood in terms of a social mechanism, and possessing rights and duties as a living factor in that mechanism. The character of a Muslim State can be judged from what the *Times of India* pointed out some time ago in a leader [i.e., front-page article] on the Indian Banking Inquiry Committee. 'In ancient India,' the paper points out, 'the State framed laws regulating the rates of interest; but in Muslim times, although Islam clearly forbids the realisation of interest on money loaned, Indian Muslim States imposed no restrictions on such rates.' I therefore demand the formation of a consolidated Muslim State in the best interests of India and Islam. For India, it means security and peace resulting from an internal balance of power; for Islam, an opportunity to rid itself of the stamp that Arabian Imperialism was forced to give it, to mobilise its law, its education, its culture, and to bring them into closer contact with its own original spirit and with the spirit of modern times.

Federal States

Thus it is clear that in view of India's infinite variety in climates, races, languages, creeds, and social systems, the creation of autonomous States, based on the unity of language, race, history, religion, and identity of economic interests, is the only possible way to secure a stable constitutional structure in India. The conception of federation underlying the Simon Report necessitates the abolition of the Central Legislative Assembly as a popular assembly, and makes it an assembly of the representatives of federal States. It further demands a redistribution of territory on the lines which I have indicated. And the Report does recommend both. I give my wholehearted support to this view of the matter, and venture to suggest that the redistribution recommended in the Simon Report must fulfill two conditions. It must precede the introduction of the new constitution, and must be so devised as to finally solve the communal problem. Proper redistribution will make the question of joint and separate electorates automatically disappear from the constitutional controversy of India. It is the present structure of the provinces that is largely responsible for this controversy.

The Hindu thinks that separate electorates are contrary to the spirit of true nationalism, because he understands the word nation to mean a kind of universal amalgamation in which no communal entity ought to retain its private individuality. Such a state of things, however, does not exist. Nor is it desirable that it should exist. India is a land of racial and religious variety. Add to this the general economic inferiority of the Muslims, their enormous debt, especially in the Punjab, and their insufficient majorities in some of the provinces as at present constituted, and you will begin to see clearly the meaning of our anxiety to retain separate electorates. In such a country and in such circumstances territorial electorates cannot secure adequate representation of all interests, and must inevitably lead to the creation of an oligarchy. The Muslims of India can have no objection to purely territorial electorates if provinces are demarcated so as to secure comparatively homogeneous communities possessing linguistic, racial, cultural, and religious unity.

Federation as Understood in the Simon Report

But in so far as the question of the powers of the Central Federal State is concerned, there is a subtle difference of motive in the constitutions proposed by the pundits of India and the pundits of England. The pundits of India do not disturb the Central authority as it stands at present. All that they desire is that this authority should become fully responsible to the Central Legislature which they maintain intact and where their majority will become further reinforced on the nominated element ceasing to exist. The pundits of England, on the other hand, realising that democracy in the Centre tends to work contrary to their interests and is likely to absorb the whole power now in their hands, in case a further advance is made towards responsible government, have shifted the experience of democracy from the Centre to the provinces. No doubt, they introduce the principle of Federation and appear to have made a beginning by making certain proposals; yet their evaluation of this principle is determined by considerations wholly different to those which determine its value in the eyes of Muslim India. The Muslims demand federation because it is pre-eminently a solution of India's most difficult problem, i.e. the communal problem. The Royal Commissioners' view of federation, though sound in principle, does not seem to aim at responsible government for federal States. Indeed it does not go beyond providing means of escape from the situation which the introduction of democracy in India has created for the British, and wholly disregards the communal problem by leaving it where it was.

Thus it is clear that, in so far as real federation is concerned, the Simon Report virtually negatives the principle of federation in its true significance. The Nehru Report, realising [a] Hindu majority in the Central Assembly, reaches a unitary form of government because such an institution secures Hindu dominance throughout India; the Simon Report retains the present British dominance behind the thin veneer of an unreal federation, partly because the British are naturally unwilling to part with the power they have so long wielded and partly because it is possible for them, in the absence of an inter-communal understanding in India, to make out a plausible case for the retention of that power in their own hands. To my mind a unitary form of government is simply unthinkable in a self-governing India. What is called 'residuary powers' must be left entirely to self-governing States, the Central Federal State exercising only those powers which are expressly vested in it by the free consent of federal States. I would never advise the Muslims of India to agree to a system, whether of British or of Indian origin, which virtually negatives the principle of true federation, or fails to recognise them as a distinct political entity.

Federal Scheme as Discussed in the Round Table Conference

The necessity for a structural change in the Central Government was seen probably long before the British discovered the most effective means for introducing this change. That is why at rather a late stage it was announced that the participation of the Indian Princes in the Round Table Conference was essential. It was a kind of surprise to the people of India, particularly the minorities, to see the Indian Princes dramatically expressing their willingness at the Round Table Conference to join an all-India federation and, as a result of their declaration, Hindu delegates—uncompromising advocates of a unitary form of government—quietly agreeing to the evolution of a federal scheme. Even Mr. Sastri who only a few days before had severely criticised Sir John Simon for recommending a federal scheme for India, suddenly became a convert and admitted his conversion in the plenary session of the Conference—thus offering the Prime Minister of England an occasion for one of his wittiest observations in his concluding speech. All this has a meaning both for the British who have sought the participation of the Indian Princes, and for the Hindus who have unhesitatingly accepted the evolution of an all-India federation. The truth is that the participation of the Indian Princes, among whom only a few are Muslims, in a federation scheme serves a double purpose. On the one hand, it serves as an all-important factor in maintaining the British power in India practically as it is; on the other hand, it gives [an] overwhelming majority to the Hindus in an All-India Federal Assembly.

It appears to me that the Hindu-Muslim differences regarding the ultimate form of the Central Government are being cleverly exploited by British politicians through the agency of the Princes who see in the scheme prospects of better security for their despotic rule. If the Muslims silently agree to any such scheme, it will simply hasten their end as a political entity in India. The policy of the Indian federation thus created, will be practically controlled by [the] Hindu Princes forming the largest group in the Central Federal Assembly. They will always lend their support to the Crown in matters of Imperial concern; and in so far as internal administration of the country is concerned, they will help in maintaining and strengthening the supremacy of the Hindus. In other words, the scheme appears to be aiming at a kind of understanding between Hindu India and British Imperialism—you perpetuate me in India, and I in return give you a Hindu oligarchy to keep all other Indian communities in perpetual subjection. If, therefore, the British Indian provinces are not transformed into really autonomous States, the Princes' participation in a scheme of Indian federation will be interpreted only as a dexterous move on the part of British politicians to satisfy, without parting with any real power, all parties concerned—Muslims with the word federation; Hindus with a majority in the Centre; the British Imperialists—with the substance of real power.

The number of Hindu States in India is far greater than Muslim States; and it remains to be seen how the Muslim demand for 33 percent [of the] seats in the Central Federal Assembly is to be met within a House or Houses constituted of representatives taken from ot help

British India as well as Indian States. I hope the Muslim delegates are fully aware of the implications of the federal scheme as discussed in the Round Table Conference. The question of Muslim representation in the proposed all-India federation has not yet been discussed. 'The interim report,' says Reuters' summary, 'contemplates two chambers in the Federal Legislature, each containing representatives both of British India and States, the proportion of which will be a matter of subsequent consideration under the heads which have not yet been referred to the Sub-Committee.' In my opinion the question of proportion is of the utmost importance and ought to have been considered simultaneously with the main question of the structure of the Assembly.

The best course, I think, would have been to start with a British Indian Federation only. A federal scheme born of an unholy union between democracy and despotism cannot but keep British India in the same vicious circle of a unitary Central Government. Such a unitary form may be of the greatest advantage to the British, to the majority community in British India, and to the Indian Princes; it can be of no advantage to the Muslims, unless they get majority rights in five out of eleven Indian provinces with full residuary powers, and one-third share of seats in the total House of the Federal Assembly. In so far as the attainment of sovereign powers by the British Indian provinces is concerned, the position of His Highness the Ruler of Bhopal, Sir Akbar Hydari, and Mr. Jinnah is unassailable. In view, however, of the participation of the Princes in the Indian Federation, we must now see our demand for representation in the British Indian Assembly in a new light. The questions is not one of [the] Muslim share in a British Indian Assembly, but one which relates to representation of British Indian Muslims in an All-India Federal Assembly. Our demand for 33 per cent must now be taken as a demand for the same proportion in the All-India Federal Assembly, exclusive of the share allotted to the Muslim states entering the Federation.

The Problem of Defence

The other difficult problem which confronts the successful working of a federal system in India is the problem of India's defence. In their discussion of this problem the Royal Commissioners have marshalled all the deficiencies of India in order to make out a case for Imperial administration of the Army. 'India and Britain,' say the Commissioners, 'are so related that India's defence cannot, now or in any future which is within sight, be regarded as a matter of purely Indian concern. The control and direction of such an army must rest in the hands of agents of Imperial Government.' Now, does it [not] necessarily follow from this that further progress towards the realisation of responsible government in British India is barred until the work of defence can be adequately discharged without the help of British officers and British troops? As things are, there is a block on the line of constitutional advance. All hopes of evolution in the Central Government towards the ultimate goal prescribed in the declaration of 20th August 1917, are in danger of being indefinitely frustrated, if the attitude illustrated by the Nehru Report is maintained, that any future change involves the putting of the administration of the army under the authority of an elected Indian Legislature. Further to fortify their argument they emphasize the fact of competing religions and rival races of widely different capacity, and try to make the problem look insoluble by remarking that 'the obvious fact that India is not, in the ordinary and natural sense, a single nation is nowhere made more plain than in considering the difference between the martial races of India and the rest.' These features of the question have been emphasised in order to demonstrate that the British are not only keeping India secure from foreign menace but are also the 'neutral guardians' of internal security.

However, in federated India, as I understand federation, the problem will have only one aspect, i.e. external defence. Apart from provincial armies necessary for maintaining internal peace, the

Indian Federal Congress can maintain, on the north-west frontier, a strong Indian Frontier Army, composed of units recruited from all provinces and officered by efficient and experienced military men taken from all communities. I know that India is not in possession of efficient military officers, and this fact is exploited by the Royal Commissioners in the interest of an argument for Imperial administration. On this point I cannot but quote another passage from the Report which, to my mind, furnishes the best argument against the position taken up by the Commissioners. 'At the present moment,' says the Report, 'no Indian holding the King's Commission is of higher army rank than a captain. There are, we believe, 39 captains of whom 25 are in ordinary regimental employ. Some of them are of an age which would prevent their attaining much higher rank, even if they passed the necessary examination before retirement. Most of these have not been through Sandhurst, but got their Commissions during the Great War.' Now, however genuine may be the desire, and however earnest the endeavour to work for this transformation, overriding conditions have been so forcibly expressed by the Skeen Committee (whose members, apart from the Chairman and the Army Secretary, were Indian gentlemen) in these words: 'Progress ... must be contingent upon success being secured at each stage and upon military efficiency being maintained, though it must in any case render such development measured and slow. A higher command cannot be evolved at short notice out of existing cadres of Indian officers, all of junior rank and limited experience. Not until the slender trickle of suitable Indian recruits for the officer class—and we earnestly desire an increase in their numbers—flows in much greater volume, not until sufficient Indians have attained the experience and training requisite to provide all the officers for, at any rate, some Indian regiments, not until such units have stood the only test which can possibly determine their efficiency, and not until Indian officers have qualified by a successful army career for the high command, will it be possible to develop the policy of

Indianisation to a point which will bring a completely Indianised army within sight. Even then years must elapse before the process could be completed.'

Now I venture to ask: who is responsible for the present state of things? Is it due to some inherent incapacity of our martial races, or to the slowness of the process of military training? The military capacity of our martial races is undeniable. The process of military training may be slow as compared to other processes of human training. I am no military expert to judge this matter. But as a layman I feel that the argument, as stated, assumes the process to be practically endless. This means perpetual bondage for India, and makes it all the more necessary that the Frontier Army, as suggested by the Nehru Report, be entrusted to the charge of a committee of defence, the personnel of which may be settled by mutual understanding.

Again, it is significant that the Simon Report has given extraordinary importance to the question of India's land frontier, but has made only passing references to its naval position. India has doubtless had to face invasions from her land frontier; but it is obvious that her present masters took possession of her on account of her defenceless sea coast. A self-governing and free India will, in these days, have to take greater care of her sea coast than [of her] land frontiers.

I have no doubt that if a Federal Government is established, Muslim federal States will willingly agree, for purposes of India's defence, to the creation of neutral Indian military and naval forces. Such a neutral military force for the defence of India was a reality in the days of Mughal rule. Indeed in the time of Akbar the Indian frontier was, on the whole, defended by armies officered by Hindu generals. I am perfectly sure that the scheme for a neutral Indian army, based on a federated India, will intensify Muslim patriotic feeling, and finally set at rest the suspicion, if any, of Indian Muslims joining Muslims from beyond the frontier in the event of an invasion.

The Alternative

I have thus tried briefly to indicate the way in which the Muslims of India ought, in my opinion, to look at the two most important constitutional problems of India. A redistribution of British India, calculated to secure a permanent solution of the communal problem, is the main demand of the Muslims of India. If, however, the Muslim demand of a territorial solution of the communal problem is ignored, then I support, as emphatically as possible, the Muslim demands repeatedly urged by the All-India Muslim League and the All-India Muslim Conference. The Muslims of India cannot agree to any constitutional changes which affect their majority rights, to be secured by separate electorates in the Punjab and Bengal, or [which] fail to guarantee them 33 percent representation in any Central Legislature. There were two pitfalls into which Muslim political leaders fell. The first was the repudiated Lucknow Pact, which originated in a false view of Indian nationalism and deprived the Muslims of India of chances of acquiring any political power in India. The second is the narrow-visioned sacrifice of Islamic solidarity, in the interests of what may be called Punjab ruralism, resulting in a proposal which virtually reduces the Punjab Muslims to a position of minority. It is the duty of the League to condemn both the Pact and the proposal.

The Simon Report does great injustice to the Muslims in not recommending a statutory majority for the Punjab and Bengal. It would make the Muslims either stick to the Lucknow Pact or agree to a scheme of joint electorates. The despatch of the Government of India on the Simon Report admits that since the publication of that document the Muslim community has not expressed its willingness to accept any of the alternatives proposed by the Report. The despatch recognises that it may be a legitimate grievance to deprive the Muslims in the Punjab and Bengal of representation in the councils in proportion to their population merely because of weightage allowed to Muslim minorities elsewhere. But the despatch of the Government of India fails to correct the injustice of the Simon Report. In so far as the Punjab is concerned—and this is the most crucial point—it endorses the so-called 'carefully balanced scheme' worked out by the official members of the Punjab Government which gives the Punjab Muslims a majority of two over Hindus and Sikhs combined, and a proportion of 49 percent of the House as a whole. It is obvious that the Punjab Muslims cannot be satisfied with less than a clear majority in the total House. However, Lord Irwin and his Government do recognise that the justification for communal electorates for majority communities would not cease unless and until by the extension of franchise their voting strength more correctly reflects their population; and further unless a two-thirds majority of the Muslim members in a provincial Council unanimously agree to surrender the right of separate representation. I cannot, however, understand why the Government of India, having recognised the legitimacy of the Muslim grievances, have not had the courage to recommend a statutory majority for the Muslims in the Punjab and Bengal.

Nor can the Muslims of India agree to any such changes which fail to create at least Sind as a separate province and treat the North-West Frontier Province as a province of inferior political status. I see no reason why Sind should not be united with Baluchistan and turned into a separate province. It has nothing in common with Bombay Presidency. In point of life and civilization the Royal Commissioners find it more akin to Mesopotamia and Arabia than India. The Muslim geographer Mas'udi noticed this kinship long ago when he said: 'Sind is a country nearer to the dominions of Islam.' The first Omayyad ruler is reported to have said of Egypt: 'Egypt has her back towards Africa and face towards Arabia.' With necessary alterations the same remark describes the exact situation of Sind. She has her back towards India and face towards Central Asia. Considering further the nature of her agricultural problems which can invoke no sympathy from the Bombay Government, and her infinite commercial possibilities, dependent on the inevitable growth of Karachi into a second metropolis of India, it is unwise to keep her attached to a Presidency which, though friendly today, is likely to become a rival at no distant period. Financial difficulties, we are told, stand in the way of separation. I do not know of any definite authoritative pronouncement on the matter. But assuming there are any such difficulties, I see no reason why the Government of India should not give temporary financial help to a promising province in her struggle for independent progress.

As to the North-West Frontier Province, it is painful to note that the Royal Commissioners have practically denied that the people of this province have any right to reform. They fall far short of the Bray Committee, and the Council recommended by them is merely a screen to hide the autocracy of the Chief Commissioner. The inherent right of the Afghan to light a cigarette is curtailed merely because he happens to be living in a powder house. The Royal Commissioners' epigrammatic argument is pleasant enough, but far from convincing. Political reform is light, not fire; and to light every human being is entitled, whether he happens to live in a powder house or a coal mine. Brave, shrewd, and determined to suffer for his legitimate aspirations, the Afghan is sure to resent any attempt to deprive him of opportunities of full self-development. To keep such a people contented is in the best interest of both England and India. What has recently happened in that unfortunate province is the result of a step-motherly treatment shown to the people since the introduction of the principle of self-government in the rest of India. I only hope that British statesmanship will not obscure its view of the situation by hoodwinking itself into the belief that the present unrest in the province is due to any extraneous causes.

The recommendation for the introduction of a measure of reform in the North-West Frontier Province made in the Government of India's despatch is also unsatisfactory. No doubt, the despatch goes farther than the Simon Report in recommending a sort of representative Council and a semi-representative cabinet, but it fails to treat this important Muslim province on [an] equal footing with other Indian provinces. Indeed the Afghan is, by instinct, more fitted for democratic institutions than any other people in India.

The Round Table Conference

I think I am now called upon to make a few observations on the Round Table Conference. Personally I do not feel optimistic as to the results of this Conference. It was hoped that away from the actual scene of communal strife and in a changed atmosphere, better counsels would prevail and a genuine settlement of the differences between the two major communities of India would bring India's freedom within sight. Actual events, however, tell a different tale. Indeed, the discussion of the communal question in London has demonstrated more clearly than ever the essential disparity between the two great cultural units of India. Yet the Prime Minister of England apparently refuses to see that the problem of India is international and not national. He is reported to have said that 'his government would find it difficult to submit to Parliament proposals for the maintenance of separate electorates, since joint electorates were much more in accordance with British democratic sentiments.' Obviously he does not see that the model of British democracy cannot be of any use in a land of many nations; and that a system of separate electorates is only a poor substitute for a territorial solution of the problem. Nor is the Minorities Sub-Committee likely to reach a satisfactory settlement. The whole question will have to go before the British Parliament; and we can only hope that the keen-sighted representatives of [the] British nation, unlike most of our Indian politicians, will be able to pierce through the surface of things and see clearly the true fundamentals of peace and security in a country like India. To base a constitution on the concept of a homogeneous India, or to apply to India principles dictated by British democratic sentiments, is unwittingly to prepare her for a civil war. As far as I can see, there will be no peace in the country until the various peoples that constitute India are given opportunities of free self-development on modern lines without abruptly breaking with their past.

I am glad to be able to say that our Muslim delegates fully realise the importance of a proper solution of what I call [the] Indian international problem. They are perfectly justified in pressing for a solution of the communal question before the question of responsibility in the Central Government is finally settled. No Muslim politician should be sensitive to the taunt embodied in that propaganda word—communalism—expressly devised to exploit what the Prime Minister calls British democratic sentiments, and to mislead England into assuming a state of things which does not really exist in India. Great interests are at stake. We are 70 millions, and far more homogeneous than any other people in India. Indeed the Muslims of India are the only Indian people who can fitly be described as a nation in the modern sense of the word. The Hindus, though ahead of us in almost all respects, have not yet been able to achieve the kind of homogeneity which is necessary for a nation, and which Islam has given you as a free gift. No doubt they are anxious to become a nation, but the process of becoming a nation is kind of travail, and in the case of Hindu India involves a complete overhauling of her social structure.

Nor should the Muslim leaders and politicians allow themselves to be carried away by the subtle but fallacious argument that Turkey and Persia and other Muslim countries are progressing on national, i.e. territorial, lines. The Muslims of India are differently situated. The countries of Islam outside India are practically wholly Muslim in population. The minorities there belong, in the language of the Quran, to the 'people of the Book'. There are no social barriers between Muslims and the 'people of the Book'. A Jew or a Christian or a Zoroastrian does not pollute the food of a Muslim by touching it, and the law of Islam allows intermarriage with the 'people of the Book'. Indeed the first practical step that Islam took towards the realisation of a final combination of humanity was to call upon peoples possessing practically the same ethical ideal to come forward and combine. The Quran declares: 'O people of the Book! Come, let us join together on the "word" (Unity of God), that is common to us all.' The wars of Islam and Christianity, and later, European aggression in its various forms, could not allow the infinite meaning of this verse to work itself out in the world of Islam. Today it is being gradually realised in the countries of Islam in the shape of what is called Muslim Nationalism.

It is hardly necessary for me to add that the sole test of the success of our delegates is the extent to which they are able to get the non-Muslim delegates of the Conference to agree to our demands as embodied in the Delhi Resolution. If these demands are not agreed to, then a question of a very great and far-reaching importance will arise for the community. Then will arrive the moment for independent and concerted political action by the Muslims of India. If you are at all serious about your ideals and aspirations, you must be ready for such an action. Our leading men have done a good deal of political thinking, and their thought has certainly made us, more or less, sensitive to the forces which are now shaping the destinies of peoples in India and outside India. But, I ask, has this thinking prepared us for the kind of action demanded by the situation which may arise in the near future?

Let me tell you frankly that, at the present moment, the Muslims of India are suffering from two evils. The first is the want of personalities. Sir Malcolm Hailey and Lord Irwin were perfectly correct in their diagnosis when they told the Aligarh University that the community had failed to produce leaders. By leaders I mean men who, by Divine gift or experience, possess a keen perception of the spirit and destiny of Islam, along with an equally keen perception of the trend of modern history. Such men are really the driving forces of a people, but they are God's gift and cannot be made to order.

The second evil from which the Muslims of India are suffering is that the community is fast losing what is called the herd instinct. This [loss] makes it possible for individuals and groups to start independent careers without contributing to the general thought and activity of the community. We are doing today in the domain of politics what we have been doing for centuries in the domain of

religion. But sectional bickerings in religion do not do much harm
to our solidarity. They at least indicate an interest in what makes the
sole principle of our structure as a people. Moreover, the principle
is so broadly conceived that it is almost impossible for a group to
become rebellious to the extent of wholly detaching itself from the
general body of Islam. But diversity in political action, at a moment
when concerted action is needed in the best interests of the very life
of our people, may prove fatal.

How shall we, then, remedy these two evils? The remedy of the
first evil is not in our hands. As to the second evil, I think it is possible
to discover a remedy. I have got definite views on the subject; but I
think it is proper to postpone their expression till the apprehended
situation actually arises. In case it does arise, leading Muslims of all
shades of opinion will have to meet together, not to pass resolutions,
but finally to determine the Muslim attitude and to show the path
to tangible achievement. In this address I mention this alternative
only because I wish that you may keep it in mind and give some
serious thought to it in the meantime.

The Conclusion

Gentlemen, I have finished. In conclusion I cannot but impress upon
you that the present crisis in the history of India demands complete
organisation and unity of will and purpose in the Muslim community,
both in your own interest as a community, and in the interest of India
as a whole. The political bondage of India has been and is a source of
infinite misery to the whole of Asia. It has suppressed the spirit of
the East and wholly deprived her of that joy of self-expression which
once made her the creator of a great and glorious culture. We have a
duty towards India where we are destined to live and die. We have a
duty towards Asia, especially Muslim Asia. And since 70 million of
Muslims in a single country constitute a far more valuable asset to
Islam than all the countries of Muslim Asia put together, we must
look at the Indian problem not only from the Muslim point of view,

but also from the standpoint of the Indian Muslim as such. Our duty towards Asia and India cannot be loyally performed without an organised will fixed on a definite purpose. In your own interest, as a political entity among other political entities of India, such an equipment is an absolute necessity.

Our disorganised condition has already confused political issues vital to the life of the community. I am not hopeless of an intercommunal understanding, but I cannot conceal from you the feeling that in the near future our community may be called upon to adopt an independent line of action to cope with the present crisis. And an independent line of political action, in such a crisis, is possible only to a determined people, possessing a will focalised by a single purpose. Is it possible for you to achieve the organic wholeness of a unified will? Yes, it is. Rise above sectional interests and private ambitions, and learn to determine the value of your individual and collective action, however directed on material ends, in the light of the ideal which you are supposed to represent. Pass from matter to spirit. Matter is diversity; spirit is light, life, and unity.

One lesson I have learnt from the history of Muslims. At critical moments in their history it is Islam that has saved Muslims and not vice versa. If today you focus your vision on Islam and seek inspiration from the ever-vitalising idea embodied in it, you will be only reassembling your scattered forces, regaining your lost integrity, and thereby saving yourself from total destruction. One of the profoundest verses in the Holy Quran teaches us that the birth and rebirth of the whole of humanity is like the birth and rebirth of a single individual. Why cannot you who, as a people, can well claim to be the first practical exponents of this superb conception of humanity, live and move and have your being as a single individual? I do not wish to mystify anybody when I say that things in India are not what they appear to be. The meaning of this, however, will dawn upon you only when you have achieved a real collective ego to look at them. In the words of the Quran, 'Hold fast to yourself; no one who erreth can hurt you, provided you are well guided' (5:104).

Two letters from Iqbal to Jinnah (1937)[5]

28th May, 1937

My dear Mr Jinnah,

Thank you so much for your letter which reached me in due course. I am glad to hear that you will bear in mind what I wrote to you about the changes in the constitution and programme of the League. I have no doubt that you fully realise the gravity of the situation as far as Muslim India is concerned. The League will have to finally decide whether it will remain a body representing the upper classes of Indian Muslims or Muslim masses who have so far, with good reason, no interest in it. Personally I believe that a political organisation which gives no promise of improving the lot of the average Muslim cannot attract our masses.

Under the new constitution the higher posts go to the sons of [the] upper classes; the smaller go to the friends or relatives of the ministers. In other matters too our political institutions have never thought of improving the lot of Muslims generally. The problem of bread is becoming more and more acute. The Muslim has begun to feel that he has been going down and down during the last 200 years. Ordinarily he believes that his poverty is due to Hindu money-lending or capitalism. The perception that equality [is] due to foreign rule has not yet fully come to him. But it is bound to come. The atheistic socialism of Jawahar Lal [Nehru] is not likely to receive much response from the Muslims. The question therefore is—how is it possible to solve the problem of Muslim poverty? And the whole future of the League depends on the League's activity to solve this question. If the League can give no such promises I am sure the Muslim masses will remain indifferent to it as before.

Happily there is a solution in the enforcement of the Law of Islam and its further development in the light of modern ideas. After a long and careful study of Islamic Law I have come to the conclusion that if this system of Law is properly understood and applied, at last the right to subsistence is secured to every body. But the enforcement and development of the Shariat of Islam is impossible in this country without a free Muslim state or states. This has been my honest conviction for many years and I still believe this to be the only way to solve the problem of bread for Muslims as well as to secure a peaceful India.

If such a thing is impossible in India the only other alternative is a civil war which as a matter of fact has been going on for some time in the shape of Hindu-Muslim riots. I fear that in certain parts of the country, e.g. N.W. India, Palestine may be repeated. Also the insertion of Jawarhar Lal's socialism into the body-politic of Hinduism is likely to cause much bloodshed among the Hindus themselves. The issue between social democracy and Brahmanism is not dissimilar to the one between Brahmanism and Buddhism. Whether the fate of socialism will be the same as the fate of Buddhism in India I cannot say. But it is clear to my mind that if Hinduism accepts social democracy it must necessarily cease to be Hinduism.

For Islam the acceptance of social democracy in some suitable form and consistent with the legal principles of Islam is not a revolution but a return to the original purity of Islam. The modern problems therefore are far more easy to solve for the Muslims than for the Hindus. But as I have said above in order to make it possible for Muslim India to solve the problems it is necessary to redistribute the country and to provide one or more Muslim states with absolute majorities. Don't you think that the time for such a demand has already arrived? Perhaps this is the best reply you can give to the atheistic socialism of Jawahar Lal Nehru.

Anyhow I have given you my own thoughts in the hope that you will give them serious consideration either in your address or in the discussions of the coming session of the League. Muslim India hopes that at this serious juncture your genius will discover some way out of our present difficulties.

Yours Sincerely,

(Sd.) Mohammad Iqbal

P.S. On the subject-matter of this letter I intended to write to you a long and open letter in the press. But on further consideration I felt that the present moment was not suitable for such a step.

Private and Confidential
Lahore
June 21st, 1937

My dear Mr. Jinnah,

Thank you so much for your letter which I received yesterday. I know you are a busy man; but I do hope you won't mind my writing to you so often, as you are the only Muslim in India today to whom the community has a right to look up for safe guidance through the storm which is coming to North-West India and perhaps to the whole of India. I tell you that we are actually living in a state of civil war which, but for the police and military, would become universal in no time.

During the last few months there has been a series of Hindu–Muslim riots in India. In North-West India alone there have been at least three riots during the last three months and at least four cases of vilification of the Prophet by Hindus and Sikhs. In each of these four cases, the vilifier has been murdered. There have also been cases of burning of the Qur'an in Sind. I have carefully studied the whole situation and believe that the real cause of these events is neither religious nor economic. It is purely political i.e., the desire of the Sikhs and Hindus to intimidate Muslims even in the Muslim majority provinces. And the new constitution is such that even in the Muslim majority provinces, the Muslims are made entirely dependent on non-Muslims.

The result is that the Muslim Ministry can take no proper action and are even driven to do injustice to Muslims partly to please those on whom they depend, and partly to show that they are absolutely impartial. Thus it is clear that we have our specific reasons to reject this constitution. It seems to me that the new constitution is devised only to placate the Hindus. In the Hindu majority provinces, the Hindus have of course absolute majorities, and can ignore Muslims altogether. In Muslim majority provinces, the Muslims are made entirely dependent on Hindus. I have no doubt in my mind that this constitution is calculated to do infinite harm to the Indian Muslims. Apart from this it is no solution of the economic problem which is so acute among Muslims.

The only thing that the communal award grants to Muslims is the recognition of their political existence in India. But such a recognition granted to a people whom this constitution does not and cannot help in solving their problem of poverty can be of no value to them. The Congress President has denied the political existence of Muslims in no unmistakable terms. The other Hindu political body, i.e., the Mahasabha, whom I regard as the real representative of the masses of the Hindus, has declared more than once that a united Hindu-Muslim nation is impossible in India. In these circumstances it is obvious that the only way to a peaceful India is a redistribution of the country on the lines of racial, religious, and linguistic affinities. Many British statesmen also realise this, and the Hindu-Muslim riots which are rapidly coming in the wake of this constitution are sure further to open their eyes to the real situation in the country. I remember Lord Lothian told me before I left England that my scheme was the only possible solution of the troubles of India, but that may take 25 years to come.

Some Muslims in the Punjab are already suggesting the holding of [a] North-West Indian Muslim Conference, and the idea is rapidly spreading. I agree with you, however, that our community is not yet sufficiently organised and disciplined and perhaps the time for holding such a conference is not yet ripe. But I feel that it would be highly advisable for you to indicate in your address at least the line of action that the Muslims of North-West India would be finally driven to take.

To my mind the new constitution with its idea of a single Indian federation is completely hopeless. A separate federation of Muslim provinces, reformed on the lines I have suggested above, is the only course by which we can secure a peaceful India and save Muslims from the domination of non-Muslims. Why should not the Muslims of North-West India and Bengal be considered as nations entitled to self-determination just as other nations in India and outside India are?

Personally I think that the Muslims of North-West India and Bengal ought at present to ignore Muslim [-minority] provinces. This is the best course to adopt in the interests of both Muslim majority and minority provinces. It will therefore be better to hold the coming session of the League in the Punjab, and not in a Muslim minority province. The month of August is bad in Lahore. I think you should seriously consider the advisability of holding the coming session at Lahore in the middle of October when the weather is quite good in Lahore. The interest in the All-India Muslim League is rapidly growing in the Punjab, and the holding of the coming session in Lahore is likely to give a fresh political awakening to the Punjab Muslims.

Yours sincerely,
(Sd) Mohammad Iqbal
Bar-at-Law

The Hindu–Muslim Problem (1924): The Shuddhi, Sanghathan, and Tanzim Movements[6]

by Lala Lajpat Rai

The aggressive Hinduism preached by the Arya Samaj was not political in its conception. That it has been strengthened by political considerations cannot, however, be denied.

This is an appropriate place for examining the origin and bearings of the Shuddhi movement of which we have heard so much of late. The movement is as old as the Arya Samaj or even the Sikh religion. The Arya Samaj claims that the religion preached by it is universal religion, and aims at bringing the whole world under its banner. In this respect its claims are as ambitious and wide as those of Christianity and Islam. There was a time when the more orthodox section of the Arya Samaj used to proclaim from the housetops that they were non-Hindus; and that they were free to eat and drink and marry with non-Hindus; and that even Hindus should undergo a certain amount of Shuddhi before they could be admitted into the Arya Samaj.

The other section, which was believed to be more political-minded, was opposed to all these claims of the Mahatma party of which Swami Shraddhanand (then Lala Munshi Ram) was the head. Shuddhi with the latter was purely the ritual of conversion, i.e. admission into their Church. It had no political significance whatsoever. For a time, Lala Munshi Ram's party maintained this attitude, and some of them attempted to put into practice what they believed in theory. It was then that the now-famous Dharmpal was made a hero. Soon after, however, they found that by insisting on this idea and putting it into practice they were bound to lose the practical sympathy of the Hindu community. This they could not afford to do, as it was the general Hindu community that greased the various mills they were running. So better counsels prevailed, and they changed their attitude.

I know it as a fact, however (as I was an active member of the Arya Samaj then), that serious efforts were made even then to bring the Malkana and other Rajputs of the United Provinces and Rajputana into the fold of the Arya Samaj. Some were actually so brought at Aligarh and in the neighbouring districts. The Malkanas, however, did not want to be 'Aryas'; what they desired was to be re-admitted into their own caste, and brotherhood on equal terms. To this the orthodox Rajputs would not agree. So the matter remained in suspense for a number of years, until the orthodox Rajputs consented to take them in. What was at the back of the latter's mind in this change of attitude, is also clear. It was the communal demands of the Muslim community, the policy of Mian Fazl-i-Husain and the Multan riots,which created the necessary atmosphere. The principle of Shuddhi has now been accepted by the Hindu Mahasabha, and I am free to confess that the idea at the back of this decision is partly political, partly communal, and partly humanitarian, the latter element being more in evidence in the Shuddhi of the untouchables.

It was, it must be confessed, only natural that the Muslims should be exasperated at this change in the attitude of the orthodox Hindus, because the change opens out an entirely new chapter in Indian history. The question raised by the movement is a fundamental one, and although one can understand and appreciate the Muslim point of view, one can see no way of stopping the movement as long as non-Hindu agencies are free to carry on their proselytizing work. The movement has come to stay, and this fact should be philosophically accepted. That it has direct political bearings cannot be denied, and the only way to minimise its importance is to do away with communal representation. For the present, the decisions arrived at by the Delhi Unity Conference may be accepted as the final word in the matter.

At this stage we might discuss the Sangathan and the Tanzim movements too. The Sangathan movement also (or to call it by its proper name, the Hindu Sabha movement) represents an old idea. The object was presented to the mind of the founder of the Arya Samaj. But the Samaj signally failed to realise it, as it went on developing its sectarian proclivities. I remember that when I was a student of the Lahore Government College in the early eighties, a Hindu Sabha was formed at the house of Raja Harbans Singh of Shaikhupura in Lahore. That Sabha died in its infancy. Then the movement was revived towards the end of the last century at the house of the late Lala Balmokand, Reis, Lahore. Even this organization, however, remained almost lifeless until the late R.B. Lal Chand put life into it.

But somehow or other, the movement never took root. It has benefitted individual members, but it has done no good to the Hindu community as a whole. It had two formidable rivals: on the political side the Indian National Congress, on the socio-religious side the Arya Samaj. Fixed between these two mill-stones, it was never able to lift its head sufficiently high to be a success. The present movement is a reaction of the Hindu-Muslim situation. There is nothing in its aims and objects or its constitution that need make it anti-Muslim, but to be frank, the fact that it is anti-Muslim is the only thing that keeps it alive.

The Khilafat Committees which were originally established to support the Khilafat agitation have regularly and systematically carried on a religious propaganda to which is directly traceable a part, at least, of the present bitterness between Hindus and Muslims. At Cocanada, it was given out that the Khilafat Committee would be used to organise the Indian Muslims. *Tanzim* is its other name. It is obviously anti-Hindu.

Personally, I would welcome both the movements, i.e. the Sanghathan and the Tanzim, if they could unite the different sections of the Hindus into one organization, in one case, and all the different sections of the Muslims, in the other; for then it would be a comparatively easy thing for the two main organizations to come to terms with each other. But the task is hopeless. In my judgment the only purpose which the two movements are likely to serve is to increase the already existing estrangement between the two communities. The Muslim movement is also intended to keep the Pan-Islamic movement going. One cannot help noticing, and noticing with regret, that while the Muslims do not open their purses for the relief of Indian sufferers from famine, floods, earthquakes, etc., and that while very little Muslim money is spent to improve the educational and economic condition of Indian Muslims, thousands and lakhs [hundreds of thousands] are sent abroad under one name or other. The phenomenon is confined to India. One finds no evidence of it in other Muslim nations like Egypt, Turkey, Morocco, Sudan, Syria, etc., etc.

As far as internal organization is concerned, both movements are bound to fail. The canker of sectarianism is as fatal in one case as in the other.

In the case of Sanghathan, the Arya Samaj and the Sanatan Dharam Sabha will not allow it to flourish and succeed. They do not seem prepared to transfer any of their functions or influence to the Hindu Sabha. In the case of Tanzim, the different Muslim sects will not unite to let it be a success. Both the movements will, however, be much advertised though, to keep alive anti-Muslim feeling in one case, and the anti-Hindu feeling in the other.

Notes

Introduction

1 Dr Yahya Michot is a Fellow of Islamic Studies at the Oxford Centre for Islamic Studies and the Faculty of Theology, Oxford University. He specializes in the works of classical Muslim theologians Avicenna and Ibn-e Taymiyya.

2 Ayesha Jalal, *Self and Sovereignty: Individual and Community in South Asian Islam since 1850*, New York, 2000, p. 170

3 Muhammad Sadiq, *A History of Urdu Literature*. Delhi: OUP, 1995.

4 Pankaj Mishra, *From the Ruins of the Empire*, London: Allen Lane, 2012; p. 258

5 Muhammad Iqbal, *The Call of the Caravan Bell*, translated by Umrao Singh Gill

6 Rajmohan Gandhi, *Understanding the Muslim Mind*, India: Penguin Books, 2013, p. 52

7 Muhammad Iqbal, *Masnavi-e Asrar-e Khudi*, Foreword, pp. 8-9

8 'To this end, he began to exalt Nietzschean-style masculine vigour and the great Islamic past in his writings,' writes Pankaj Mishra. 'Like many Islamic modernists who harked back to classical Islam, Iqbal became a critic of Sufism and the mystical and folk traditions within Islam that advocate the rejection of the ego and the self, and even of Islamic sects like the Ahmadi.' Pankaj Mishra, *From the Ruins of the Empire*, London: Allen Lane, 2012; p. 258

9 Gandhi, op. cit, p. 53

10 Muhammad Sadiq argues that Iqbal got ideas of Islamic internationalism from his predecessors like Jamal uddin Afghani. 'Picked up out of the old armoury of Islamic dogmas, it had been brandished about in a spectacular

way by Jamaluddin Afghani. Iqbal took it from him and gave it a new edge. His optimism is the result of his unshaken faith in the survival and value of Islam as a way of life; but here too, he was heartened by the nascent revival in the Islamic world.'

11 Gandhi, op. cit, p. 51. Quoted from Malik (ed). *Iqbal.*

12 'To the student of psychology this switch over to Persian is symptomatic of an unconsciously waning interest in India and things Indian, and a growing absorption in Islam. He must have come to feel that Persian was somehow nearer to the heart of Islam than Urdu.' Muhammad Sadiq, p. 450

13 Syed Sulaiman Nadvi (1884–1953) was an eminent Indian historian, biographer, littérateur and scholar of Islam. He co-authored *Sirat-un-Nabi* and wrote *Khutbat-e Madras.*

14 Sir Sir Ross Masood (1889–1937), son of Syed Mahmood and grandson of Sir Syed Ahmed Khan, was the vice-chancellor of Aligarh Muslim University starting in 1929. He was educated at Aligarh Muslim University and Oxford University.

15 Sh. Abdul Qadir, *Iqbal: The Great Poet of Islam*, Lahore: Sang-e Meel Publications, 2003, p.28

16 Muhammad Sadiq, op. cit., p.450

17 In 1912, Tagore sailed from India to England with a collection of English translations—the 100 or so poems that became the anthology Gitanjali, or 'song offerings'. He lost the manuscript on the London tube. Famously, it was found in a left luggage office. Then—decisively—WB Yeats met Tagore, read his poems and became his passionate advocate (while pencilling in suggestions for improvements). Ian Jack, 'Rabindranath Tagore was a global phenomenon, so why is he neglected?', May 7, 2011, *Guardian, http://www.theguardian.com/commentisfree/2011/may/07/rabindranath-tagore-why-was-he-neglected*

18 Qadir, Iqbal, op. cit, p. 62, from *Asrar-e Khudi/Kulliyat*

19 Sh. Abdul Qadir, op. cit, p. 61

20 'He warned his readers against the intoxicating effects of the wine of the poetry of Hafiz of Shiraz as it led to inaction'. Sh. Abdul Qadir, op. cit, p. 61

21 Shafiq Ali Khurram says that Iqbal's interpretation of Rumi was, however, based on an understanding that the spirit of Devotional Sufism (represented by Rumi, Bu Ali Qalandar, Nizamuddin Aulya, Mian Mir and others) was not necessarily the same as that of metaphysical mysticism

(such as Ibn-ul-Arabi and Al-Jili). Iqbal's understanding of Rumi was, therefore, independent of classical interpretations of the master. Also, a Persian masnavi written by a master of Devotional Sufism from the 14th Century India, Bu Ali Qalandar, was yet another role model which Iqbal had used as a role model for his own work.

22   Jalaluddin Rumi, better known simply as Rumi, was perhaps the finest Persian poet of all time and a great influence on Muslim writing and culture. His poetry is still well known throughout the modern world, and he is one of the best selling poets in America. Jalaluddin Rumi was born in 1207 in Balkh in present-day Afghanistan. Increasing Mongol incursions when he was around the age of eleven forced his family to leave Afghanistan, who travelled to Baghdad, Mecca, Damascus and finally settled in Konya in Turkey. Rumi lived here for most of his life. *http://www.bbc.co.uk/religion/religions/islam/art/rumi_1.shtml*

23   Qadir, op. cit, p. 63-64

24   C.M. Naim, In *Iqbal, Jinnah and Pakistan: The Vision and the Reality* *http://www.columbia.edu/itc/mealac/pritchett/00litlinks/naim/ambiguities/13iqbaljinnah.html*

25   Letters of Iqbal to Jinnah, Lahore: Sh. Muhammad Ashraf, n.d., p. 23. Letter dated 21 June 1937.

26   The only immediate response in 1930 was from Chaudhry Rahmat Ali and his associates at Cambridge who were themselves not taken seriously. 'We don't have Jinnah's letters to Iqbal, but reading between the lines of Iqbal's correspondence one gathers the impression that,' writes C.M. Naim. 'Thus Iqbal's idea went a-begging for a long while, as did Chaudhry Rahmat Ali's Pakistan Scheme. Their time came only when the nature of the political arena changed and it became expeditious for the Muslim League in its strategy to overcome the regional groups and emerge as the authoritative voice of the Muslims of India.'

27   Quaid-i-Azam Muhammad Ali Jinnah: Speeches as Governor General of Pakistan 1947-1948, Karachi: Government of Pakistan, Ministry of Information and Broadcasting, n.d., pp. 6-10.

28   Ibid, p.p. 8-9

29   Edward Thompson, *Enlist India for Freedom*, London: Victor Golancz Ltd., 1940, p. 58

30   Javed Iqbal, 'Afterword' in *Stray Reflections: The Private Notebook of Muhammad Iqbal*, edited by Javed Iqbal, Lahore: Iqbal Academy Pakistan, 1961. pp. 174-175

31 Dr Javed Iqbal, *Ideology of Pakistan*. Lahore: Sang-e Meel Publications, 2011. p. 133

Chapter 1: The Son of an Untutored Philosopher

1   Was it a pigeon or a dove? Or was it a colourful bird? There are conflicting accounts about this bird.

2   Greek historical texts mention of the city of Sialkot dating back to before 327 BC when the city was known as Sagala. It represented the eastern-most outpost and expansion of the Hellenic Empire created by Alexander the Great. The Greek historians state that the city was one of the most productive Silk regions of the Achaemenid Empire. Sákala or Sagala was the capital, or one of the capitals, of the Indo-Greek Kingdom which broke-away from the Greco-Bactrian Kingdom during the Euthydemid Dynasty the Indo-Greek king, Menander, ruled in Sialkot during the 2nd century. Popular legends attribute the foundation of Sialkot city to Raja Sala – the uncle of the Pandavas. According to Punjabi folk-lore, the early history of Sialkot is closely interwoven with the traditions of Raja (King) Sáliváhan, his son, Raja Rasálu, and his foe, Raja Húdi. A popular belief is that the city was re-founded by Raja Sáliváhan or Sálbán when it became a part of Kashmir. Raja Sáliváhan built a fort (Sialkot Fort) and the city and gave the place its present name. It is believed that the word 'Sialkot' means the 'Fort of the Sia'. Sialkot became part of the Muslim Sultanate of Delhi under Shahabuddin Ghauri in 1185, and later on, it became part of the Mughal Empire.

3   Sh. Abdul Qadir, 'Dr Sir Muhammad Iqbal' in *Iqbal: The Great Poet of Islam*, ed.Muhammad Hanif Shahid, Sang-e Meel Publications, Lahore, 2003.

4   Dr Javed Iqbal, *Zinda Rood*, Vol. 1.

5   Later on it was named as Iqbal Manzil.

6   Dr Javed Iqbal, op. cit, Vol. 1.

7   Since Nur Muhammad was born after many prayers and invocations of Pirs and Faqirs, his parents had his nostrils pierced to save him from the evil eye, as the custom went in those days. Because of this people called him Natthu. He died in 1930.

8   Dr Javed Iqbal, op. cit, Vol. 1.

9   Munshi Muhammad Din Fauq, Editor of *Akhbar-e Kashmiri*, Lahore, 1932. This is mentioned by Dr Muhammad Baqar in an essay, Iqbal ke

Ajdad ka Silsila-e Aliya, in *Allama Iqbal: Hayat, Fikr-o-fan*, compiled by Dr Saleem Akhtar, 2012, Sang-e-Meel Publications, Lahore.

10 The unclean, the untouchables, an euphemism for Muslims.

11 Dr Javed Iqbal, op. cit.

12 The meaning of 'Sapru' is controversial. According to one definition, it denotes a boy who shows mental perspicacity of an adult. Others says it denotes that group of Kashmiri Brahmins who took to Islamic reading and writing and won the confidence of Muslim leaders. Yet another explanation connects the Saprus with ancient Iran's kinfg Shahpur. By that definition, Saprus are those Iranis who migrated much before the Islamic period to Kashmir and became a part of the Brahmin community because of their intellectual abilities. See *Iqbal ki Ibtedai Zindagi* by Dr Syed Sultan Mahmood Hussain.

13 Letter of Allama Iqbal to Munshi Muhammad Din Fauq, 16 January 1934; Iqbal also mentions linguist Diwan Tek Chand, who was Commissioner in Punjab in this connection. Tek Chand told Iqbal in Ambala that the word Sapru is related to Iran's ancient king Shahpur and the Saprus are in fact Iranians, who came to Kashmir much before Islam's coming and settled down in Kashmir and were embraced by the Brahmin community because of their intelligence and brilliance. However, according to Dr Muhammad Baqar, there is hardly an historical evidence to back this claim.

14 In Kashmir, Lol or Lala or Laj is a word that denotes love or respect when used for a person.

15 Iqbal's letter to his brother Shaikh Ata Muhammad; 15 October 1925

16 Dr Javed Iqbal, op. cit.

17 Shaikh Baba Nasruddin was one of the chief disciples or followers of Shaikh Nuruddin Wali. He was born in a wealthy and influential Hindu family. They had named him Raotar (Wrestler in Kashmiri). He converted to Islam when Shaikh Nuruddin cured him of his chronic indigestion.

18 Shaikh Nuruddin Wali was one of Kashmir's famous rishis. He was the son of Shaikh Salar Din and Sudra Haji. He was born in a village called Kaimoh in 1378. He had four chief disciples (khalifa).

19 Sh. Abdul Qadir, in *Iqbal: The Great Poet of Islam* says that Iqbal's grandfather Shaikh rafiq left his ancestral village of Looehar in Kashmir in 1857 and settled in Sialkot along with his three brothers.

20 'Dr Sir Muhammad Iqbal' in *Iqbal: The Great Poet of Islam* by Sh. Abdul Qadir, edited by Muhammad Hanif Shahid, Sang-e Meel Publications, Lahore, 2003.

21 This statement is referred to Josef Korbel in 'Dr Sir Muhammad Iqbal' in *Iqbal: The Great Poet of Islam* by Sh. Abdul Qadir, edited by Muhammad Hanif Shahid, Sang-e Meel Publications, Lahore, 2003.

22 This is according to William Moorcroft (1767–27 August 1825), an English explorer, who visited Kashmir in 1824. This has been quoted by Dr Javed Iqbal, op. cit.

23 This is according to Baron Schonberg, a traveler, who visited the valley. He is quoted in Dr Javed Iqbal, op. cit.

24 Beji died in 1914.

25 Shaikh Ata Muhammad was the eldest son of Shaikh Noor Muhammad. He was born in 1860. After completing his education, he qualified as an engineer and served as SDO in the Military Department. He died on 22 December 1940 at the age of 80 years.

26 Dr Javed Iqbal, op. cit.

27 There has been controversy around Iqbal's date of birth. Khurram Ali Shafique writes in his book, *Iqbal: His Life and Our Times* (Lahore: Iqbal Academy Pakistan, 2014): 'I was born on the 3rd of Dhu Q'ad 1294 A.H. (1876 A.D.)', Iqbal wrote in the 'Lebenslauf' of his Ph.D Thesis (Below). Iqbal usually quoted 1876 as the year of his birth approximately but the Islamic date actually corresponded to November 9, 1877 A.D. as pointed out in *Rozgar-i-Faqir* (Vol. 2) in 1963 and later ratified by two special committees appointed for this purpose by the Bazm-i-Iqbal in late 1972 and the Federal Ministry of Education in 1974. The mistaken date of birth, February 22, 1873, was first mentioned in the Lahore-based Urdu daily *Inquilab* on May 7, 1938 (sixteen days after Iqbal's death) and it later gained currency through Iqbal's first standard biography written by the editor of the same newspaper in 1955. The entry in the Municipal Register of Sialkot, on which this date was based is now seen as unrelated to Iqbal. Other dates regarded as Iqbal's date of birth include December 29, 1873 (propounded in 1971 by a family member who later relegated), 1875 (mentioned on Iqbal's Middle School Certificate) and December 1876 (miscalculated by Iqbal and his brother from the Islamic date actually corresponding to November 9, 1877).

28 Iqbal is their fourth child to survive infancy. He was preceded by a brother, Shaikh Ata Muhammad, and two sisters, Fatima and Talat. He was followed by two more sisters, Karim and Zainab.

29 Noor Muhammad had seven children, but only six of them survived. The eldest was Shaikh Ata Muhammad, who was born in 1859. Iqbal was born eighteen years after Ata Muhammad.

Chapter 2: A Pair of Leeches

1 'I do not remember ever seeing anything with my right eye,' he is reported
  to have said later. Hameed Ahmad Khan (1974) *Iqbal ki Shaksiyat aur Shaeri*
  quoted in Iqbal: His Life and Our Times by Khurram Ali Shafique.
2 *Iqbal ki Ibtedai Zindagi* by Dr Syed Sultan Mahmood Hussain
3 'The 1857 revolt was one of the turning points of Syed Ahmed's life. He
  clearly foresaw the imperative need for the Muslims to acquire proficiency
  in the English language and modern sciences if the community were to
  maintain its social and political identity, particularly in Northern India. He
  was one of those early pioneers who recognized the critical role of education
  for the empowerment of the poor and backward Muslim community. In
  1875, Sir Syed founded the Madarsatul Uloom in Aligarh and patterned
  the MAO College after Oxford and Cambridge universities that he visited
  on a trip to London in 1869. His objective was to build a college in tune
  with the British education system but without compromising its Islamic
  values.' Afzal Usmani on Sir Syed Ahmed Khan *http://aligarhmovement.
  com/sir_syed*
4 Dr Javed Iqbal in *Zinda Rood*, Vol. 1.
5 Maulvi Syed Mir Hasan (18 April 1844–25 September 1929) was a
  scholar of Arabic and Persian. He recognized and forecast Iqbal's poetic
  talent and greatness. He was a friend of Iqbal's father. He also a friend of
  Sir Syed Ahmed Khan and actively supported his movement. He played
  a great role in Iqbal's early formation as a poet and scholar, a clay that was
  further shaped by Iqbal's mentor Professor T W Arnold. In 1923, when
  Iqbal was knighted, he also made sure that the government conferred the
  title of Shamsul Ulema on Mir Hasan. When Mir Hasan died, Iqbal paid
  his tribute to his great teacher in *Iltija-I Musafir, Bang-e Dara*.
6 *Iqbal: His Life and Our Times* by Khurram Ali Shafique
7 *Iqbal ki Ibtedai Zindagi* by Dr Syed Sultan Mahmood Hussain
8 Iqbal's mother also played an important role in the development of Iqbal.
  Iqbal loved her dearly. She was the reason for Iqbal's visits to Sialkot. When
  Iqbal studied in London, she used to wait for his letter.
9 In *Zinda Rood*, Dr Javed Iqbal refers to Abdul Majeed Salik and Atia Faizi
  as sources.
10 Rajmohan Gandhi, *Understanding the Muslim Mind*.
11 Dr Syed Sultan Mahmood Hussain, *Iqbal ki Ibtedai Zindagi*

Chapter 3: Seeds of Mysticism

1   The narration is based on Atiya Begum's account of the incident in *Iqbal* by Atiya Begum. Atiya Faizi and Iqbal became friends while studying in England, and their friendship survived after they returned to India.

2   Iqbal related this incident to Atiya Faizi a few days after she met him in Europe. Begum, ibid, pp. 3–5.

3   'Seeking knowledge was inherent in the family, and for this purpose his father had spent several months in seclusion under the guidance of a saint and all that was known to him was imparted to his young son, Iqbal, not quite equipped for the responsibility of receiving higher knowledge. But the seed was there and the watering was done by Iqbal himself--wisely or unwisely the result was shown.' Begum, ibid. p. 4.

4   Probably Saeikh Noor Muhammad was a murid of Qazi Sultan Mahmood (Qadriya) and Iqbal was associated with this silsila right from his childhood. For Iqbal his father was like his Pir—the source of his spiritual sustenance.

5   In *Rumuze-e Bekhudi*, Iqbal narrated this incident about his father.

Chapter 4: The Birth of a Poet

1   *Iqbal ki Ibtedai Zindagi* by Dr Syed Sultan Mahmood Hussain

2   There is no exact evidence when he started composing poetry but most of his biographers claim that it all began from a very early age.

3   Mahmood Hussain, op. cit.

4   Iqbal continued to pay Karim Bi a monthly stipend for the rest of his life. Iqbal had two children from Kareem Bi: Meraj Begum was born in 1896 and Aftab Iqbal in 1898. Meraj Begum died at the age of 19 in 1915. Kareem Bi passed away in 1946, nearly eight years after Iqbal's death. Aftab, who eventually became a barrister, became increasingly estranged to his father until all contact was severed between them in 1920. He died in 1979.

5   Dr Javed Iqbal, *Zinda Rood*, Vol. 1

6   Those who could not physically reach him used to establish a relationship of master and disciple with him through correspondence. Ghazals would go to him through Dak and come back to the sender (poet) with corrections. This practice was so popular that Daagh had to keep a separate staffed department to attend to large volumes of corrections in poetry.

7   He became a disciple of Daagh when he was in the first year of F.A. and
    the period of guidance spanned almost three years (1893 -1896).
8   Shaikh Abdul Qadir in the Preface to *Bang-e Dara: In his own lifetime*,
    Daagh saw Iqbal rise as a great poet and used to take pride in the fact that
    he had once mentored him
9   Dr Javed Iqbal, op. cit.
10 Later on, Scotch Mission College came to be known as Murray College,
    after BA classes were added to it.

Chapter 5: A Scholar in Lahore

1   *Tehband*: A loose one-piece garment extending downward from the waist
    and not joined between the legs.
2   At that time, Oriental college was situated in the campus of Government
    College and some classes between the two institutions were shared.
3   1897 is when Iqbal passed the BA exam, according to Khurram Ali
    Shafique.
4   This is according to the 1906 calendar of Punjab University, as quoted in
    Zinda Rood Vol. 1. p. 162
5   In the B.A. exam, only 105 candidates had successfully passed and four
    had passed in first division.
6   To manage the mushairas in Lahore, a literary association was formed
    whose President was Madan Gopal Barrister and secretary was Khan
    Ahmed Hussain Khan. The latter was the editor of a magazine called
    Shabab-e Urdu.
7   *http://iqbalurdu.blogspot.sg/2011/02/hamala-bang-e-dra-1.html*
8   He had gifted his sitar to one of his Hindu friends.
9   *http://iqbalurdu.blogspot.sg/2011/03/bang-e-dra-028-zohed-aur-rindi.html*

Chapter 6: A Patriotic Poet

1   What if this did not happen? What if Iqbal became an assistant
    commissioner? Would he still go on to joined politics in his later career?
    Would it have changed the course of Indian history?
2   Arnold works as the provisional principal until 1903 and then he returns
    to Government College. In 1904, he retires from his job and goes back to
    England.

3   Pervez Tahir, Introducing Iqbal the Economist in *The Pakistan Development Review*, 40:4 Prt II (Winter 2001) 1167-1176

4   His first research paper, 'The Doctrine of Absolute Unity as Expounded by Abdul Karim al-Jili', was published in the *Indian Antiquary*, Bombay, in September 1900.

5   The translation part of his job was performed by bringing out an abridged urdu version of the popular American textbook on political economy by Walker (1888). The Oriental College Report for 1901-02 confirms translation of Walker's book and a new work on political economy under preparation *'The translation of Walker'* is not traceable.

6   Iqbal, Shaikh Muhammad (n.d.) *Ilmul Iqtisad* [*The Science of Economics*]. Lahore: Khadimul-Taleem Steam Press of Paisa Akhbar. First published 1904. 2nd edition (1961), Karachi: Iqbal Academy; Reprinted (1977), Lahore: Iqbal Academy Pakistan; 2nd Reprint (1991), Lahore: Aina-i-Adab. Urdu.

7   Khurram Ali Shafique, *Iqbal: His Life, Our Times*

8   For a long time, therefore, the year of publication was thought to be 1903, although other dates have been mentioned between 1900–03. But the controversy now stands resolved on the basis of reliable evidence and 1904 is the commonly agreed year of publication. (Pervaiz Tahir)

9   The claim is justified but it is not the first work in Urdu. Before the publication of *Ilmul Iqtisad* in 1904, a number of celebrated works of economics had been translated in Urdu. These included: Rev. Francis Walyland's *Elements Political Economy* (1837), translated by Pandit Dharam Narain in 1845; Nassau William Senior's *An Outline of the Science of Political Economy* (1836), translated by Babu Ramkali Chaudhri and Roy Shankar Das in 1865; first thirteen chapters of John Stuart Mill's *Principles of Political Economy with Some of Their Applications to Social Philosophy* (1848), again translated by Pandit Dharam Narain in 1869. Even some of Jevons was translated by Maulvi Muhammad Zakaullah in 1900.

10   Pervez Tahir, *Introducing Iqbal the Economist* in *The Pakistan Development Review*, 40:4 Prt II (Winter 2001) 1167-1176: Reading the preface gives one a clear idea of Iqbal's thoughts on the economic organization of man and resources in the society. Iqbal writes in the preface of the book: 'The science of economics discusses the ordinary business of human life and its objective is to investigate the matter as to how people get their income and how they use it. Thus in one respect its subject matter is wealth and in another respect it is a branch of that vast body of knowledge whose

subject matter is man himself. It is an accepted point that man's ordinary business has a great influence on his habits, conduct and his way of life. So much so that even his mental faculties cannot wholly remain free of this influence. There is no doubt that the religious principle too has been extremely influential in the spate of human history. But it is also borne out by every day experience and observation that the business of making a living is all the time with man, quietly moulding his visible and inner faculties. Just imagine the extent to which human behaviour is affected by poverty, or put another way, the inadequate satisfaction of the necessities of life. Poverty has a huge impact on human faculties, nay, many a time it covers the shiny bright mirror of human spirit with so much rust that its being is equated with nothingness in moral as well as sociocultural terms. The first teacher and philosopher Aristotle thought that slavery is a necessary element for the establishment of human civilisation. But religion and present day education have emphasised the instinctive freedom of man and the civilised nations felt gradually that this barbaric class distinction, instead of being a necessary element to establish civilisation, disestablishes it and exercises an extremely despicable influence on every aspect of human life. In the same way the question has arisen in the present age whether poverty is also a necessary element in the global system. Is it not possible that every individual is free from the suffering of poverty? Can it not be that the heart-rending calls of those quietly groaning all over the place silence for ever and the sad spectacle of poverty that frightens a caring heart, disappear from the face of the earth like a blot on the landscape? To give a categorical answer to this question is not the task of economics because, to some extent, the answer depends on the moral abilities of human nature for whose discovery the experts in this science do not have any particular method in their hands. But since the answer also largely depends on the events and outcomes which enter the sphere of inquiry of economics, this science is therefore of immense interest to man and its study is very nearly among the necessities of life. The study of this science and reflecting on its results is particularly important for the Indians, as poverty is becoming a common complaint here. Due to the lack of universal education, our country is completely unaware of her weaknesses and again of the socio-cultural factor, the knowledge of which is judged as a panacea for national welfare and prosperity. History of man is witness to the fate befalling nations who neglected their socio-cultural and economic conditions. In a valuable speech made fair recently the Mahraja of Baroda has observed that adjusting our present economic condition is the ultimate prescription for all our ills and our destruction is guaranteed if this prescription is not applied. Thus if the people of India wish to retain their name in the comity of nations, it is necessary for them to seek awareness of the principles of this important science to find out which factors are obstructing the rise of the country. My aim in writing these pages is to explain in an intelligible manner the most important principles of this science and also to discuss at places the extent to which these general principles apply to the present condition of India. I will not consider my brain-cudgelling to have gone waste if these lines encourage even one person to ponder over these matters.'

11 Khurram Ali Shafique, *Iqbal: His Life, Our Times*

12 The title was later changed to 'the Indian Song' (*'Tarana-i-Hindi'*) but that was insignificant, since the poem was always going to be remembered by its first line, imprinted on the hearts of even those Indians who did not know Urdu: Khurram Ali Shafique, op. cit.

13 Apparently, the line was inspired by the first two lines of German national anthem, 'Deutschland, Deutschland über alles, / Über alles in der Welt,' – (Germany, Germany, above everything, / Above everything in the world,): Shafique, op. cit.

14 See Abdullah Qureshi, *Baqiyat-e Iqbal*.

15 http://iqbalurdu.blogspot.sg/2011/03/bang-e-dra-17-aftab.html

16 It is also possible that Arnold had offered Iqbal the idea of pursuing a PhD in Islamic philosophy and tasaw'uf. However, the idea to become a barrister was his own.

17 When Mirza Jalaluddin was returning from England, Shaikh Abdul Qadir asked him to guide Iqbal in case he wanted to collect more information about how to come over to England. Iqbal consulted with Jalaluddin before leaving for England. This was their first meeting and they became friends after Iqbal's return from England.

18 Dr Javid Iqbal, *Zinda Rood*.

19 When he reached England, he was wearing a suit. Iqbal put on a felt hat only during his stay in England and did not wear it in India. (Ali Bakhsh to Javed Iqbal)

20 *http://iqbalurdu.blogspot.sg/2011/03/bang-e-dra-12-parinde-ki-faryad.html*

21 Khwaja Hasan Nizami (1878–1955) was a Sufi of the Chishti Islamic order, a Delhi author and journalist during the Indian independence movement, who advocated the ecstatic Sufi mystic practices, as much as the demure

religious laws. He supported the Islamic tablighi-mission and the pan-Islamic movement, while promoting, at the same time a joint Indian nation of Hindus and Muslims. *https://www.mpib-berlin.mpg.de/en/research/ history-of-emotions/projects/emotion-and-power/khwaja-hasan-nizami*

22   The Traveler's Request, Allama Iqbal poetry *http://iqbalurdu.blogspot. sg/2011/03/bang-e-dra-049-iltajaay-musafir.html*

Chapter 7: Bombay

1   By 1864, there were 31 banks, 16 financial associations, 8 land companies, 16 press companies, 10 shipping companies, 20 insurance companies as against 10 in 1855, and 62 joint stock companies where none had existed in 1855!

2   By 1911 motorised taxis were already plying in Bombay.

3   The Bombay that Iqbal comes across in 1905 already contains a lot of the characteristics that Bombay will come to be associated with in the later decades. For example, in his 1990 book, *India—A Million Mutinies Now*, Naipaul describes 'Bombay as a crowd'. He complains of the city's slow moving traffic because of the crowd, and turns up his nose at the money culture of Bombay. 'With industrialization and economic growth people had forgotten old reverences,' he says in the book's opening chapter. 'Men honored only money now.'

'From the beginnings of the city,' writes Suketu Mehta in *Maximum City* (2004), nearly a hundred years after Iqbal reaches Bombay, 'there was a Bombay culture, unique in India. Bombay is all about transaction—dhandha. It was founded as a trading city, built at the entrance to the rest of the world, and everybody was welcome as long as they wanted to trade.'

There is another thing about early Bombay, as Mehta points out, worth noticing. 'Nobody back then came to Bombay to live there for ever; it was just a way station, between paradise and hell. You came to Bombay to pass through it.'

4   Dr Javed Iqbal, *Zinda Rood*

5   According to the Encyclopaedia Britannica, Young Turks was a coalition of various reform groups in the early twentieth century that led a revolutionary movement against the authoritarian regime of Ottoman sultan Abdülhamid II, which culminated in the establishment of a constitutional government. After their rise to power, the Young Turks introduced programs that promoted the modernization of the Ottoman

Empire and a new spirit of Turkish nationalism. Their handling of foreign affairs, however, resulted in the dissolution of the Ottoman state. h*ttp:// global.britannica.com/EBchecked/topic/654123/Young-Turks*

6   Abdülhamid II, (born Sept. 21, 1842, Constantinople [now Istanbul, Turkey]—died Feb. 10, 1918, Constantinople), Ottoman sultan from 1876 to 1909, under whose autocratic rule the reform movement of Tanzimat (Reorganization) reached its climax and who adopted a policy of pan-Islamism in opposition to Western intervention in Ottoman affairs. *http:// global.britannica.com/EBchecked/topic/931/Abdulhamid-II*

7   Javed Iqbal, op. cit.

8   The Russo-Japanese War (1904–05) was a military conflict in which a victorious Japan forced Russia to abandon its expansionist policy in the Far East, becoming the first Asian power in modern times to defeat a European power. The Russo-Japanese War developed out of the rivalry between Russia and Japan for dominance in Korea and Manchuria. *http:// global.britannica.com/EBchecked/topic/514017/Russo-Japanese-War*

9   Dadabhai Naoroji (4 September 1825–30 June 1917), known as the Grand Old Man of India, was a Parsi intellectual, educator, cotton trader, and an early Indian political and social leader. He was a Member of Parliament (MP) in the United Kingdom House of Commons between 1892 and 1895, and the first Asian to be a British MP. He is also credited with the founding of the Indian National Congress, along with A.O. Hume and Dinshaw Edulji Wacha. His book, *Poverty and Un-British Rule in India* brought attention to the draining of India's wealth into Britain (Wikipedia)

Chapter 8: A Journey to the West

1   *Encounters with Destiny: Autobiographical Reflections* by Javed Iqbal (Translated from Urdu by Hafeez Malik and Nasira Iqbal), Sang-e Meel Publications, Lahore, 2012.

2   Sir William Muir (27 April 1819–11 July 1905) was a Scottish Orientalist and colonial administrator. In 1837 he entered the Bengal Civil Service. During the Mutiny he was in charge of the intelligence department there. In 1865 he was made foreign secretary to the Indian Government. In 1867 Muir was knighted (K.C.S.I.), and in 1868 he became lieutenant-governor of the North Western Provinces. In 1876, after his retirement, he became a member of the Council of India in London. It was chiefly through his

exertions that the central college at Allahabad, known as Muir Central College, was built and endowed, which later became a part of the Allahabad University.

3   Muir's early book, *Life of Mahomet*, was criticized in a contemporary review in *The Times* for 'propagandist writing' with Christian bias and for 'odium theologicum'. Contemporary historian E.A. Freeman praised the book as a 'great work', yet questioned its conjectural methodology, particularly the 'half timid suggestion' made by Muir that Muhammad had fallen under the influence of Satanic inspiration. In the final chapters of Life, Muir concluded that the main legacy of Islam was a negative one, and he subdivided it in 'three radical evils': First: Polygamy, Divorce, and Slavery strike at the root of public morals, poison domestic life, and disorganise society; while the Veil removes the female sex from its just position and influence in the world. Second: freedom of thought and private judgment are crushed and annihilated. Toleration is unknown, and the possibility of free and liberal institutions foreclosed. Third: a barrier has been interposed against the reception of Christianity.'

4   Perhaps he was referring to Sahabi Astar Abadi, the famous Iranian poet and quatrain composer.

5   *Encounters with Destiny: Autobiographical Reflections* by Javed Iqbal (Translated from Urdu by Hafeez Malik and Nasira Iqbal), Sang-e Meel Publications, Lahore, 2012.

6   Iqbal, ibid.

7   Muhammad al-Qasim ibn Ali ibn Muhammad ibn Uthman al-Hariri, popularly known as al-Hariri of Basra (1054–1122) was an Arab poet, philologist, man of letters and official of the Seljuk Empire. *Encyclopedia of Arabic Literature*, Volume 1, edited by Julie Scott Meisami, Paul Starkey

8   The Suez Canal is an artificial sea-level waterway in Egypt, connecting the Mediterranean Sea and the Red Sea. Opened in November 1869 after 10 years of construction work, it allows ship transport between Europe and eastern Asia without navigation around Africa. The northern terminus is Port Said and the southern terminus is Port Tawfiq at the city of Suez. Ismailia lies on its west bank, 3 km (1.9 mi) from the half-way point. http://en.wikipedia.org/wiki/Suez_Canal

9   Iqbal, op. cit.

Chapter 9: Iqbal in England – London and Cambridge

1   Lindsey German and John Rees, *A People's History of London*, Verso, 2012.

2   R. Barltrop, *Jack London: The Man, the writer, the rebel* (London 1978).

3   German and Rees, op. cit.

4   German and Rees, op. cit

5   Ramchandra Guha, *Gandhi Before India*, Allen Lane, 2013.

6   In 1892, Sir Frederick Leigh Croft, a business associate of Jinnahbhai
     Poonja, offered young Jinnah a London apprenticeship with his firm,
     Graham's Shipping and Trading Company. However, soon after his
     arrival in London, Jinnah gave up the apprenticeship in order to study
     law, enraging his father, who had, before his departure, given him enough
     money to live for three years. The aspiring barrister joined Lincoln's Inn.
     (Wikipedia)

7   Not much detail on Iqbal's life in Europe is available. He did not keep a
     dairy. Whatever we know about Iqbal is through the writings of his friends
     and contemporaries like Atiya Faizi and Shaikh Abdul Qadir.

8   Most probably Thomad Arnold had guided him in making this suggestion,
     says Saeed A. Durrani in his essay, 'Encountering Modernity: Iqbal at
     Cambridge' in Muhammad Suheyl Umar and Dr Basit Bilal Koshul (eds),
     *Muhammad Iqbal - A Contemporary: Articles from the International Seminar
     held at The University of Cambridge* (June 19-20, 2008); Celebrating the
     Centenary of Iqbal's Stay in Europe (1905-08); Iqbal Academy Pakistan,
     2010

9   It was submitted in mid-March 1907 with the title: 'The Development of
     Metaphysics in Persia', for which he got a distinction in his BA degree by
     research on 13 June 1907

10   Durrani, op. cit.

11   After he returns to India from England, he would keep on his
     correspondence with Nicolson and McTaggart. After having translated
     Iqbal's Asrar-e Khudi Nicholson asks him if he had changed his position
     with regard to Existentialism. Iqbal later on writes an essay on McTaggart's
     philosophy too.

12   This literary journal was started by Sir Abdul Qadir in April 1901. Qadir
     was Iqbal's friend, and together they spent two years in England. Qadir
     was a lawyer, judge of the High Court (Punjab),Minister for Education,
     Member of the Council for the Secretary of the State for India and editor

of the *Observer*. His journal published all the Urdu masterpieces of Iqbal's poetry.

13 According to Dr Javed Iqbal (*Zinda Rood*), in German universities, a student is required to attend lectures for one and a half years to three years, depending upon the caliber of the scholar. The final dissertation is expected to be presented in German language. But Iqbal was exempted from all these conditions on the recommendation of his professors in Cambridge. The only condition was that he had to get his viva voce done in German and for that he had to learn the language.

14 Ramchandra Guha, *Gandhi Before India*, Allen Lane, 2013.

15 According to Dr Javed Iqbal (*Zinda Rood*), in those days, he visited London to attend the dinners at Lincoln's Inn or to write the first part exam of Barrister. He would stay either with Sir Abdul Qadir or stay in a house near his house.

16 In Europe only the Jews were particular about eating kosher meat.

17 Javed Iqbal, *Zinda Rood*

18 The thesis is published in 1908 by Luzac & Co., London. The work of scholarship introduces Iqbal to Europe. It is later translated into Urdu as *Falsafah-i Ajam*.

19 Syed Bilgrami (1851–1911), born into a noble family of Bilgram, was known for his courtesy and hospitality, and was known for his grand parties. He knew ten languages including Arabic, Persian, Marathi and Sanskrit. He worked for Salar Jung of Hyderabad State and went with him to England. In Europe he learned many European languages and in 1879 he returned to India to serve the Hyderabad State's railways and mines departments. In 1901, he resigned from the Hyderabad State and went to England. He was appointed a professor of Marathi language at Cambridge University in 1902. In the same year, he also worked for the India Office Library, London. He has many books to his credit including Gustav Le Bon's two books on Indian and Islamic civilisation (he translated them from French into Urdu). He died in India in Bilgram.

20 The Swadeshi Movement, the most successful of the pre-Gandhian movements, was part of the Indian independence movement and it played a role in developing Indian nationalism. It was primarily an economic strategy aimed at removing the British Empire from power and improving economic conditions in India by following the principles of swadeshi (self-sufficiency in Hindi). Strategies of the Swadeshi movement involved boycotting British products and the revival of domestic products and

production processes. The movement, that started with the partition of Bengal by the Viceroy of India, Lord Curzon, in 1905 and continued up to 1911, was the strongest in Bengal. It was also called vandemataram movement.Its chief architects were Aurobindo Ghosh, Lokmanya Bal Gangadhar Tilak, Bipin Chandra Pal and Lala Lajpat Rai. Gandhi, at the time of the actual movement, remained loyal to the British Crown (Wikipedia).

Chapter 10: Atiya Begum

1 Atiya Begum (popularly know as Atiya Faizi) was born in 1887 in Istanbul. In 1912, two years after Iqbal's return to India, she married Fyzee Rahamin who was a painter. 'Atiya Begum had a deep love and command of the arts, music, literature, and philosophy. She was fluent in several languages: English, Urdu, Persian, Gujarati, German, French and Turkish. It is clear that Iqbal held Atiya Begum in great esteem, for example, he showed her the manuscript of his doctoral dissertation. In fact, he sought his advice on several occasions regarding his poetry and wordly affairs; also confiding in matters of the heart. After the creation of Pakistan, Atiya Begum migrated to Pakistan and died in Karachi on 4 January 1967.' Rauf Parekh in the Preface to *Iqbal* by Atiya Begum, Oxford University Press, 2011, Karachi, Pakistan. Most of Iqbal's life in England and Germany has been recreated from Atiya's book, and this narrative also closely follows hers.

2 They both loved philosophy and literature and a friendship developed between the two that lasted as long as Iqbal lived. It was not a perfect relationship and both regarded each other with great respect yet there were periods of misunderstanding and coldness between the two.

3 Notes of Rauf Parekh in *Iqbal* by Atiya Begum, Oxford University Press, 2011, Karachi, Pakistan.

4 *Iqbal* by Atiya Begum, Oxford University Press, 2011, Karachi, Pakistan.

5 During her stay in London, Atiya Begum wrote letters back home and her sister Zohra Begum (1866-1940) got the selected text of these letters published as a travel account in *Tehzeeb-e-Niswan*, a magazine for women, published from Lahore. Later these missives were published in book form titled, *Zamana-e-Tehseel* (Mufeed-e-Aam Press, Agra, 1922). Notes by Rauf Parekh in *Iqbal* by Atiya Begum (OUP, Karachi, 2011), p. 109.

6 Khwāja Shams-ud-Dīn Muhammad Hāfez-e Shīrāzī, known by his pen

name Hāfez (1325–1389), was a Persian poet. His collected works are regarded as a pinnacle of Persian literature.

7   It was either 21 April or 22 April 1907. Atiya has used two dates in two places in her memoir.

8   Sarojini Naidu, born as Sarojini Chattopadhyay also known by the sobriquet as The Nightingale of India, was a child prodigy, Indian independence activist and poet. Naidu served as the first governor of the United Provinces of Agra and Oudh from 1947 to 1949; the first woman to become the governor of an Indian state. She was the second woman to become the president of the Indian National Congress in 1925 and the first Indian woman to do so. (Wikipedia)

9   One of the books Iqbal had published in Lahore before coming to England.

Chapter 11: Heidelberg, Germany

1   Some Iqbal experts say that Iqbal has expressed his joy of finding a beloved in this letter, and the beloved he means here is not Atiya but Emma Wegenast.

2   Letter of Iqbal to Atiya, Lahore, 17 July 1909

Chapter 12: Emma Wegenast

1   'It is well known that the poet-philosopher Muhammad Iqbal had a deep admiration for Germany, German thought, German poetry and there are innumerable instances in his writings, in his poems, in letters and in recorded conversations with him which indicate clearly that the works of German philosophers and poets have been a source of great inspiration to him. Foremost among them was Goethe to whom he refers again and again of whom he says, though not a prophet, he has a book namely 'Faust', and whom he compares to Ghalib the great poet of Urdu and Persian of the nineteenth century and to that illustrious sage of the East, Maulana Jalal al Din Rumi. In a poem in the *Payam i Mashriq* Iqbal imagines Goethe meeting Rumi in paradise and reciting Faust to him. Rumi listens and extols Goethe as one who has really understood the Great Secret. In bringing Goethe and Rumi together, Iqbal brought together not only two of the greatest spirits of the East and West, but also the two men who have influenced him more than anyone else in his career as a thinker and as a poet.' M. A. H. Hobohm, Muhammad Iqbal and Germany. 'A

Correspondence of the Heart' *http://www.allamaiqbal.com/publications/journals/review/oct00/08.htm*

2   Saeed A. Durrani in his essay, 'Encountering Modernity: Iqbal at Cambridge' in Muhammad Suheyl Umar and Dr Basit Bilal Koshul (eds), *Muhammad Iqbal - A Contemporary: Articles from the International Seminar held at The University of Cambridge* (June 19-20, 2008); Celebrating the Centenary of Iqbal's Stay in Europe (1905-08); Iqbal Academy Pakistan, 2010

3   Muhammad Iqbal, *Masnavi-e Asrar-e Khudi*, Foreword, pp. 8-9

4   'Fraulein Wegenast was in her twenties when she and Iqbal met and we have it on the authority of Begum Atiya Fayzee that she was very beautiful and highly accomplished, polished young lady.' M.A.H. Hobohm, Muhammad Iqbal and Germany—'A Correspondence of the Heart' http://www.allamaiqbal.com/publications/journals/review/oct00/08.htm

5   Muhammad Ikram Chugtai, 'Iqbal and Wegenast' in *Allama Iqbal: Hiyat, Fikr-o-Fun*, edited by Saleem Akhtar, Lahore: Sang-e Meel publications, 2012.

6   'Pension Scherer', one of those highly respectable boarding houses for students—so common in German university towns before the advent of the students hostel tower blocks. M.A.H. Hobohm, Muhammad Iqbal and Germany—'A Correspondence of the Heart' *http://www.allamaiqbal.com/publications/journals/review/oct00/08.htm*

7   Iqbal may still have had her in mind when he offered his personal definition of beauty a little later: 'A woman of superb beauty with a complete absence of self-consciousness is probably the most charming thing on God's earth.' (Khurram Shafique)

8   Emma was quite evidently the muse, but the influence of German romantic poets need not be overlooked either – Iqbal studied Goethe's *Faust* in original German in the company of Emma herself. 'Our Soul discovers itself when we come into contact with a great mind,' he wrote in a personal reflection in 1910, which was published in 1917. 'It is not until I had realized the Infinitude of Goethe's mind that I discovered the narrow breadth of my own.' (Khurram Shafique)

9   According to Hobohm, Wegenast's collected letters were gifted by her, in the early sixties, shortly before her death, to the Pakistan German Forum, a bilateral cultural association of which at the time the late Mr. Mumtaz Hasan was President while he (Hobohm) its honorary General

Secretary. The Pakistan German Forum, being an organisation worked to promote and strengthen cultural relations between the two countries, was fully aware that Muhammad Iqbal is the greatest cultural link that exists between Germany and Pakistan. 'It was only natural, therefore, that when Mr. Mumtaz Hasan and I were invited to visit Germany in the summer of 1959, we made it a point not only to visit the cities and universities of Heidelberg and Munich where Iqbal had stayed and studied in 1905 and 1906 but to make every effort and attempt to trace any person still alive who had met Iqbal during his days in Germany,' writes Hobohm. 'It was in the pursuit of this aim that with the help of friends we were able to find and to contact Miss Emma Wegenast to whom our attention had been drawn by references to her in Begum Atiya Fayzee's book on Iqbal. Although we could not meet Miss Wegenast personally, a correspondence developed between Mr. Mumtaz Hasan and her. As a result of this correspondence she made over to the Forum the letters she had received from Iqbal with the request to pass them on to any archive in Pakistan where they could be accessible to scholars engaged in research into Iqbal's life and work. Mr. Mumtaz Hasan was kind enough to prepare for me a complete set of photocopies which he gave to me along with two original letters. Since, I had to leave Pakistan on transfer soon after, I do not know the present whereabouts of the letters that were donated by Miss Wegenast.' M. A. H. Hobohm, Muhammad Iqbal and Germany—'A Correspondence of the Heart' *http://www.allamaiqbal.com/publications/journals/review/oct00/08. htm*

10 'Iqbal was very fond of her (Emma)—there is no doubt about that— but as the letters reveal, it was a pure and innocent fondness,' writes M.A.H. Hobohm. 'I have the feeling when reading the letters, that to Iqbal Fraulein Emma Wegenast was the embodiment of all that he loved and respected of all that he was so strongly attracted by, in German culture, in German thought, in German literature, perhaps in German life as a whole. Iqbal addresses her throughout very formally as 'Mein liebes Fraulein Wegenast' or 'My dear Fraulein Wegenast' with only the 'Mein' hinting at his fondness for her.' But it is fondness coupled with respect, for in all the letters written in German and they all belong to the first period when his memories of her were the freshest and his feelings for her must have been the strongest, he always uses the formal and respectful 'Sie' in addressing her, not once lapsing into the intimate 'Du'. The letters do not reveal anything sensational.

They are rather ordinary letters as any two friends would exchange among themselves: no deep thoughts, no poetry, and yet they answer some of the questions about Iqbal which were still open and they certainly throw further light on Iqbal's feelings for my country.' M. A. H. Hobohm, Muhammad Iqbal and Germany—'A Correspondence of the Heart' *http://www. allamaiqbal.com/publications/journals/review/oct00/08.htm*

11 No one knows what these storms were and what kind of independence Iqbal referred to.

12 'They are altogether 27 in numbers including two postcards. They cover two distinct periods, namely the year from 1907 to the outbreak of the Great War in 1914 and the years from 1931 to 1933. The long silence between these periods is only interrupted once by a letter written in 1919.' M. A. H. Hobohm, Muhammad Iqbal and Germany—'A Correspondence of the Heart' *http://www.allamaiqbal.com/publications/journals/review/oct00/08. htm*

Chapter 13: Return to India

1 'In his preface to the *Payam-i Mashriq*, the book in which Iqbal's art probably reached the height of its power and perfection, he writes these Lines: 'The *Payām-i Mashriq* owes its inspiration to the Western Divan of Goethe, the German 'Philosopher of Life', about which, Heine, the Israelite poet of Germany says: 'This is a nosegay presented by the West to the East as a token of high regard. This Divan bears testimony to the fact that the West, being dissatisfied with its own spiritual life is turning to the bosom of the East in search of spiritual warmth.' The *Payam-i Mashriq* is Iqbal's response to Goethe's West-Ostlicher Divan on the title page of which —I should like to recall to our memory— Goethe had written in his own hand the following words in Arabic language and script: 'Ad-Dīwān Sharqī lil Mu'allif al-Gharbī'—An Eastern Divan by a Western Author.' M. A. H. Hobohm, Muhammad Iqbal and Germany --'A Correspondence of the Heart' *http://www.allamaiqbal.com/publications/journals/review/oct00/08. htm*

2 Ayesha Jalal, *Self and Sovereignty: Individual and Community in South Asian Islam since 1850*, New York, 2000, p. 170

3 Iqbal wrote something on these lines in a letter in 1921 to the editor of Naqeeb, Waheed Ahmed.

4   'To this end, he began to exalt Nietzschean-style masculine vigour and
     the great Islamic past in his writings,' writes Pankaj Mishra. 'Like many
     Islamic modernists who harked back to classical Islam, Iqbal became a
     critic of Sufism and the mystical and folk traditions within Islam that
     advocate the rejection of the ego and the self, and even of Islamic sects
     like the Ahmadi.' Pankaj Mishra, *From the Ruins of the Empire*, London:
     Allen Lane, 2012; p. 258

5   In Islam, Iqbal saw 'a successful opponent of the race idea, which is probably
     the hardest barrier in the way of the humanitarian ideal.'

6   Muhammad Iqbal, *The Call of the Caravan Bell*, translated by Umrao Singh
     Gill.

Chapter 14: A Wretched Soul

1   Dr Javed Iqbal, *Zinda Rood*.

2   Iqbal, ibid.

3   In 1775, Goethe was invited, on the strength of his fame as the author of
     The Sorrows of Young Werther, to the court of Carl August, Duke of Saxe-
     Weimar-Eisenach, who would become Grand Duke in 1815. The Duke
     at the time was 18 years of age, to Goethe's 26. Goethe went on to live in
     Weimar for the rest of his life and over the course of many years, he held
     a succession of offices, becoming the Duke's chief adviser.

4   Iqbal accords high regard to Aurangzeb in his private diary: 'The history of
     the preceding Muslim dynasties had taught Aurangzeb that the strength
     of Islam in India did not depend, as his ancestor Akbar had thought, so
     much on the goodwill of the people of this land as on the strength of the
     ruling race.'

5   Khurram Ali Shafique says that in his private correspondence, Iqbal has
     said that he believed himself to have a keen insight into the destiny of
     nations, and that some of his poems were intended to be prophesies. 'I
     have written a few verses at the end [of that poem], which have been
     corroborated by the [breaking out of] the war between Turkey and Italy,'
     he wrote on October 6, 1911, to the senior poet Akbar Allahabadi, whom
     he had begun to see as a kind of mentor.

6   Nazım Pasha, the chief of staff of the Ottoman army was held responsible
     of the failure and was assassinated in 1913 by Young Turks.

7   Khurram Ali Shafique writes: 'Despair, anger and disillusionment from
     personal life may have become distilled with the political setbacks of the
     Muslim world, and produced that extraordinary pressure which resulted in
     the cathartic outcome of 'The Complaint'—his greatest poem until then,
     and one of his most famous ever.'
8   *http://iqbalurdu.blogspot.sg/2011/04/bang-e-dra-105-shikwa.html*
9   Accoridng to Khurram Ali Shafique, in his poems, he also speaks against
     the concept of 'territorial nationalism'. 'The homelands of modern nations
     appeared to him like so many idols for so many tribes—Germany for
     Germans, Britain for British, and so on. 'The idol-maker of civilization
     has presented new idols in this age,' he declared in the poem, 'Patriotism'.
     'Chief among these new idols is country . . .' He implores his Muslim
     audience to break this idol, and to make Islam their homeland.
10   Hobohm, op. cit

Chapter 15: The Three Wives

1   Later on, the poem was translated into German and Italian too. In Sadiq's
     words, Nicholson's translation brought Iqbal 'a rather tardy recognition in
     the form of a knighthood in 1922'. Many believe had Iqbal found a more
     publicly famous champion just as Tagore had found in W.B. Yeats, he
     would have been better known in the West and could have possible won
     the Nobel Prize too.

Chapter 16: Knighthood

1   The Muslims regarded the Caliph (Khalifa) of Turkey as their spiritual
     head. The Caliph was in-charge of protecting the Islamic holy lands.
2   Bipan Chandra and others, *India's Struggle for Freedom*. Delhi: Penguin
     Books India, 1988, p. 184
3   Chandra, ibid., p. 184
4   Chandra, ibid., p. 185
5   Chandra, ibid., p. 184
6   Chandra, ibid., p. 186
7   Chandra, ibid., p. 187
8   Chandra, ibid., p. 189
9   Muhammad Salim, *Allama Iqbal Ki Siyasi Zindagi*, Lahore: Sang-e Meel
     Publications, 2001.

10 Salim, ibid., p 11
11 Salim, ibid., p 15
12 See Khurram Ali Shafique: Iqbal's knighthood in recognition of his literary stature was announced on January 1, 1923. 'Thereafter, he printed his name on his stationery as Dr Sir Muhammad Iqbal. The nationalist press denounced him, completely disregarding his right to remain aloof from Non-Cooperation Movement of Gandhi. Since this was a time when the British Raj was at the height of unpopularity, Iqbal may not have taken a favour from the government but given one by accepting the title.'
13 *http://iqbalurdu.blogspot.sg/2011/04/zarb-e-kaleem-160-mashriq.html*

Chapger 17: A Tulip in the Wilderness

1 Rafi-ud Din Hashmi, ed., *Khutut-I Iqbal*, pp. 165-166.
2 Dr Hafeez Malik, *Iqbal in Politics*, Lahore: Sang-e Meel Publications, 2009. pp. 27
3 Muhammad Rafiq Azad, ed., *Guftar-e Iqbal* (Lahore: The Iqbal Academy, 1961).
4 Azad, op. cit.
5 Malik, op. cit., p. 37
6 *Zamindar,* 24 October 1926
7 Malik, op. cit., p. 38
8 Faqir Sayyid Wahid-ud-Din, *Ruzgar-i Faqir*, Karachi: Line Art Press, 1966. pp. 103-104
9 Malik, op. cit., p. 49

Chapter 18: On the Path of Separatism

1 See Appendix for Lala Lajpat Rai's views on these movements
2 Satish Chandra Mittal, *Freedom Movement in Punjab*, 1905-29
3 http://mehmal.blogspot.sg/2007/06/religious-extremism-in-pakistan-part-v.html
4 According to Muhammad Miyan (Jamiat al Ulama kia hai?), the Jamiat al Ulama-e-Hind was successful in converting more than 2,000 non-Muslims and winning back 11,000 apostates.
5 Dr Hafeez Malik, *Iqbal in Politics*, Lahore: Sang-e Meel Publications, 2009. pp. 52
6 Considering that separate electorates posed the main hindrance to

improving Hindu-Muslim relations, Jinnah proposed that if the Hindus agreed to providing certain safeguards, the Muslims would give up this demand. Consequently, the proposals were formally approved at a conference held by the Muslims in 1927 at Delhi, and are now called 'The Delhi Proposals': The fundamental philosophy of the Delhi proposals was that there should be a balance of power between the Hindus and the Muslims. Their rights should be protected in each other's provinces, no matter who was in majority or minority.

7   Malik, op. cit., p. 55
8   Malik, op. cit., p. 59
9   The Indian demand was the revision of the diarchy state of government.
10 Malik, op. cit., p. 59
11 Malik, op. cit., p. 60
12 The Nehru Report, compiled in August 1928, was a memorandum outlining a proposed new dominion status constitution for India, prepared by a committee of the All Parties Conference chaired by Motilal Nehru with his son Jawaharlal acting as secretary. There were nine other members in this committee, including two Muslims. However, the final report was signed by only eight persons: Motilal Nehru, Ali Imam, Tej Bahadur Sapru, M.S. Aney, Mangal Singh, Shuaib Qureshi, Subhas Chandra Bose, and G.R. Pradhan.

Chapter 19: A Turn in the South

1   *Qiyas* (analogical deduction) is the extension of a Shari'ah value from an original case, or *asl*, to a new case, because the latter has the same effective cause as the former. The original case is regulated by a given text, and qiyas seeks to extend the same textual ruling to the new case.
2   Dr Hafeez Malik, *Iqbal in Politics*, p. 88
3   Shaikh Ata Allah, ed., *Iqbal Namah*, Vol 1. p. 155
4   American historian of science, Toby E. Huff, has said: 'From the 8th century to the end of the 14th, Arabic science was probably the most advanced science in the world, greatly surpassing the West and China.' Toby E. Huff, *The Rise of Early Modern Science*. Cambridge: Cambridge University Press, 1993. p. 48
5   Malik, op. cit., p. 99
6   Bashir Ahmed Dar, *Letters and Writings of Iqbal,* pp. 50-51.
7   The Nizam accepts the invitation but is not able to make it to the Punjab.

Chapter 20: A Poet's Vision for a Muslim State

1   Jinnah was shouted down by the delegates at the 1920 session of the
     Congress in Nagpur, and passed Gandhi's proposal, pledging Satyagraha
     until India was free. Because of the action of the Congress in endorsing
     Gandhi's campaign, Jinnah resigned from it, leaving all positions except
     in the Muslim League.
2   On the other hand, Lala Lajpat Rai's and Chaudhry Rahmat Ali's idea of
     an amalgamated Muslim state envisaged exchange of population. Rahmat
     Ali was a student at Cambridge University, and he called his suggested
     state Pakistan.
3   Malik, op. cit., p. 142
4   Malik, op. cit., p. 144
5   Lala Lajpat Rai advocated the exchange of population from the partitioned
     areas while Iqbal did not.
6   He suggested that India be divided into three zones—Muslim Zone, Hindu
     Zone and Zone of Indian states.
7   Malik, op. cit., p. 145
8   The Hindu Mahasabha was founded in 1914 in Amritsar and established
     its headquarters in Haridwar. Its early leaders were Pandit Madan Mohan
     Malaviya and Lala Lajpat Rai. In the late 1920s, the Mahasabha came
     under the influence of nationalist Vinayak Damodar Savarkar, a former
     revolutionary who opposed the secularism of the Congress. Under Savarkar,
     the Mahasabha became a more intense critic of the Congress and its
     policy of wooing Muslim support. In 1925, Mahasabha's former member
     Dr Keshav Baliram Hedgewar left to form the Rashtriya Swayamsevak
     Sangh, a Hindu volunteer organisation that abstained from active politics.
     RSS grew faster all across India and became a competitor for the core
     constituency of the Mahasabha.
9   'Proceedings of the Minority Sub-Committee of the First London Round
     Table Conference,' pp. 43-44.
10   Minority Sub-Committee's meeting on 1 January 1931.

Chapter 21: A Bloody Year: 1931

1   The British government in India issued invitations to delegates of the
     Round Table Conference in August 1931. They were supposed to reach
     London by September and the Conference was to start on October 1.

2   According to the Encyclopaedia Britannica, social democracy is a political
     ideology that advocates a peaceful, evolutionary transition of society from
     capitalism to socialism using established political processes. Based on 19th-
     century socialism and the tenets of Karl Marx and Friedrich Engels, social
     democracy shares common ideological roots with communism but eschews
     its militancy and totalitarianism. Social democracy was originally known
     as revisionism because it represented a change in basic Marxist doctrine,
     primarily in the former's repudiation of the use of revolution to establish
     a socialist society.

3   Malik, op. cit., p. 185
4   Malik, op. cit., p. 186
5   Malik, op. cit., p. 187
6   Malik, op. cit., p. 190

Chapter 22: London Once More

1   Who proposed Iqbal's name as an attendee? According to Azim Hussain,
     the recommendation came from his father Sir Fazl-e Hussain, an old
     class-mate of Iqbal.
2   Dr Hafeez Malik, *Iqbal in Politics*, Lahore: Sang-e Meel Publications,
     2009. pp. 194
3   The Merriam-Webster dictionary defines Pan-Islamism as 'a political
     movement launched in Turkey at the end of the 19th century by
     Sultan Abdul-Hamid II for the purpose of combating the process of
     westernization and fostering the unification of Islam'.
4   Afghani's movement was also labeled as Pan-Islamism. Iqbal was not sure
     if Aghani wanted to
5   Malik, op. cit., p. 195
6   Malik, op. cit., p. 195
7   Malik, op. cit., p. 201
8   Malik, op. cit., p. 201
9   Malik, op. cit., p. 201–02

Chapter 23: London, Rome, Egypt and Palestine

1   Established in 1914, the National League looked after the British war
     efforts, and after the War, opposed Soviet Union and advocated 'Muslim-
     British Friedhsip'.

2   Dr Hafeez Malik, *Iqbal in Politics*, Lahore: Sang-e Meel Publications, 2009. pp. 210

3   Lord Irwin was the Viceroy of India between 1926-31.

4   Muhammad Hamza Faruqi, *Safar Nama-i Iqbal*, pp. 50-52. quoted in Dr Hafeez Malik, *Iqbal in Politics*, Lahore: Sang-e Meel Publications, 2009. pp. 211

5   Malik, op. cit., p. 213

6   Malik, op. cit., p. 214

7   The Catacombs of Rome are underground burial places. At least forty have been discovered so far, out of which six are Jewish. Though most famous for Christian burials, either in separate catacombs or mixed together, they began in the 2nd century AD, mainly as a response to overcrowding and shortage of land. (Wikipedia)

8   Malik, op. cit., p. 214

9   Amanullah Khan (June 1892–25 April 1960) was the Sovereign of the Kingdom of Afghanistan from 1919 to 1929, and he led Afghanistan to independence over its foreign affairs from the United Kingdom. He was the first Afghan ruler who attempted to modernize Afghanistan on western designs. However, he did not succeed in this because of a popular uprising by Habibullah Kalakani and his followers. On 14 January 1929, Amanullah abdicated and fled to then neighbouring British India while Afghanistan fell into a civil war. From British India he went to Europe where he died in Zürich, Switzerland, in 1960.

10 There are many stories around Iqbal's meeting with Mussolini and all of them cannot be true.

11 The meeting between Mussolini and Iqbal described here is based on three different accounts by Ghulam Rasul Mehr (who did not accompany Iqbal in the meeting), Sir Malcolm Darling (who met Iqbal in Lahore in 1934) and Faqir Sayyid Wahiduddin.

12 On October 3, 1911, Italy attacked Tripoli, claiming to be liberating the Ottoman Wilayats from Istanbul's rule. Despite a major revolt by the Arabs, the Ottoman sultan ceded Libya to the Italians by signing the 1912 Treaty of Lausanne. From 1922 to 1928, Italian forces under General Badoglio waged a punitive pacification campaign but fighting with the Libyan resistance intensified during after Mussolini became the dictator of Italy. After a much-disputed truce on 3 January 1928, the Italian policy in Libya reached the level of full scale war. By 1934, Libya was fully pacified and the new Italian governor Italo Balbo started a policy of integration

between the Libyans and the Italians, that proved fully successful.

13 Faqir Sayyid Wahiduddin, *Ruzgar-i Faqir*, Vol I, pp. 48-49, as quoted by Dr Hafeez Malik, Iqbal in Politics, Lahore: Sang-e Meel Publications, 2009. pp. 217

14 Malik, op. cit., p. 214

15 Malik, op. cit., p. 214

16 Malik, op. cit., p. 223.

Chapter 24: Paris and Spain

1 Louis Massignon (July 25, 1883–October 31, 1962) was a Catholic scholar of Islam and a pioneer of Catholic-Muslim mutual understanding. He was the single most influential figure in the twentieth century in regard to the church's relationship with Islam. He focused increasingly on the work of M. K. Gandhi, whom he considered a saint. He is responsible, among the Catholics, for designating Islam an Abrahamic Faith. There is a growing consensus among scholars that his tireless research, esteem for Islam and Muslims, and the cultivation of key students in Islamic studies and largely prepared the way for the positive vision of Islam articulated in the Lumen Gentium and the Nostra Aetate at the Second Vatican Council. Although a Catholic himself, he tried to understand Islam from within and thus had a great influence on the way Islam was seen in the West; among other things, he paved the way for a greater openness inside the Catholic Church towards Islam as it was documented in the pastoral Vatican II declaration Nostra Aetate. (Wikipedia)

2 In 1914, Massignon had edited and published Hallaj's *Kitab al-Tawasin*. In 1922, he published his seminal work on Hallaj, *La Passion d'al-Hosayn ibn Mansour al Hallaj*.

3 Dr Hafeez Malik, *Iqbal in Politics*, Lahore: Sang-e Meel Publications, 2009. pp. 251.

4 Henri Bergson (1859–1941) was one of the most famous and influential French philosophers of the late 19th century-early 20th century. Although his international fame reached cult-like heights during his lifetime, his influence decreased notably after the second World War. While such French thinkers as Merleau-Ponty, Sartre, and Lévinas explicitly acknowledged his influence on their thought, it is generally agreed that it was Gilles Deleuze's 1966 *Bergsonism* that marked the reawakening of

interest in Bergson's work. Stanford Encyclopedia of Philosophy *http://plato.stanford.edu/entries/bergson/*

5 In a letter to Sir William Rothstein, Iqbal wrote in 1933: 'I met Bergson in Paris and we had very interesting conversation on philosophical issues. Bergson stated that Berkeley's philosophy can be summed up that in intellect matter is completely revealed but not in mind.'

6 Stanford Encyclopedia of Philosophy http://plato.stanford.edu/entries/bergson/

7 Iqbal's letter to Atiya Faizi, 29 May 1933.

8 UNESCO http://whc.unesco.org/en/list/313

Chapter 25: The Last Days

1 Dr Hafeez Malik, *Iqbal in Politics*, Lahore: Sang-e Meel Publications, 2009. p. 309

2 Khurram Ali Shafique writes in *Iqbal: His Life and Our Times*: 'This was the only instance when Iqbal accepted stipend from a prince. He politely stopped Sir Ross from seeking additional support from three other potential patrons.'

3 Later, Mayo Road was renamed as Iqbal Road.

4 'In September 1934, Iqbal's well-known work, *Musafer*, was published and its royalty along with the royalty of other works were transferred to Javed's name, and necessary documents were filed with the Registrar.' *Iqbal in Politics* by Dr Hafeez Malik; Lahore: Sang-e Meel Publications, 2009. p. 310.

5 Khurram Ali Shafique, *Iqbal: His Life and Our Times,* and *Iqbal in Politics* by Dr Hafeez Malik; Lahore: Sang-e Meel Publications, 2009.

6 After a while, Javed felt, these kisses became perfunctory, a matter of routine. (*Iqbal Baap ki Haisiyat Se* in *Allama Iqbal–Hayat, Fikr-o-Fan*)

7 Later, she became Mrs. Doris Ahmad. She retuned to Germany in 1962.

8 Rafiq Dogar in *Allama Iqbal: Hayat, Fikr-o-Fan*, compiled by Dr Saleem Akhtar. Lahore: Sang-e Meel Publications, 2012.

9 The sixth book of his poetry, *Gabriel's Wing* (*Baal-i-Jibreel*) was in Urdu and was self-published in January 1935 from Lahore. His seventh book of poetry, *The Blow of Moses* (*Zarb-i-Kaleem*) was sub-titled 'a declaration of war against the present age'. It was self-published from Lahore in July 1936. It was dedicated to Nawab Hamidullah of Bhopal in gratitude

for the financial support offered to the poet. *What Then Is To Be Done, O Nations of the East? With the Masnavi 'The Traveller'* (1936) was the long title of the eighth book of Iqbal's poetry (in Persian, it was '*Pas Cheh Bayed Kerd Aye Aqwam-i-Sharq Maa Masnavi Musafir*'). It was a masnavi in two parts. The ninth, and the last, book of Iqbal's poetry was *The Gift of Hijaz* (Armughan-i-Hijaz), published from Lahore in November 1938, seven months after the author's death. It comprised of Persian quatrains and Urdu poems. (Khurram Ali Shafique, *Iqbal: His Life and Our Times*)

10 *The Reconstruction of Religious Thought in Islam* (1934): A revised second edition of the lectures came out from Oxford University Press in May 1934 as *The Reconstruction of Religious Thought in Islam* (dropping the 'Six Lectures on' from the title). Revisions in the text were minor, except the addition of a completely new lecture that had been delivered at London at the request of the Aristotelian Society in 1932. (Khurram Ali Shafique, *Iqbal: His Life and Our Times*)

11 Malik, op. cit., p. 311

12 Khurram Shafique, *Iqbal: His Life and Our Times*: 'Jinnah was one Muslim leader of British India whose personal magnanimity matched Iqbal's lofty imagination, and the two became inseparable in the popular Muslim imagination after Jinnah's return to India.'

13 Shaikh Ata Allah, ed., *Iqbal Nama*, Vol. I, pp. 313-4, quoted in *Iqbal in Politics* by Dr Hafeez Malik; Lahore: Sang-e Meel Publications, 2009. p. 316

14 Malik. op. cit., p. 311

15 Malik. op. cit., p. 312

Chapter 26: A Politician and a Patriot

1 Sayyid Nazi Niazi, *Iqbal Ke Hadur Mein*, p. 103 quoted in *Iqbal in Politics* by Dr Hafeez Malik; Lahore: Sang-e Meel Publications, 2009. p. 313

2 Jawaharlal Nehru, *The Discovery of India*.

3 The historical meet is recounted by Ashiq Hussein Batalvi in his Urdu book '*Last Two Years of Iqbal*'.

4 Iqbal was extremely concerned on the economic plight of poverty-affected Muslims. In one of his many missives to Jinnah, he pointedly mentioned it. The one dated 28th May 1937 warned Jinnah that the success of Muslim League depended on providing a solution to economic plight of Muslims.

5 Malik. op. cit., p. 313

6   Niazi (op. cit.) in *Iqbal in Politics* by Dr Hafeez Malik; Lahore: Sang-e Meel Publications, 2009. p. 314

7   Nehru family confidant, Mian Iftikhar-ud-Din switched sides later, as Pakistan became a reality. The statements attributed to him during the Iqbal-Nehru meeting were later disowned by his wife who was also present when the meeting took place.

8   Niazi, quoted in *Iqbal in Politics* by Dr Hafeez Malik; Lahore: Sang-e Meel Publications, 2009. p. 314

9   Niazi, quoted in *Iqbal in Politics* by Dr Hafeez Malik; Lahore: Sang-e Meel Publications, 2009. p. 314

10 '... Iqbal was certainly right in holding that I was not much of a politician, although politics had seized me and made me its victim,' Nehru wrote in his book, *The Discovery of India*.

Chapter 27: The Time of This Faqir Has Come

1   In his poem, Qalandar Ki Pehchaan, he says:

> *Meher-o-mah-o-anjum ka mahasib hai qalandar*
> *Ayyam ka markab nahin, rakin hai qalandar*

> Like a steed's, a dervish holds the reins of time in his hands,
> The sun, stars and moon he brings to book with speed!

2   This is Iqbal's wit on display again. Here, he makes a pun on the name Javed. 'I would rather that you become Javed!' The name Javed means 'immortal' or 'eternal' in Persian.

3   'An Address to Javed' from *Javed Nama*

4   This might have been composed a few months earlier; *Iqbal in Politics* by Dr Hafeez Malik; Lahore: Sang-e Meel Publications, 2009. p. 313

5   Khurram Ali Shafique, *Iqbal: His Life, Our Times*

6   He died of cardiac asthma on 21 April 1938.

7   Westward, in the direction of the Kaaba in Mecca.

8   This entire episode is based on an essay by Dr Javed Iqbal, 'Iqbal—Ek Baap Ki Haisiyat Se' in *Allama Iqbal: Hayat, Fikr-o-Fan*, compiled by Dr Saleem Akhtar.

9   With the permission of the Punjab governor, Iqbal was buried on a spot to the left of the steps leading to the Badshahi mosque in Lahore. His body was lowered into the grave on the evening of 21 April, 1938. The construction of a mausoleum on the grave started in 1946.

Epilogue

1   Iqbal considered Palestine a Muslim problem. He said in a statement in
    1937 that in the light of history, Palestine ceased to be a Jewish problem
    long before the entry of Caliph Umar into Jerusalem more than 1300 years
    ago. In his opinion, the issue of Palestine has a emerged as a 'problem of
    both a reliogious and political nature' since the abolition of the Khilafat.
    Dr Hafeez Malik, *Iqbal in Politics*. Pp. 272-273.

2   Iqbal followed the upheavals in Xinjiang (Chinese Turkistan) with great
    concern in 1932-33. 'Turkistan is a vast country divided into three parts,
    one of which is ruled by Russia, the other by Afghanistan, and the third
    by China,' Iqbal wrote after attending a lecture in England on this theme.
    'In 1914, there was a great deal of discontent in Chinese Turkestan owing
    to the appointment of Chinese magistrates in that country and an attempt
    made by the Chinese Government to impose the Chinese language on the
    population which is almost wholly Muslim. But matters did not come to a
    head then. As far as I know, the present revolution in that country began
    in 1930 under the leadership of a 17-year old Muslim boy named Chong
    Ying ... My apprehension is that the revolution in Chinese Turkestan
    may develop into a Pan-Turanian movement is borne out of the trend of
    thought in central Asia ...' Dr Hafeez Malik, *Iqbal in Politics*, pp. 268-269.

3   'How many Muslims has the United States killed in the past thirty years,
    and how many Americans have been killed by Muslims? Coming up
    with a precise answer to this question is probably impossible, but it is also
    not necessary, because the rough numbers are so clearly lopsided,' writes
    Stephen M. Walt in *The Foreign Policy* in a 2009 article, *Why they Hate
    Us?*. According to his own rough calculations, US suffered 10,325 fatalities
    whereas Muslim fatalities were around 288,000 (between 1990-2003).
    *http://www.foreignpolicy.com/posts/2009/11/30/why_they_hate_us_ii_how_
    many_muslims_has_the_us_killed_in_the_past_30_years*

4   'The question we might want to ask ourselves today is whether contemporary
    Europe is confronting a Muslim question similar to the Jewish question
    170 years ago. Is European antipathy towards Muslims comparable to that
    first stage of hatred towards Jews, a hatred that culminated in one of the
    darkest pages of human history?' writes Sarah R. Farris in an article, *On
    anti-Semitism and Islamophobia in Europe*'In spite of the obvious differences
    between the two contexts, the success of the far right during the recent
    elections in several European countries seems to suggest that the answer

is a resounding yes. The victory of these parties attests to the incredible gains made by Islamophobic propaganda in the last ten years. In France, the president of the National Front, Marine Le Pen - who obtained one quarter of all votes - has asked school canteens to stop offering Muslim children alternatives to pork. In Britain, the UK Independence Party campaigned against the construction of mosques and became the biggest winner in the elections, with an astonishing 27.5 percent of the vote.' 5 June, 2014. *http:// www.aljazeera.com/indepth/opinion/2014/06/anti-semitism-islamophobia-europ-20146414191330623.html*

5   Iqbal was convinced that solidarity among the Muslim peoples was the only possible hope for the survival of Islam. He saw everywhere around him the collapse and decay of the Muslims, and he could see that soon there might be no trace of independent Islam left in the world. Javed Iqbal, 'Afterword' in *Stray Reflections: The Private Notebook of Muhammad Iqbal*, edited by Javed Iqbal, Lahore: Iqbal Academy Pakistan, 1961.

6   'More than 40 years ago, in the famous film, 'Garam Hawa' starring Balraj Sahani, the agony of a lower middle class Muslim family in search of a house was shown. Today, the situation is worse. They (Muslims) feel marginalized in the job market, in bank loan distribution, in educational institutions and of course in living together with the Hindus. The educated middle class Hindus feel uneasy with having Muslims as members of their cooperative housing society and the Muslims feel physically and psychologically insecure. This divide is growing and the 2014 elections do not hold a promise of 'Happy Days'. Indeed, not only the idea, but the reality of a secular society is under siege...' writes Kumar Ketkar in, *The Soul of Man Under Secularism, NDTV, 2 July 2014*. He adds, 'For the first time the number of Muslim members of Parliament has been reduced to a single digit. The BJP does not have a single Muslim MP. The only Muslim minister, Najma Heptulla is a non-elected member of the party, and she has complicated the issue of 'minority community' by saying that only the Parsis can be considered a minority. Even the Parsis were not impressed by Najma's statement.' *http://www.ndtv.com/article/opinion/the-soul-of-man-under-secularism-551585*

7   Ranu Jain, 'Educational backwardness among Muslims in India—A Case of Misrepresentation' in *Religion, Power and Violence—Expression of Politics in Contemporary Times*, Ed. Ram Punyani, New Delhi: Sage, 2005; p. 273.

8   'I have always questioned the secularism-communalism divide in India's political discourse as a false dichotomy. It is majoritarianism that needs

to be contested by taking a firm stand on minority rights and federalism as intrinsic features of India's democracy,' says historian Ayesha Jalal to interviewer Ather Farouqi ('It Is Majoritarianism That Needs To Be Contested'). 'India's minorities, and Muslims in particular, have to overcome internal divisions and forge wider and more effective links with relevant civil society organizations in order to be heard and heeded. Tragic episodes in contemporary history cannot be wished away and must be remembered if they are not to be repeated.' http://www.outlookindia.com/article/-It-Is-Majoritarianism-That-Needs-To-Be-Contested/291165

9   Justice Iqbal begins US visit with Innovation, Dr Javed Iqbal, *A Collection of Preserved Letters*, Lahore: Sang-e Meel Publications, 2012. p. 243

10   Javed Iqbal, 'Afterword' in *Stray Reflections: The Private Notebook of Muhammad Iqbal*, edited by Javed Iqbal, Lahore: Iqbal Academy Pakistan, 1961.

11   Occupy Wall Street was a protest movement that began on September 17, 2011, in Zuccotti Park, located in New York City's Wall Street financial district. The movement was aimed at issues such as social and economic inequality, greed, corruption and the perceived undue influence of corporations on government—particularly from the financial services sector. (Wikipedia)

12   A French economist whose bestselling book *Capital in the Twenty-First Century* (2013), emphasizes the themes of his work on wealth concentrations and distribution over the past 250 years. The book argues that the rate of capital return in developed countries is persistently greater than the rate of economic growth, and that this will cause wealth inequality to increase in the future. To address this problem, he proposes redistribution through a global tax on wealth. (Wikipedia)

13   *Zamindar*, 24 June, 1923, quoted in Dr Javed Iqbal, *Ideology of Pakistan*, Lahore: Sang-e Meel Publications, 2011; pp. 132-133.

14   Muhammd Safiq, *A History of Urdu Literature*. Delhi: Oxford University Press, 1984. p 455

Appendix

1   His first research paper, 'The Doctrine of Absolute Unity as Expounded by Abdul Karim al-Jili', was published in the *Indian Antiquary*, Bombay, in September 1900.

2   Sh. Abdul Qadir, *Iqbal—The Great Poet of Islam*, Lahore: Sang-e Meel
      Publications, 2003.p.28

3   Muhammad Sadiq, op. cit., p.450

4   Source: Speeches, Writings, and Statements of Iqbal, compiled and edited
      by Latif Ahmed Sherwani (Lahore: Iqbal Academy, 1977 [1944], 2nd ed.,
      revised and enlarged), pp. 3-26. This version has been slightly edited for
      classroom use. *http://www.columbia.edu/itc/mealac/pritchett/00islamlinks/
      txt_iqbal_1930.html*

5   Source: G. Allana, Pakistan Movement Historical Documents (Karachi:
      Department of International Relations, University of Karachi, nd [1969]),
      pp. 129-133. *http://www.columbia.edu/itc/mealac/pritchett/00islamlinks/
      txt_iqbal_tojinnah_1937.html*

6   *http://www.columbia.edu/itc/mealac/pritchett/00islamlinks/txt_
      lajpatrai_1924/10part.html*

Bibliography

Afzal, Muhammad Rafique (Urdu). *Guftar-i-Iqbal* [The Speeches of Iqbal]. 1969. Lahore: Idara-i-Tehqiqat Pakistan, 1986

Ahmad, Jamil-ud-Din (ed.). *Historic Documents of the Muslim Freedom Movement*. Lahore: Publishers United, 1970.

Akhtar, Saleem (ed.) (Urdu). *Allama Iqbal: Hiyat, Fikr-o-Fun*. Lahore: Sang-e Meel publications, 2012

Ali, [Dr] Parveen Shaukat. *The Political Philosophy of Iqbal* (Second Edition). Lahore: Publishers United, 1978

Alvi, Amjad Saleem, ed. (Urdu). *Iqbaliat-i-Mehr*. Lahore: Mehr Sons Pvt. Ltd., 1988

Begum, Atiya, Parekh Rauf. *Iqbal*. Karachi: Oxford University Press, 2011

Chaghatai, M. Ikram. *Goethe, Iqbal and the Orient* [Revised]. 1999. Lahore: Iqbal Academy Pakistan, 2003

Chandra, Bipan, Mukherjee, Mridula, Mukherjee, Aditya, Panikkar, K N and Mahajan, Sucheta, *India's Struggle for Independence*. New Delhi: Penguin Books, 1989

Dar, B.A. (Compiled and Edited by). *Letters of Iqbal*. Lahore: Iqbal Academy Pakistan, 1978

Durrani, Saeed Akhtar (Urdu). *Iqbal Europe Mien*. Lahore: Iqbal Academy Pakistan, 1985

Gandhi, Rajmohan. *Understanding the Muslim Mind*. India: Penguin Books, 2013

German, Lindsey and Rees, John. *A People's History of London*. London: Verso, 2012

Guha, Ramchandra. *Gandhi Before India*. Delhi: Allen Lane, 2013

Hasan, Dr Riffat. *The Sword and the Sceptre*. Lahore: Iqbal Academy Pakistan, 1977

Husain, Dr Sultan Mahmood (Urdu). *Allama Iqbal kay Ustaad Shamsul Ulema*

Maulvi Syed Mir Hasan [*The Teacher of Allama Iqbal, Shamsul Ulema Maulvi Syed Mird Hasan*]. Lahore: Iqbal Academy Pakistan, 1981

Hussain, Dr Syed Sultan Mahmood. *Iqbal ki Ibtedai Zindagi.* Lahore: Iqbal Academy, 1989

Jalal, Ayesha. *Self and Sovereignty: Individual and Community in South Asian Islam since 1850.* New York: Routledge, 2000

Iqbal, Shaikh Muhammad. *Ilmul Iqtisad* [*The Science of Economics*]. Lahore: Sang-e Meel Publications, 2011 (reprint).

Iqbal, Dr Sir Muhammad ['Iqbal M.A., S. M.']. *The Development of Metaphysics in Persia.* London: Luzac & Co., 1908

Iqbal, Dr Sir Muhammad ['Sir Mohammad Iqbal']. *The Reconstruction of Religious Thought in Islam.* London: Oxford University Press, 1934

Iqbal, Dr Sir Muhammad. *Stray Reflections, the Private Notebook of Muhammad Iqbal; also includes: 'Stray Thoughts'.* Dr. Javid Iqbal (Ed.). 1961. Lahore: Iqbal Academy Pakistan, 2006

Iqbal, Dr Sir Muhammad. *Letters and Writings of Iqbal.* B.A. Dar (Ed.). 1967. Lahore: Iqbal Academy Pakistan, 1981

Iqbal, Dr Sir Muhammad ['Iqbal'] (Urdu). *Kulliyat-i-Iqbal Urdu* [Complete Poetical Works of Iqbal in Urdu]. Lahore: Shaikh Ghulam Ali and Sons, 1973.

Iqbal, Dr Sir Muhammad. *Speeches, Writings and Statements of Iqbal* (Third Edition). Latif Ahmad Sherwani (Ed.). 1977. Lahore: Iqbal Academy Pakistan, 1995

Iqbal, Dr Sir Muhammad ['Allama Muhammad Iqbal']. *Discourses of Iqbal.* Shahid Husain Razzaqi (Ed.). 1979. Lahore: Iqbal Academy Pakistan, 2003

Iqbal, Dr Sir Muhammad ['Iqbal'] (Urdu). *Kulliyat-i-Iqbal Urdu* [Complete Poetical Works of Iqbal in Urdu]. Lahore: Iqbal Academy Pakistan, 1990

Iqbal, Dr Sir Muhammad. *Letters of Iqbal to Jinnah, Foreword by Quaid-e-Azam.* Mohammad Jehangir Alim (Ed.). Faisalabad: Daera Maaref-i-Iqbal, 2001 (Based on work published in 1943)

Iqbal, Dr Javid (Urdu). *Zindah Rud* [The Living Stream]. Revised Edition. Lahore: Sang-e-Meel Publications, 2008

Iqbal, Dr Javid. *Ideology of Pakistan.* Lahore: Sang-e Meel Publications, 2011

Iqbal, Javid. *Encounters with Destiny: Autobiographical Reflections* (Translated from Urdu by Hafeez Malik and Nasira Iqbal). Lahore: Sang-e Meel Publications, 2012

Malik, Dr Fateh Muhammad. *Reconstruction of Muslim Political Thought.* Islamabad: National Book Foundation, 2013

Malik, Dr Nadeem Shafiq (Compiled and Edited). *The All India Muslim League and Allama Iqbal's Allahabad Address, 1930 (Archives of the Freedom Movement, Volumes No.153 & 154)*. Lahore: Iqbal Academy Pakistan, 2013

Malik, Hafeez (Ed.). *Iqbal, Poet-Philosopher of Pakistan*. New York: Columbia University Press, 1971

Malik, Hafeez. 'The Marxist Literary Movement in India and Pakistan'. *The Journal of Asian Studies*, Vol. 26, No. 4, August 1967, pp.649-664. Association for Asian Studies. Retrieved from http://www.jstor.org/stable/2051241 on February 5, 2014

Malik, Dr Hafeez. *Iqbal in Politics*. Lahore: Sang-e Meel Publications, 2009

Mishra, Pankaj. *From the Ruins of the Empire*. London: Allen Lane, 2012.

Niazi, Syed Nazeer (Urdu). *Iqbal Kay Huzoor*. Lahore: Iqbal Academy Pakistan, 1971

Piketty, Thomas, (translated by Arthur Goldhammer). *Capital in the Twenty-First Century*. Paris: Editions du Seuil, Harvard University Press, 2014

Punyani, Ram. Religion, Power and Violence—Expression of Politics in Contemporary Times. New Delhi: Sage, 2005

Qadir, Sh. Abdul. *Iqbal—The Great Poet of Islam*. Lahore: Sang-e Meel Publications, 2003.

Qaiser, Dr. Nazir. *Creative Dimensions of Iqbal's Thought*. Lahore: Iqbal Academy Pakistan, 2012

Sadiq, Muhammad. *A History of Urdu Literature*. Delhi: Oxford University Press,1995

Salim, Mohammad (Urdu). *Allama Iqbal Ki Siyasi Zindagi*, Lahore: Sang-e Meel Publications, 2001

Schimmel, Dr. Annemarie. *Gabriel's Wing*. 1963. Lahore: Iqbal Academy Pakistan, 1989

Shafique, Khurram Ali, *Iqbal: His Life and Our Times*. Lahore: Iqbal Academy Pakistan, 2014.

Tanvir, Hina (Tr.). *Javidnama* (abridged). Dr. Sir Muhammad Iqbal. Lahore: Iqbal Academy Pakistan, 2006

Thompson, Edward. *Enlist India for Freedom*. London: Victor Golancz Ltd., 1940

Umar, Muhammad Suheyl and Koshul, Dr. Basit Bilal (ed.), *Muhammad Iqbal - A Contemporary: Articles from the International Seminar held at The University of Cambridge* (June 19-20, 2008)

Wolpert, Stanley. *Jinnah of Pakistan*. 1984. Karachi: Oxford University Press, 1989.

Acknowledgements

Like most biographies, this work too rises from the shoulders of many biographies and specialist studies of Iqbal. In the writing of this biography, I have benefitted from the scholarly works of Dr Javid Iqbal, Dr Hafeez Mallik, Rajmohan Gandhi and Khurram Ali Shafique, just to name a few. I also owe a debt to Pankaj Mishra who included Allama Iqbal in his seminal work, *From the Ruins of Empire*, which inspired me to take a crack at this long-cherished dream.

Along the way, I have received help from my friends Mohammad Sajjad, Najmul Hoda, and Farah Bashir who kindly read different parts of the manuscript and offered advice whenever I reached out to them. I am extremely grateful to Dr Muhammad Suheyl Umar, Director of Iqbal Academy Pakistan, who offered me his learned suggestions and guidance, and allowed us to use valuable pictures of Iqbal from the vaults of the academy.

In getting this project started and finished, I owe special thanks to Jayapriya Vasudevan, my agent, to Meru Gokhale, my publisher, who showed great courage in supporting this project, to Fazal Rashid, my meticulous and challenging editor, and the entire production and marketing team at Random House India, including Caroline Newbury. I thank Pia Hazarika, who designed the cover. Gratitude is also due to many friends and well-wishers who have kept me inspired while I was working on this project: Moazzam Sheikh, Krishna Udayasankar, Mirza Rizwan, Monideepa Sahu, Anu Kumar, Rajeev

Jayaswal, Rajeev Yerneni, Abdullah Khan, Lai Kwok Kin, P.N. Balji, Saba Syed Hafeez, Reyaz Ahmed, Jawaid Iqbal, and Teng Fang Yih.

My heartfelt thanks are also due to my parents, my brothers, sisters, and in-laws for their encouragement and best wishes. I can't tell you how much I cherish your presence, love and support.

Finally, a zillion thanks to my wife Shabana and daughter Zara for providing me a sanctuary to read and write, for tolerating my intolerable absences, both physical and mental. Each word of this book that has arisen from my heart owes its existence to your endurance of the unkindness of daily life—a burden that you have claimed to yourself to allow me to indulge in my delusions.